D0025287

Post-War British Drama

In this extensively revised and updated edition of her classic work, *Look Back in Gender*, Michelene Wandor pinpoints the symbiotic relationship between gender and theatre in a provocative look at key representative British plays from the last fifty years.

Repositioning the playtext at the heart of theatre studies, Wandor surveys plays by Ayckbourn, Beckett, Churchill, Daniels, Friel, Hare, Kane, Osborne, Pinter, Ravenhill, Wertenbaker, Wesker and others. Her provocative mix of historical and aesthetic reasoning ranges over many gender-based issues including:

- the imperative of gender in the playwright's imagination
- the function of gender as a major determinant of structural and narrative drives
- the impact of socialism and feminism on post-war British drama, and an understanding of feminist dynamics in drama
- the causes of the differences in the representation of the family, sexuality and the figure of the mother before and after 1968
- the impact on drama of the slogan that the 'personal is political'

Wandor's nuanced argument is central to any thorough analysis of contemporary theatre, offering an analytical framework to illuminate recent drama, and challenging the playwrights of the future.

Michelene Wandor is a playwright and critic. She is a prolific radio dramatist, and is Senior Lecturer in Creative Writing at the University of North London. Her previous publications include *Carry On, Understudies* (1986) and *Gardens of Eden* (poetry, 1999).

Post-War British Drama

Looking back in gender

Michelene Wandor

London and New York

First published 2001 by Routledge
11 New Fetter lane, London EC4P 4EE

Simultaneously published in the USA and Canada
by Routledge
29 West 35th Street, New York, NY 10001

Routledge is an imprint of the Taylor & Francis Group

© 2001 Michelene Wandor

Typeset in Goudy by BC Typesetting, Bristol
Printed and bound in Great Britain by
TJ International Ltd, Padstow, Cornwall

British Library Cataloguing in Publication Data
A catalogue record for this book is available from the British Library

Library of Congress Cataloging in Publication Data
Wandor, Michelene.
   Post-war British Drama: looking back in gender/Michelene Wandor.
   p.   cm.
   Includes bibliographical references (p.   ) and index.
   1. English drama – 20th century – History and criticism.
   2. Sex role in literature. 3. Feminism and literature – Great Britain –
   History – 20th century. 4. Literature and society – Great Britain –
   History – 20th century. 5. World War, 1939–1945 – Great Britain –
   Influence. 6. Domestic drama, English – History and criticism.
   7. Family in literature. I. Title.

   PR739.S45 W34 2001
   822'.91409–dc21   00-069925

ISBN 0–415–13855–8 (hbk)
ISBN 0–415–13856–6 (pbk)

Contents

Acknowledgements   x
Introduction   1

PART I

1 The imperative of gender   15

Orlando's tea-party   15
To be or not to be (gendered)   17
The imperative of gender   21

2 The imperative of context: family and gender   27

After the war was over   27
Public and private   35

PART II

3 The 1950s   41

Good causes. Displacement: kitchen sink and psyche   41
LOOK BACK IN ANGER
Men, authority and the state   48
WAITING FOR GODOT
Political causes: Communism and the Jewish family   50
CHICKEN SOUP WITH BARLEY, ROOTS, I'M TALKING ABOUT
JERUSALEM

The outsider at the door   58
THE BIRTHDAY PARTY
Voices from the distaff side: mother and daughter   60
A TASTE OF HONEY
Women and myth   63
THE SPORT OF MY MAD MOTHER
Women and emancipation   67
EACH HIS OWN WILDERNESS, PLAY WITH A TIGER
Men and the military   71
SERJEANT MUSGRAVE'S DANCE

4 The 1960s   76

Military homosexuality   77
A PATRIOT FOR ME
Behind the lace curtains   80
ENTERTAINING MR SLOANE
Suburbia fights back   81
LOOT
Respectable lesbians   82
THE KILLING OF SISTER GEORGE
Beginning to come out   86
STAIRCASE
Urban violence   87
SAVED

**5 The Lady Macbeth syndrome – The 1950s and
1960s: conclusions**   91

6 *The Royal Smut-Hound* by Kenneth Tynan   98

PART III

7 New contexts   115
Sexual politics   115
Alternative theatres   121
Who works where: writers and the rest   130

Gender and playwriting 132
Cross-dressing and gender 136
*Feminist dynamics: radical, bourgeois and socialist
    feminism* 140

8 A theatrical legacy 148

Mother on a pedestal – a doubtful chivalry 148
THE MOTHER

PART IV

9 The 1970s 157

Whose territory? 157
VAGINA REX AND THE GAS OVEN
On female territory 159
RITES
Womb envy 162
OCCUPATIONS
Whose public school? 164
SLAG
The sexual psyche 166
AC/DC
Whose sexual freedoms? 168
LAY-BY
Biology and property values 170
OWNERS
Gender and creativity: the Ophelia syndrome 173
TEETH 'N' SMILES
Gender and the Left 176
DESTINY
Rites of passage 179
ONCE A CATHOLIC
Utopias 181
CLOUD NINE
Daring loves 185
BENT

Chronicling gender   187
THE ROMANS IN BRITAIN

10 **The 1970s: conclusions**   190

PART V

11 **The 1980s**   197

Ireland, imperialism and language   197
TRANSLATIONS
Taking gender out of the ring   199
TRAFFORD TANZI
Foreign customs   202
TIBETAN INROADS
Cleaning up the act   204
STEAMING
The right legacy   207
MAYDAYS
Pornographics   212
MASTERPIECES
Myth revisited   217
THE LOVE OF THE NIGHTINGALE

12 **The 1980s: conclusions**   220

PART VI

13 **The 1990s**   225
Down on the estate   225
BEAUTIFUL THING
New urban disaffection   227
SHOPPING AND FUCKING
Intellectual life   229
COPENHAGEN
New brutalism   232
CLEANSED

14 The 1990s: conclusion   235

PART VII

15 Turning the tables   241

16 Coda   253
   Serendipities and alter egos   253
   PASSION PLAY
   Home and away   255
   HOUSE and GARDEN

   Epilogue   260

   Select bibliography   261
   Index   266

Acknowledgements

Thanks to Roxana and Matthew Tynan for permission to reproduce *The Royal Smut-Hound* by Kenneth Tynan. Thanks to Celia Mitchell and Ernie Eban for their help. Thanks also to Nick Hern who was indirectly responsible for sending me down this road.

Introduction

In the quick forge and working-house of thought.
(William Shakespeare, *Henry V*)

This book is a revised and updated version of *Look Back in Gender*. That book was itself the culmination of a phase of work which began for me in 1981 with *Understudies*, continued with an updated version, *Carry on, Understudies* (1986) and was followed by *Look back in Gender* (1987). During this time I also edited five anthologies of plays: *Strike While the Iron is Hot* (Journeyman Press, 1980), and the first four volumes of *Plays by Women* (Methuen, 1982–1985).

These books came out of my own situation; the hybrid and, in Britain, the sometimes difficult position of being on both sides of the creative fence. At the turn of the 1960s to 1970s I began writing poetry, plays and short stories, and from 1971 to 1982 I worked on *Time Out* magazine (founded in 1968) as poetry editor, and theatre, book and film reviewer. At the same time I became heavily involved in socialist-feminism, its constantly developing theory, debate and creativity.

The heady mix of politics and art which characterised much of that time had its objective correlative in the abolition of theatre censorship in Britain in 1968. It meant then that as a working/beginning playwright, it was relatively easy to get plays put on in the variety of theatre spaces – makeshift, converted, new – which rapidly appeared. Although since 1979 my main dramatic work has been for radio, in 1987 I inadvertently became a statistic in theatre history, when my dramatisation of Eugene Sue's *The Wandering Jew*, at the Lyttelton Theatre, was the first work by a British woman playwright to appear on one of the South Bank's main stages (plays by women – and there are very few of those – tend to be put on at the Cottesloe).

As the 1970s progressed, feminist theatre practitioners began pointing out the gender imbalance in contemporary theatre and campaigning for change, researching into lost and/or forgotten plays by women. In my journalism and reviews I alternately enthused about the presence of new plays/performance styles by women, wrote my own plays, and puzzled about how to understand and evaluate this new work. Alongside my utopian hopes for a new kind of theatre, I became concerned that the ephemerality of live performance might mean that this work could all disappear. It had to be documented, and it had to be published.

In practice, of course, this was not so easy. Some of the left-wing/ alternative presses published plays. Methuen, then the main drama publisher in this country, evolved a cheaper and quicker turn-round for publishing plays, in pamphlet-like booklets, stapled rather than bound. My initial drive was to try and find a way to publish other plays. I self-published some short plays of my own and those of a fellow writer, Dinah Brooke, but my impetus was not merely a selfish one. Value judgements and historical endurance immediately came into the discussion when I proposed editing an anthology of new plays by women writers. Nick Hern, the drama editor at Methuen, shunted me sideways into the project which became *Understudies*. *Understudies* was a monograph about theatre and sexual politics in Britain in the 1960s and 1970s, published as part of Methuen's Theatrefile series, whose aim was to 'deal with recent developments in modern theatre not yet discussed in book form, and to approach them in a fresh, even unconventional form'. My aim then was threefold.

First, I was eager to document, describe and try to categorise some of the radical and exciting work in theatre initiated by women and gay people who were part of, and influenced by, the socialist, feminist and gay liberation movements of the time, the groupings of people involved in 'sexual politics'. For many, this also involved questioning the working structures of theatre, and aiming to democratise the way plays were made, the audiences to whom they performed, and the purposes for which their drama was created.

Essentially, this movement, variously styled 'alternative', 'political', 'fringe' theatre, was passionately engaged in living and demonstrating the way art and politics were in symbiotic relationship with each other. *Understudies* also discussed the sexual division of labour in theatre, how it was – and still is – ideologically underpinned. The book foregrounded the work of women and gay people, contextualising it within the theatre industry at large, and in its more immediate context of the fringe/socialist theatre movement of the time.

My second aim was to clear a space so that the work of contemporary women playwrights could begin to become better documented than they (we) have been throughout history. This was, of course, part of my own political agenda as playwright and critic; to demonstrate the male dominance of the stage play, and to be part of the drive to increase the number of women playwrights.

As I engaged with these plays, I had to think about the influences feeding into them, and – like anyone reading or seeing a play – to begin to evaluate whether I thought they were interesting/good/ effective/original. What was their relationship with the dominant culture in which they were inevitably intervening? A theoretical frame- work was needed which could make sense of this work.

My third aim, therefore – taking up the smallest amount of space (ten out of the book's eighty-eight pages) laid the foundations for a gender- based framework with which to critique the work of male playwrights in the 1970s, and suggested a method of discussing, in a more cogent theoretical way, the relationship between feminism, the 'gendered' imagination (of men and women), the aesthetics of theatre(s) and how, if at all, this impinges on the use/manipulation of theatrical form, the creation of meanings, and finally, on the issue of the theatrical canon, the process of value judgement itself. Does simply introducing new content, new perspectives, and exploring and inventing new theatrical forms necessarily result in 'good', effective, art or imaginative polemic? What effect does redressing the imbalance of the under-, mis- and non-representation of certain kinds of people by the dominant culture have on our critical vocabulary? These questions were there in my mind, but in the climate of the time they took a relative second place to documenting the new, the now, to shifting some of the signposts of modern theatre.

The two embryonic critical strands from *Understudies* were developed separately. In *Carry on, Understudies*, I applied a more extensive model of the three basic dynamics of feminism: radical feminism, bourgeois feminism and socialist-feminism. I suggested ways in which these three different feminist 'dynamics' could be read off against the aesthetic, narrative and theatrical drives of plays in which women were at the centre of the action. Given that such plays were in any case mainly written by women, this critical approach tended to apply more easily to plays by women writers. At the same time, in analysing plays by male writers, I offered an analysis of the way the gender dynamic in their plays (both in narrative and themes) reinforced (textually and subtextually) male-centredness.

I was particularly concerned then about the ways in which labels such as 'feminist drama', 'women's theatre', 'feminist playwright', 'feminist theatre', 'gay theatre', 'gay plays', 'feminist aesthetic' were being aired. It made a kind of common sense to talk and write in this way, but it did not really confront the fundamental historical or aesthetic issues. It became a kind of Good Housekeeping sign of approval if you were excited by the work, and a term of abuse if you disliked it. 'Feminist' could be used to market work or to denigrate it, but analytically it went only so far. A work of art can never be totally explained by slapping a polemical label on it, or the allegiances of its author. If one likes the message of a play, one may forgive its weaknesses, but it is also possible to dislike the message and still be emotionally affected, theatrically impressed. I wanted to 'cut a rigorous swathe' through what I saw as lazy thinking, which would 'be useful to academics, students, theatre practitioners, critics and audiences'. Nothing like aiming high.

The second strand was the gender-based critique which I used in *Look Back*. Here I was working with the notion of the 'imperative of gender' in the imaginative world of the play (and by implication in the imagination of the writer), and the gender dynamic in the drive or narrative of the play itself. This notion of the 'gender dynamic' provides a way of looking at gender-based relations and their impact on the subject matter and themes of plays. 'Gender' thus becomes a crucial issue in any play, as important as the class, race, geographical location of the play, and its action and relationships. It affects the focus of the play, its narrative drive, its representational priorities; above all, its themes and meanings, what the play says as well as what it does. It enables us to make sense of the ways in which public/private worlds, personal/political issues are represented on stage. I also developed the notion of 'feminist dynamics' from *Understudies* into a more rigorous conceptual framework, in order to provide a way of analysing and evaluting the way women playwrights were using different forms to explore women's experiences, their relationships to one another, to men and to their world. The aim of this was to connect political ideology (conscious or not) with imaginative realisation, going beyond the linearities of 'plot' or the one-dimensional messages of what individual characters 'said' or 'did', to the structural dynamic of the work, its form and its overall argument and message(s).

Since these two books were written, the attention paid to the relationship between gender and theatre has developed almost beyond recognition. Performance and gender studies sprinkle the academic field. More forgotten plays by women writers have been published. A few more contemporary women playwrights are now a fixed part of the theatrical map. Much exciting theory has explored the relations between gender and performance, and the complex process of signification to which the male/female body gives rise on stage. Most of the theory has inevitably come from women (and some men) working in academia, with a scattering of texts from women theatre practitioners – the latter tending to consist of experiential interviews or commentaries, the former engaging in theoretically contextualised exegesis. The discourses of semiotics, psychoanalysis, reception theory, analyses of the theatre industry, film theory are all immensely stimulating and provocative. This has revealed an interesting conundrum, which I believe is to do not only with the different priorities of academia versus theatre practice, but also with a fundamental question about the nature of text.

This book unabashedly repositions the written text at the centre of play analysis. In order not to be misunderstood, I want to emphasise that non-text-based (or partially text-based) theatre can be (and often is) exciting, innovative, challenging to unspoken/unconscious assumptions, can shock and please, can move and challenge. A greater understanding of the meanings generated by the onstage signs can enhance theatrical pleasure and illuminate drama.

However, I am concerned that the proliferation of performance studies, and the love affair which theatre academics inevitably have with live performance, should not collapse the written text into just one feature among many. The pressure to come up with the 'new' can gravitate frighteningly quickly from description via theory to prescription. To overstate my position: the fundamental meanings generated by a written play text remain the same, irrespective of the what and how of the performative realisations. It is a complex, political and theoretical imperative within the academy to argue for the study of 'performance' as a valid and serious subject, for 'drama' and 'theatre' to be seen as complementary to each other. In the immediacy of the moment of live performance the two appear to be enmeshed as one, but the reality is that there is always also the existence of the written text as a discrete entity; discrete in a way which the performance can never be.

This is clear as soon as one tries to pin down what performance actually is. Is it the first time a piece is played to an audience? Is it the video of the stage performance, which itself is at least at one remove and is no longer live theatre? Which performance anyway, since each one will be subtly different? Is 'performance' in the imagination of the reader? In the imagination of the audience? And so it goes on. Are we eventually dealing in meanings which will emerge from statistical surveys, answers to questionnaires? Meanwhile the text is published, and the 'performance' goes on to have many lives. Of course, this is precisely what is so exciting about live performance, and why we must constantly try to pin it down, but we must also realise that this will never be possible, not in the way in which a text can be identified, and then argued over.

This is not an argument for old-fashioned 'study' of the text, exclusively away from the stage. In fact, it derives partly from my own experiences as a performer, with the knowledge of how much detailed care and work goes into exploring the text before, during and after rehearsal. No significant decisions about how to realise a play on stage can be made before the play is understood, and the source for that is the text, the cultural sources to which it refers, and then the text again. Texts must therefore be 'read' on the page as well as 'read' into the performance process, and then 'read' again by the audience. Inevitably, the process of understanding is also, to some extent, ongoing: during rehearsals, and even in actual performances, new nuances of meaning can strike performers and audience, but always within an already established conceptual context.

The text is not merely a 'blueprint' for performance. It is the starting point, and it remains after the live performance is done. It exists as a literary text in its own right, available for analysis and argument and debate as to its meanings. This text demands special ways of reading; it has its own special internal conditions. It consists primarily of dialogue, which itself constitutes interaction in the moment. I have taught playwrighting workshops for many years, and one of the hardest things to convey and internalise is the understanding that theatre 'happens' between the lines, as it were, in the space where the inter-action happens between the voices/characters. Thus to be able to 'read' a play involves coming to terms uniquely with an understanding of subtext, of what is not 'said', but is conveyed emotionally in inter-action, in the actions (emotional, historical and physical) of the play.

Central to this process of understanding is the contradiction between the two simultaneous time schemes which confront us in the theatre. The play runs in real time – i.e., between 7.30 and 10 p.m. – but its own internal time can span millennia, dart around in history and geography, or enter the surreal. We make sense of this contradiction via the suspension of disbelief which enables the process, but also because in some way we enact the 'sense' of the play by being guided by its narrative, a narrative that is centrally defined as a cumulative relationship between cause and effect.

Every play, I would contend, no matter what its form, realistic or surreal, reveals a dominant narrative drive, simply by virtue of being sequential in time. This may sometimes contradict the 'real' theatrical time within the play, but the experience of watching a play in finite, real clock time means that there will always be some sequence of events which asserts narrative. Even when the stage time darts backwards and forwards, we still reconstruct it for ourselves as sequential. The play tells some kind of sequential story, it makes connections between cause and effect, some explicit, some subtextual. It is the sum of these that constitutes what it 'says' about the experiences/ themes it represents. This will operate in performance, just as it operates in the reading of the text on the page. Productions can always show texts in new lights, with new interpretations, but there is a limit to how far one can stray from the basic template of meaning. It has to be a very rare production indeed which can overturn the dominant, structural drives of a play's narrative and meaning. I should stress here that this is irrespective of the play's form. Within recent writing there has been some debate about whether realism is an inherently 'reactionary' form, and (implicitly) whether simply challenging linear, realistic narrative is the only way to write radical, critical plays. This is obviously an untenable position. It has been clear to me from the early 1970s onwards that there are no absolute ideological conclusions to be drawn about a play's meanings based on form alone. This underpins the historical and analytical writing from the first edition of *Understudies* (1981), through my other critical writing and in my own plays for theatre and radio.

The debates about form will doubtless continue to run; but my analyses of the plays, which range over a wide variety of manipulations of stage conventions (theatrical form) are predicated on the theoretical premise and practical experience that it is content which determines form. 'Content' here refers to choice of subject matter, the playwright's point of view as refracted through an analysis of the play's dominant meanings. 'Form' refers to the historical conventions which identify the means with which the content is built, argued (emotionally as well as rationally) and structurally framed. It follows, therefore, that it does not matter whether a play is 'Brechtian', naturalistic, surreal or performance art; it will still consist of an 'argument', a point of view, a 'message'. It is the *how* of it which a sound analysis yields.

Theatrical productions will always be shaped by the structural imperative of the play. The 1999 revival of John Osborne's *Look Back in Anger* at London's National Theatre is an interesting case in point. Ignoring most of the stage directions (in my view always a valid step, and one which most directors take anyway), the final scene had Alison returning, beating Jimmy with her fists and, instead of the couple clasping each other at the end, playing their game of bears and squirrels, the final lines were spoken with the two at a cool distance, facing away from one another, weary, exhausted. The sense at the end was of a couple together again, but with Alison for the first time expressing real anger, and thus implying that the apparent reconciliation was not an entirely happy one. Ambiguity was introduced in the physical action accompanying the texted dialogue, which remained the same.

The introduction of ambiguity of this kind (as in the way various productions of Shakespeare's *The Taming of the Shrew* have tried to subvert the representation of Katherine) may appear to make the play's 'case' less clear-cut, but with all the dialogue and drive of the text intact, no more than a slight ambiguity can be introduced, and this is merely an extension of the artistic licence of any director. The most that a director and cast can do – exciting as this may be – is to raise a possible question about the couple's future, or suggest that Katherine is resisting the inevitable submission towards which her written fate drives her. In itself this is a step of major artistic gender-awareness, but it can never turn the play's meanings upside-down. New plays are needed for that.

How the textual meanings are read is, of course, a product of the reading imagination/interpretation. My approach derives from a grounding in Leavisite textual analysis from the 1950s and 1960s, recast in the (en)light(enment) of Marxist-feminist thought about the relationship between culture, the individual, history and society in the 1970s, with parts gleaned from structuralism, semiotics and anything else that has sparked into view since, and an overwhelming passion for the quicksilver moment of the experience of live performance, in which the meticulously prepared can paradoxically play hostess to the spontaneous. At the risk of being accused of eclecticism (which I would take as a compliment), I happily inhabit twin worlds, in which the dramatic text, as the subject of this book, is knowingly held in suspension in relation to the living excitements and complexities, unpredictable discoveries, which happen during the creation of a piece of live performance. I am, if you like, a reconstituted Leavisite, a radical traditionalist, an untraditional radical. I should add that I have seen every play discussed in this book at least once.

There is one final cautionary comment. The theatre has a relatively high profile in the dramatic arts, and radio and television relatively low profiles. Only playwrights who have made a career in the theatre are taken seriously, as part of the literary landscape. There are occasional rare exceptions – the television dramatist, the late Dennis Potter, for example. Very few playwrights actually manage to make a continuous career in the theatre, and we have to be aware that we are discussing a very pressurised and preciously small number of playwrights in any given period. Theatre audiences are statistically tiny, yet we have to take these playwrights seriously, since it is from this small number that the contemporary canon is formed, plays receive repeat productions, get filmed, shown on television, are on examination syllabuses, and are therefore read and performed, and so on. Theatre continues to be at the cutting edge of exploration, experiment, and nothing can ever replace the special excitement of the live theatrical event.

I find myself in a series of recurring contradictions. I recognise the vitality of the unpublished, undocumented theatre. Along with many other women and men, I have hopefully contributed to a process of documentation which helps include this work in histories and books. As part of this process, I am aware of being part of, intervening in, both journalistic critical writing and broadcasting, and academic publications. To this end, and because I think we must constantly re-examine our given canons, all the plays chosen for this book have been published, and most would, I believe, be considered part of our contemporary canon. They thus fall into the category of 'high art' radical, contemporary drama, beginning from the post-war watershed of 1956, through the abolition of theatre censorship in 1968, the post-Thatcher years after 1979, into the 1980s and 1990s and up to the turn of the twenty-first century.

I should explain my own attitude to the concept of the canon: wary is how I would best describe it. I am not alone; any writer interested in the under- and misrepresentation of social groups understands very well the relative partiality of the canonic tip of the iceberg. As a playwright, I know only too acutely how the decision-making process works, and how contemporary plays progress into history and therefore towards some kind of hierarchical ordering. Artistic directors make decisions about which playwrights are commissioned, and then which plays are produced. Publishers then decide which plays are worth publishing.

These decisions are likely to coincide with links between certain theatres and publishers, the status of that theatre in the profile of the arts, and whether it gets widely reviewed in the national press. Not surprisingly, three theatres front this process: the Royal Court, the Royal Shakespeare Company and the Royal National Theatre. It can never be stressed too heavily that our contemporary theatre is *not* a writers' theatre (though paradoxically it is known by its writers), but a *directors'* theatre. They are the decision makers, more or less at the mercy of the imperatives of the commercial versus subsidy battle for survival.

However, that is, pragmatically, what we have to deal with. The best-known, high-profile plays are the ones most likely to be reviewed, be seen and then receive further productions. It is therefore these plays which demand our attention; their process of canonisation demands our analysis, as does our challenge to this canon, by publishing other plays, by documenting other kinds of challenging theatre, by making spaces for new voices of all kinds. Critiques of the canon are responding to the challenge of what is taken to be the typical excellence of our theatrical culture. Commentary should never dismiss these plays, since they become embedded in our imaginations and form the way we think and imagine anew.

In this book I have deliberately chosen not to present a lightning tour of nearly half a century of British drama, by briefly summarising the *oeuvres* of individual playwrights, with a phrase or two for each important play. Nor have I analysed the entire output of a selected number of playwrights – this work is far better done in monographs and biographies. Each play is analysed in terms of the way content and form engage with the play's theme(s), to focus particularly on the way that what it is 'about' is crucially entirely contingent on the imperative of gender, as well as the gender dynamic.

I have chosen a series of exemplary texts, high-flying case studies, exemplary moments in the history of post-war British drama. Inevitably someone's favourite play or playwright will be omitted. Of course, books such as this help confirm the contemporary canon. The play which most people discuss becomes the play which most people know, becomes . . . and so on. But my aim is critical in the best sense of the word, and interventionist. If we can see these plays in new lights, we can also be enlightened about what our theatre needs.

The analysis demonstrates how the imperative of gender in the writer's imagination (conscious or not) shapes the gender dynamic in the play itself, and how this is one of the determinants of plot, storyline, interrelationship, theme and outcome. Most pragmatically, this is reflected in the way men and women are represented in plays, why it is crucial that they *are* men and women (male and female), and in the way the family and sexuality (sexualities) have been reflected in our contemporary drama.

This is all the more intriguing, as the gamut of work from which I am choosing has been created during a time when all writers (even when they see themselves as individually apolitical) have been working with the post-Brechtian consciousness of the relationship between the individual and society. When this is joined with one of the most important slogans taken up by feminism, that 'the personal is political', we have an intriguing overarching question about the drama of the past fifty years. In the process of politicisation to which the theatre has been subject since the 1950s, what has happened to the 'personal'? How have the self-styled radicals among our playwrights interpreted the 'political' in the imaginative worlds of their plays?

In discussing only about forty plays out of the thousands written and produced in the past fifty years, I am defining what I think are the dominant trends among playwrights, most of whom theatres and critics have considered most important, and therefore I am suggesting an ideology which, while it does not amount to a 'school' of thought, is certainly an imaginative trend, a pattern of dominant theatrical representation. My main conclusions about these trends, which surprised me in the first version of *Look Back in Gender*, have not changed fundamentally, but I hope that the revision of the contexts of this work, the additional plays discussed and the tone of the text will reinvigorate the insights for anyone interested in the rich heritage of our theatre in the second half of the twentieth century.

Part I

Chapter 1

The imperative of gender

Orlando's tea-party

> The sound of the trumpets died away and Orlando stood stark naked. No human being, since the world began, has ever looked more ravishing. His form combined in one the strength of a man and a woman's grace.
>
> Orlando had become a woman – there is no denying it. But in every other respect, Orlando remained precisely as he had been. The change of sex, though it altered their future, did nothing whatever to alter their identity. Their faces remained, as their portraits prove, practically the same. . . Many people . . . holding that such a change of sex is against nature, have been at great pains to prove 1) that Orlando had always been a woman, 2) that Orlando is at this moment a man.
>
> (*Orlando* by Virginia Woolf, 1928)

The story of Orlando is the tale of a person who spends the first half of his life as a man. With the godlike sleight of hand of the novelist, Virginia Woolf waves her magic words and Orlando becomes a woman for the second half of her life. This new life (Orlando is not a transsexual in our modern sense) would remain mere fairy-tale fantasy were it not for the claim that despite the 'change of sex', 'Orlando remained precisely as he had been. The change of sex, though it altered their future, did nothing whatever to alter their identity'.

Here we have the classic nature-versus-nurture nexus in a nutshell; and a pretty big nutshell at that. A pretty big nexus as well. Woolf's contention is that whether Orlando is labelled 'male' or 'female' according to mere biological characteristics, his or her social character, feelings, desires and actions remain almost the same. For her, biology is by no means everything, and indeed, as far as intellectual and creative capacities go, irrelevant. Woolf's imagination has often been collapsed into the notion of 'androgyny', the idea that somewhere there is a kind of being which transcends gender, or a person who is made up of a mixture of 'masculine' and 'feminine' characteristics (not a totally original idea, since philosophies of yin and yang, and even Jungian ideas, embody the same desire to come to terms with the vexedness of such gendered and apparently oppositional categories). It seems to me that one can just as well use Orlando as the starting point for a very different kind of understanding of the nature of gender-based difference. It is possible to be both biologically gendered (indeed, impossible not to be!), and to explore and interrogate the interface between biological givens and the social constructs of gender within which we all live (differently in different cultures).

Such an approach is provocative and inspiring. It implies that in principle (as well as in reality) there need be virtually no limits to the imaginative capacities of men and women. Whatever the biological differences, social and cultural being admits of a variety of possibilities, uninhibited by biological determinism. In social and political terms, however, this is still a revolutionary thought. To take one crucial example: women give birth, women breast-feed. Although men are fathers, their physiological investment is relatively minor; but this does not mean (and never has exclusively meant) that women are incapable of a variety of work occupations alongside motherhood, nor that men are emotionally or practically incapable of loving and nurturing a child. We can talk of visions of a world in which alongside biological differences of various kinds (procreation, strength, health), systematic and oppressive exploitation and oppression on grounds of gender alone are eliminated.

Somehow, however, this visionary possibility must be balanced with the knowledge that, like it or not, we are each contextualised in our lives, and are necessarily (among other things) socially male or female. This is one of the fundamental starting points in how we experience the world, how we are part of it, and how we imagine with and away from it. In terms of drama, some of the burning questions relate to how possible it is to 'imagine' being, feeling, what it is to function, as a member of the opposite sex. Out of this come issues such as whether men can 'write' women, or women 'write' men. In principle, of course, no writer needs to have lived every experience about which he or she writes, but in practice the point of departure is not quite so apocalyptic, as we shall see from this analysis of post-war British drama.

The imagination is – to stretch a point from Karl Marx – both every-where in chains (to its material roots), and everywhere free. Social customs – censorship, self-limitation – both compound the challenge and difficulty of re-imagining what is, and imagining or suggesting what might be. To even begin to think about this is to acknowledge that large changes need to be made in our social and gendered division of labour. Within our current social structures an equalising participa-tion in the world of work and family are made as difficult as possible. Maternity and paternity leave are still largely minimal, and childcare facilities and encouragement of the division of labour within families is negligible. It costs money, it implies a fundamental shift not just in the mind-set of working life, but also in notions about the family and the social and sexual division of labour, both emotionally and practically.

We know that in all cultures, at all times, being born male or female implies the possibility of certain social roles, and carries with it assump-tions about feelings and identity. The division of labour based on gender shifts across cultures and across time, but it is fundamentally and historically rooted in (but not necessarily ultimately determined by) differences about which we still argue. Are men and women different and equal? Are men and women different and unequal? Or a bit of both? Is it all genetic? Is it all social? Is it a bit of both? Where does the power lie? Do men and women become custodians of different kinds of social and emotional power? Do we like it as it is? Do we want to change it? If so, how much? And how?

We can see from this how profoundly political Virginia Woolf's *Orlando* is by implication. To enter fully into her imaginative world and allow it to influence ours, we must take on board these very basic questions about gender and the way gender (aspects of maleness and femaleness) is represented in art. By doing so, we acknowledge that gender roles are as much about power relations as are those of class, race and social position, and with this acknowledgement comes the exciting prospect of investigating and understanding how the gender dynamic works in the imagination. Here the world of the imagination means the world of drama.

To be or nor to be (gendered)

> . . . there is nothing either good or bad, but thinking makes it so.
> (*Hamlet*, Act 2, Scene 2)

Imagine that Hamlet is a woman. I don't mean imagine an actress playing the part of Hamlet, à la Sarah Bernhardt, and adequately filling both
breeches and the character's tragic emotional range. I mean, imagine
what would happen if Shakespeare's play was called *Hamlette, Princess
of Denmark*, where the central character does an Orlando and becomes
a woman. The text remains the same, except that where relevant, pronouns are changed from 'he' to 'she', from 'him' to 'her'. This is a relatively simple matter, since English is not a gendered language, but if we
do this, what happens to our understanding of the play, our assumptions
and its meanings?

In Act 1, Scene 1, the ghost of Hamlette's father appears with an
important message. Here the change of sex nudges the beginnings of
a question about historical relationships between men and women.
Hamlette is obviously on very comfortable terms with the soldiers.
Let us assume that she has always been a tomboy, that she has grown
up with them. They know each other well, and she is the only person
– indeed, the most relevant person – with whom they can communicate
about the ghost.

In Act 1, Scene 2, Hamlette is asked by her mother and uncle/
stepfather not to return to her studies in Wittenberg. It is clear that
Hamlette is upset at the way her mother has remarried so quickly,
thus betraying the memory of her father. When the line 'Frailty, thy
name is woman' comes, its impact is modified by the fact that a
woman is generalising about her own sex. When spoken by a man,
it could read as an accusation (ironic, perhaps, in view of the male
Hamlet's later vacillations); when spoken by a woman, it might add a
tinge of fearful anticipation – i.e. if all women are frail, and her
mother is frail, might Hamlette not fear such frailty in herself as well?
Social assumptions about frailty being a female characteristic are
tapped in different ways, depending on whether they are about a man
or a woman, spoken by a man or a woman, to a man or a woman.

Social assumptions about gender are further highlighted when
Hamlette confers with fellow students Marcello and Horatio. Further
vital questions about historical accuracy arise. First of all, there was
no 'real' historical figure called Hamlette, unless we can discover a
lost Holinshed chronicle which has the alternative story. Second, at
the time when the play is set, only men studied at universities. If royal
women were educated, they were tutored in private, and then largely
according to a code which prepared them for regal wifehood, not
combat, courtiership and politics. The friendship, loyalty and camaraderie between Hamlette and Horatio is absolutely central to the

story, and we have to ask why Shakespeare is flouting social convention, and showing a woman whose relationship to the world conforms more to male than female social behaviour.

After all, one would expect Hamlette to have been brought up more like Ophelia – reading, singing and embroidering, rather than studying and sword-fighting. Thus we have a play in which a woman is being groomed for the throne, whose intellect is formally trained, and who, if she partakes in 'manly' activities, has to dress like a man. Unlike figures in other Shakespeare plays, Hamlette does not cross-dress as a disguise, but simply in order to do the job. We do not know, of course, whether during her time off she reverts to wearing women's clothes. Does all this mean that the play leans towards satire, allegory, political subversion? Or, if it is dealing in cross-dressing, is it then one of the comedies?

In Act 1, Scene 3, the issue of gender takes on explicit – and daring – sexual implications. Laertes and Ophelia discuss Hamlette and her supposedly fickle affections for Ophelia. Clearly, when Hamlet is a man, heterosexual marriage and the question of a successor to the throne become vital. However, if it is Hamlette who has a relationship with Ophelia, we have (1) an actual or potential lesbian relationship, and (2) a society in which this is seen as the norm, since no one objects to the relationship on these grounds. There is thus a problem about a successor to the throne of Denmark. If, however, 'love' between Hamlette and Ophelia is that of a same-sex intense and non-sexual friendship (along Hamlet/Horatio lines), then the tensions which follow are not involved with matters of marriage and succession, but of friendship and some kind of real or imagined betrayal. Or, to follow the 'frailty' theme, and take a psychoanalytic tack, Hamlette is displacing on to Ophelia her own ambivalence at being a woman.

In Act 1, Scene 4, the ghost urges Hamlette to avenge the murder of her father by her uncle. A woman is entrusted with the honourable and onerous task of setting a corrupt state to rights, and exacting justice for personal moral transgression. Hamlette is that unusual female heroine, a woman in line for political power, entrusted with consequent moral and ethical dilemmas. She stands out as female in a historical line-up which is overwhelmingly male. As a tragic heroine she is very different from, say, Sophocles' Antigone. The latter's dilemmas and actions are conceived as personal; she chooses to avenge the injustice meted out to her brother. Antigone is defending personal honour, not purging the state of a political corruption which has led to instability. She is a member of the ruling class, but she does not rule and does not want to rule. She is a custodian of moral conscience (a common use of women in plays both ancient and modern), not of realpolitik. Hamlette, on the other hand, carries the dimension of personal moral conscience (how to avenge her father), but she does so as a potential king (queen), and her actions therefore have greater overall portent, straddling both the personal and the political, the private and the public.

One could continue through the play and analyse the gender reversals at every moment (which would have to happen if these ideas were applied to a real production), but the main point has been made. Keep the text exactly as it is, change the gender of the main figure and therefore the occasional pronoun, and we have altered the meanings created on the basis of assumptions about history, society and gender contained in the text. We are challenging not only the knowledges and ideologies from which Shakespeare wrote the play, but also those of our own time. It goes – almost – without saying that staging the play on the basis of the above modifications would have to produce relevant performative interpretations.

There are, however, certain limits to these imaginative parameters. If the text remains the same, the attributes of gender (expansive and confining at the same time) are likely to strain at the edges. At the very least, Hamlette is a woman in a man's world, involved in an ambiguous and anguished relationship with another woman, destined for queenship since there is no visible male successor, and challenged to prove her validity for the job by avenging her father's murder. It is fortunate that the other characters are not aware she is a man, or she might have been punished for seeking to step outside her given social role. Of course. That's it. Hamlette is really a woman who has always resented her oppression, and since her mother brought her up as a boy, and therefore a more valid heir to the throne, she is a cross-dressing heroine whose anguish is always private and inner, since no one else must know that she is really a woman. Only Gertrude knows the real truth – hence the painful scene between mother and daughter.

At this point the playwright in me has already taken over from the critic. How does the play end now? With reconciliation between the two women? Telling the court the truth, whereupon they cheer the prospect of having such an honourable queen, who then forges an alliance with Fortinbras? Perhaps she even marries Fortinbras, thus linking nations and families in a right royal tradition. To do this, of course, Hamlette would have to remain alive at the end of the play – and here the imaginative exercise of transformation reaches beyond the outer limits of the given text.

But these very limits illustrate that comprehension based on gender, testing that comprehension by reversal, quickly leads one to realise that we have to imagine a different world, with different conventions and different points of view, and therefore possibly a different text. The task in this exercise is not to rewrite Shakespeare. It is to show that, in its turn, our newly imagined world based on a reconception of gender, highlights the nature of the originally imagined world – Shakespeare's play called *Hamlet*, which, like any other play, is dependent for its creation as much on the imperative of gender as on other kinds of social and historical determinant.

The imperative of gender

> Poets must be
> Either men or women, more's the pity.
>
> (Elizabeth Barrett Browning, *Aurora Leigh*)

Gender is one of the primary imaginative imperatives. The forms of representation of the human self are influenced/determined by what we know about our lived social realities, as well as imagined possibilities. 'Characters' will be – by and large – male or female. In my playwriting classes, the issue of gender-based decisions is always fascinating and stimulating. In drama in particular, we try out different gender options in the early stages of writing. This always provokes insights for the writers: at the very least, they become usefully self-conscious about how and why they make their decisions. Inevitably, playing around with gender ascription produces different relational possibilities, different plot lines, different stresses on themes and issues, whatever the form of the play.

In prose fiction it dovetails with questions about narrative and point of view. In prose you can play around with avoiding gendered pronouns, of creating a being who could be either male or female, but the immediacy of theatre, with the presence of the body and the voice, means that the signs of gender are always more transparent: body shape, the tessitura of the voice, movement, even before the stuff of the play proper comes into it.

Cross-dressing plays with these ambiguities palpably, physically and immediately. Even if one were able to create an onstage figure whose voice and body gave no explicit clues, the look and sound would still inevitably relate to social images of male and femaleness; if you create a body with no bumps, are you simply aping the straight male shape? If you project a voice which hovers in the alto range, there will still be associations in the spectator's aural compass to relate it to a high male voice or a low male voice. We can never be free of these imperatives on either side of the footlights.

Gender attribution is hooked into the way the imagination represents social, emotional and material reality. A critical response to that reality attempts to question or subvert it, and still refer to gender. It is one of the major determinants of meaning, giving the lie to the notion that great drama, by having simply 'universal' meanings, transcends gender (and other social determinants, such as race and class).

It is certainly true that powerful drama, rooted in specific time, place and social experience, exploiting the excitement and immediacy of the theatre, can communicate to people who come from very different and varied backgrounds, but this does not mean that the supposed accolade of 'universal' should be used to deny the specificity of the imaginative. After all, just as a playwright does not need to have experienced everything about which he or she writes, neither does the spectator's life have to be a mirror image of any character. Our imaginations can project, absorb and make links with very diverse experiences, since they are all coiled around the power of the theatrical experience, and the contact between performance and audience.

Until very recently the concept of the imperative of gender has been absent from our received traditions of dramatic criticism and commentary, and yet ironically, the relationship between gender and drama has been a controversial issue from the very beginnings of theatre. Women were explicitly excluded as performers from official religious drama, from Greek drama and from the British stage until relatively recently (officially from 1660). This is a direct outcome of social and political power being primarily in the hands of men, with concomitant taboos against women appearing in public, outside the confines of family (nuclear or extended) life. It was not thought proper (indeed, it still is not in some quarters) for women to take on public roles in either politics or religion – only men could communicate with God (or gods). The occasional historical exception merely proved the rule. Anthropological research about matriarchies and cultures in which women did take more public institutional responsibility has shown that new practices, based on male dominance, took over; while knowledge about matriarchal societies may rightly fuel proof that women have ruled, it does not alter the reality of male dominance in the majority of world cultures today.

Women were therefore also officially excluded from theatre, and from other arts – such as religious music. In 'high art' drama women were considered immoral if they appeared on stage (until relatively recently the terms 'actress' and 'whore' were considered to be almost synonymous). There were, of course, always exceptions: women took part in folk and prehistoric religious drama, and were involved in the Commedia dell'Arte family/theatre troupes of the Renaissance; there were women trouvères and troubadours, the plays of the tenth-century nun Hrosvitha herald the beginnings of a known tradition of women playwrights, and of course, from the latter part of the seventeenth century, women first officially acted on stage in Britain. Other women also began to make their mark as playwrights: the best known of these was the British Aphra Behn, and today a small number of women playwrights on the theatrical landscape is at least a presence. More recent research has uncovered a whole range of plays by women writers to add to our knowledge of the past – reclaiming work which has, *pace* historian Sheila Rowbotham, been 'hidden from history'.

Inevitably the presence (or otherwise) of women in theatre links with their (our) position in society as a whole. The position of women has changed considerably since the seventeenth century. Bursts of increased theatrical activity from women have tended to coincide with periods when political and social changes, alongside radical political movements, created a climate in which women could, and demanded to, participate. The Restoration, with its relatively liberal approach to the arts, helped sanction the validity (though not without moral outcry) of women's presence in the public spaces of theatre. Actresses appeared officially on stage for the first time, and women writers began to enter the arena of professional theatre. Individual women, and feminist movements since the eighteenth and nineteenth centuries, coinciding with the rise of utopian socialism and later with our modern socialist movement, have challenged the traditionally subordinate aspects of women's social roles, and theatre has taken its place as one of the institutions affected.

In the twentieth century we have witnessed two substantial waves of feminism: the suffragette movement, which finally resulted in women achieving the vote on the same terms as men in 1928, and the Women's Liberation Movement of the late 1960s to 1970s. The latter was both a part of, and a rebellion within, radical student, youth and class-based political and cultural struggles of the time.

The imperative of gender is as fundamental to the imaginative world of the play and to its meaning as historical period, class or social

position, geography (setting) and race. The gender (biological given) of
a character defines not only his or her 'sex', but also implies imaginative
assumptions about his or her place in the world and relationships,
and, as a result, the meanings which arise – as the exercise with
Hamlet demonstrates. Stage personae must necessarily be either male
or female – *pace* Elizabeth Barrett Browning. Look at the form and
gender dynamic of the piece, analyse its meaning and arguments,
discuss the theatrical, staging implications, the way bodies move in
the theatrical space, the significance of props and other stage furniture,
and the subtlety compounds. The cross-dressing and cross-ageing in
Caryl Churchill's *Cloud Nine*, a polemical and theatrically provocative
device, demonstrated this via its subversion of our gender- and age-
based expectations. This – along with the work of many others in
theatre – is merely the most recent sign of the way our gender aware-
nesses shift through history.

The home-grown British tradition of pantomime, for example, has
arguably both a subversive and reinforcing function for the imperative
of gender. It can act as a safety-valve (through exaggeration, caricature,
laughter) for worries about gender identity, and it can also demonstrate
transgression – men and women defying convention. It can also, of
course, appear to validate the worst kinds of misogyny through male
impersonation of women, mother-in-law jokes, and enhance a complex
cluster of homo-erotic responses in the female role of principal boy –
traditionally played by a woman, in a latter-day equivalent of the earlier
tradition of the 'breeches part' – women disguised as men, displaying
alternative shapely calves. Cross-dressing always in some way challenges the status quo, even if it is ultimately recouped.

An acceptance of the imperative of gender leads to a very different
approach to analysing drama. It does not exclude other kinds of
analysis. Rather, it augments them with an approach which enables
us to understand the specificity of the gender dynamic in any given
play. This in turn enables us to see whether the play is 'about' men or
women, how the play makes both distinctions and relationships
between the sexes, how it represents (in whatever form) social realities,
and, indeed, how these very social realities are realised and defined in
terms which are gendered.

The first half of this book sets up the context for post-war British
drama, with particular reference to the changes in gender roles and
expectations. Against this backdrop, plays from the 1950s and 1960s
are discussed in terms of form, content, male and female authorship.
With the abolition of theatre censorship in 1968 (represented here

by Kenneth Tynan's brilliantly acerbic piece), a new, politically up-for-grabs theatre burgeoned. A small number of the plays discussed may no longer be in print, may merely be described in books such as this, but they are vital landmarks for some of these freer imaginings, and provide a brief glimpse into the climate of sexual exploration and political analysis of the time.

Particularly significant for the second half of this book are the notions which derive from feminism. No analysis of the imperative and dynamic of gender could exist without the influences of feminism as a political movement and of the critiques and analyses generated by women engaged with feminism. Again, I provide a theatrical, cultural and political backdrop for this half of the book, along with a brief account of the different feminist dynamics to help enable an analysis of some of the plays written by women. This is particularly important, since to call every woman playwright a 'feminist' simply because she is a woman and/or writes about women may be high in feel-good celebratory factor, perhaps even in wishful thinking, but it is not analytical and does not enable us to examine in depth what is really going on in the work. It also stresses the importance of not reading off the writer's life from the work. Reading off fiction as biography is one of literary criticism's major weaknesses (sins on a bad day); at best it is interesting, important for the knowledge we have of the writer as thinker/citizen (should we stop listening to Wagner because he was anti-Semitic?), but it will never explain to anyone what the writing is actually about. The fascinating business of interviewing playwrights will tell us what they think they might be doing or have done, will tell us everything about where they think they are, but it will necessarily be inconclusive when it comes to understanding their work. Intention is, in the end, irrelevant, and the post-modernist declaration that the author is dead (*pace* Barthes) can be modified here: the author is not dead, merely somewhere else.

Ambitiously, then, this book proposes a more comprehensive way of analysing, first, contemporary drama, and second, providing the basis of a methodology for all drama, through an understanding of the imperative of gender in the imagination and the play, the gender dynamic within each play, and the relational representations of male- and female-ness in the stage world. Most dramatic texts (as we shall see) were and are authored by men, and this is enough to say that we must look at drama for what it is: we must consciously engender post-war British drama.

We cannot understand the representation of women without understanding the representation of men, and equally we cannot understand the representation of men without seeing the symbiotic links with the representation of women. This does not deny any of the more specialised theoretical developments discussed later in the book; the reverse is the case. It enables them to be incorporated and included, rather than fighting for the one true angle. The fact that this is now possible is due to the specificity of the changes in British society and culture after the Second World War.

Chapter 2

The imperative of context
Family and gender

> A generation of cultural contortionists.
> (Sheila Rowbotham, *A Century of Women*, 1997, p. 281)

After the War was over

The Labour government which came into power at the end of the Second World War, established the Welfare State, the National Health Service and through the 1944 Education Act made it possible for the first time for everyone to be able to benefit from education at all levels. The transition from war to peace also involved a major shift in gender-based employment. The fighting armed services consisted almost entirely of men – women in the armed forces taking on largely servicing roles. As a consequence, the patterns of domestic employment altered, with women working in industries which the men had left. During both world wars, women have ironically benefited in many ways, receiving extra state support, job, education, nursery and welfare opportunities denied them in the preceding peacetime.

After the war, the traditional division of labour was largely re-established, with women shunted back into the home to 'liberate' jobs for men, and men returning to take up their roles as the major breadwinners. Women, of course, did continue to work outside the home, as they always have, but the shift returned to conventional ideology and practice. The informing agenda involved reuniting families, and re-establishing the family unit as the cornerstone of personal life and social reconstruction. In many ways all these changes were genuinely revolutionary, improving the material conditions of people's lives, and creating a climate in which opportunities and aspirations could soar.

Extensive rehousing programmes created estates and blocks of flats which were more spacious and had more amenities than pre-war housing stock. However, at the same time, there were other, disruptive consequences. The closeness and security of many working-class communities were eroded, and extended families no longer lived close to one another. This had important implications, not only for the day-to-day relationships within communities and extended families, but also for ideas about privacy, and the nature of the home to which everyone could aspire.

New technological consumer affluence brought many labour-saving devices: vacuum cleaners, fridges, more efficient stoves and so on. Matching advertising campaigns emphasised the self-sufficiency of each family unit, and one of the effects of this, while making housework easier, was to isolate each individual woman at the centre of her family unit. The modern nuclear family had come fully into being. Even here, the conventions became that work within the home, the domestic maintenance, was done by the woman, and the outside, the structural maintenance, by the man.

These new patterns of family life generated ideologies to match. Although the reality was that large numbers of women still worked outside the home (effectively doing two jobs, one at home and one outside), women's magazines went into overdrive during the 1950s, extolling domestic craft skills and the virtues of the feminine wife and mother. In particular, graduate women were the object of a barrage from psychologists and the media on the ideals of wife and motherhood as an alternative 'career' for the educated woman, in which she not only nurtured her children in time-honoured fashion, but also acted as informal educator. Helping your child to play with educational toys and to learn to read at an early stage were all part of the new liberal maternal skills encouraged in mothers during the late 1950s and early 1960s.

At the same time, new scientific advances in improved forms of contraception meant that women were no longer as inevitably tied to child-bearing roles as their mothers had been. Whereas for men sexual pleasure and procreation had always more easily been separate options, for the first time women were approaching a situation where those options could become a biological and social reality for them too. The 'Swinging Sixties', as the decade was labelled, had many of its cultural roots in Britain, and really did make it possible for women to have more sexual freedom than before, and therefore potentially more sexual power.

For men, wartime service had meant they had to look after themselves, effectively acquiring 'domestic' skills if they did not already have them, developing a nurturing element alongside the more macho heroic image of the soldier. In Britain, two years of military National Service continued to be compulsory for men until the end of the 1950s. The experiences of fighting, the trauma alongside the heroism involved in enacting the realities of national defence, were then subject to adjustments when men returned home. After such a long period at war, with the entire population geared towards a war economy, and with survival at both individual and national level, death, injury, material hardship permanently part of life, the changes to peacetime were certainly a relief, leading to new and better lives. People no longer lived at the point of everyday crisis but allowed new aspirations, which in their turn generated new conflicts.

By the end of the 1950s the impact of a post-war economic boom was evident. With the expansion of higher education, new professional groupings were expanding and being created. An increase of mass consumer goods brought a mass-distributed culture, from television, the cinema and rock and roll, much of it heavily American influenced. A new consumer group – young people – wanted its own pleasures, its own culture, and increasingly, its own lifestyles.

The changes, as has been noted, were in some ways paradoxical. For example, images of sexuality and the family were very often in conflict with one another. The cosy, safe sexuality of family life represented in women's magazines and much popular culture was contrasted with a more aggressive kind of extra- or pre-familial sexuality represented by the American *Playboy* magazine, with its pneumatic female pin-ups, and its appeal to a new kind of male-imaged reader – affluent, virile, fast-living. The conflict was there both for men and women, although with different social and political consequences for each.

The apparent comfort of the new consumerism evolved against the backdrop of threats to world peace in the form of the nuclear deterrent. The Campaign for Nuclear Disarmament (CND) and the university-based New Left, which were both founded during the 1950s, reflected a political concern for more than material, local lifestyle improvement. CND, campaigning for nuclear disarmament to ensure world peace, while initiated by people in positions of some social authority, soon drew its membership from the working classes and lower-middle classes. The New Left initiated a renewed interest in Marxist theory, drawing on European writing while pin-pointing the contradiction between the so-called liberal values of a society which created aspirations in its young, only to dampen them by expecting intellectual professionals to slot into a bureaucratised and technologised capitalism.

On a more personal front, the changes were acknowledged by increasing debates about sexuality, the family and individual choice. In 1974, the Finer Report commented retrospectively on some of these issues:

> The 1950s and 1960s witnessed the cumulative removal of customary and legal restraints on certain forms of sexual behaviour, and upon their public portrayal in print or by the visual arts or for commercial purposes. Legal restrictions on the freedom of married people to escape from the bonds which used to be defended as essential safeguards for the integrity of monogamous marriage have been relaxed, and the sexual freedom of men and women has been enlarged.
>
> (Vol 1, 1974, p. 7)

However, in time-honoured fashion, aspects of the law were lagging behind practice and demand. It took until the late 1960s for state reforms to go through, acknowledging the changes already happening in people's lives. In 1967 an Abortion Act and an Act partially legalising male homosexuality were passed (female homosexuality has never been illegal – popular myth has it that when the first anti-homosexual legislation was passed in 1885, Queen Victoria was so horrified at the mere thought of lesbianism that she refused to believe it existed, and therefore could not be made illegal). In 1969 the Divorce Reform Act eased conditions for divorce, and in 1970 the Equal Pay Act proposed that equal pay for men and women should become a reality by the end of 1975. This still has not happened, and is compounded by the complexity that where jobs are defined as 'women's' jobs, the base pay levels still tend to be particularly low anyway.

The signs of growing female discontent with the contradictions of women's situation also began to surface during this time. In America, Betty Friedan wrote a book, *The Feminine Mystique*, published in 1962, identifying what she called 'the problem with no name'. Analysing and quoting from the experiences of suburban housewives, she dissected the American domestic dream, pin-pointing the symptoms of what she saw as a profound identity crisis for women. In Britain, sociologist Hannah Gavron conducted research on housebound working- and middle-class mothers. The results were published in 1966 under the title *The Captive Wife*. The book explored the boredom, isolation and frustration women felt in their materially comfortable cocoons.

Inevitably, advances, tensions and contradictions in personal life were reflected in, and responded to, in fiction. In post-war British drama this spurred the beginnings of a change in the way the family was represented in the standard West End theatre play. John Elsom, in his book *Post-War British Theatre* (1979), commented on West End plays put on during the 1950s by a consortium of theatre managements called 'the Group': 'Many new plays seemed to be set in opulent houses in Sussex and Kent. . . . The Group catered predominantly to the metropolitan, middle-class audiences' (pp. 18, 36).

However, even these plays were beginning to reflect some of the dislocations experienced in the family:

> Many comedies after the war had shown middle-class families in difficulties, either financial ones . . . marital ones or generation squabbles. . . . These problems, however, could be solved (and usually were) and they did not challenge the basis of middle-class life. The comedies of middle-class decline were not radical in the sense that they attacked the bourgeoisie from the standpoint (say) of a Brechtian Marxist, but they did present a picture of seedy snobbery, of sexual hypocrisy and of social failure unredeemed by idealism.
>
> (p. 93)

The commercial, West End theatre was only able to pay lip-service to these new social pressures, with its focus on middle-class people – a reflection also of the nature of the West End theatre audience. In other areas of theatre – and in other parts of the country – a more grass-roots theatre began to emerge. Some of those responsible for plays about ordinary, working-class people had also been involved in the left-wing theatre movements of the 1930s and 1940s – Unity Theatre, which consisted of people involved in a range of socialist ideologies, particularly the British Communist Party, was a focus for much of this work. Joan Littlewood at the Theatre Royal in Stratford, East London in the 1950s, and Peter Cheeseman at Stoke-on-Trent in the 1960s, drew in local audiences, aiming to transform the constituency of theatre from both sides of the footlights. They turned the theatre's attention to the lives and histories of ordinary people as the subject matter for drama. Cheeseman evolved a distinctive brand of documentary theatre about local people, and Littlewood developed a vibrant theatre about ordinary people, drawing on popular entertainment forms such as music-hall at Stratford, and building up local support, although regular radical theatre-goers also pilgrimed their way across London.

My own theatre-going roots straddled many of these developments, old and new. From Chingford – not an area known for the vibrancy of its artistic culture – my grammar school English teacher organised regular treks at the end of the 1950s on trains and buses across town to the Old Vic, where we perched miles up in the narrow, uncomfortable gallery and saw a fresh-faced young Judi Dench play Ophelia during the Old Vic's five-year project of presenting all of Shakespeare's plays. This lent an extra impetus to my school acting; playing Goneril in the school production of *King Lear*, I could imagine myself on the way to greater things.

Alongside this, my brother regularly took me to Stratford, to absorb Delaney, Behan and plays which rang with spontaneity and energy. Here the seats were faded red plush, the theatre badly needed paint and polish, but the excitement was undeniable. As a teenager, I had no idea that new cultural barriers were being breached; for me it was an extension of a passion for theatre which I had discovered, when, at the age of 11, I took part in a play-reading of *The Man Who Came to Dinner*, on a summer evening at the top of a hill in a village in Israel. I remember very little of the experience, except that, to evoke a sense of occasion, the producer had us all reading our parts from behind a curtain, while the audience 'listened', as if they were sitting by a radio, to a play being broadcast by the BBC.

At the cutting edge of professional theatre, the influences of Stanislavsky and Lee Strasberg's school of Method acting were loosening up the classical traditions of English performance to incorporate styles of acting rooted in naturalism, drawing on the emotional experiences of the performers, and enabling voices from all classes and regions to find a space on stage. This dovetailed with the new voices emerging in contemporary writing, and was also linked with changes in the star system still operating in West End theatre during the 1950s. The aural landscape and social class of the new theatre began to reverberate. Even though John Elsom may slightly overstate the case, the fact remains that during the 1950s and 1960s the convention of RP (Received Pronunciation) was being challenged: 'Within ten years suave actors had been replaced by rough ones as heroes, metropolitan accents by regional ones, complacent young men by angry ones, stylish decadents by frustrated "working class" anti-heroes' (*Post War British Theatre*, p. 34).

It took a little longer for the same process to affect actresses. Sheila Allen, who left the Royal Academy of Dramatic Art in 1951, noted the restrictions on actresses:

> The current heroine at that time was five foot, four inches; a sort of fluffy little blonde, light, effervescent. I was five foot seven and a half inches, and I was told at drama school that I would have problems because I was very tall. By the mid-sixties that had changed – with leading ladies like Vanessa Redgrave and Glenda Jackson, now you could be a heroine and it didn't matter so much what you looked like.
>
> (Interview with the author, quoted in *Carry On, Understudies*,
> p. 95)

At drama schools original accents were no longer exclusively ironed out into well-spoken southern cadences at the expense of other accents. However, even today, RP remains the cornerstone of mainstream performance in theatre, television and radio.

One playwright, whose influence straddled the new voices of the 1950s through to the radical drama post-1968, was Berthold Brecht. He visited London with his Berliner Ensemble in 1956, boosting the democratising approaches of people like Joan Littlewood, and also bringing the beginnings of a more deep-rooted philosophy of theatre into British thinking. In his focus on an 'epic' theatre, he redefined the nature of historical drama for the post-war period. Challenging the bourgeois theatre, with its stress on the individual hero (*sic*) and dilemmas, he asserted that theatre must develop an awareness of the individual's social and political context, making connections between individual experience and consciousness and economic and social formation.

Brecht's desire to challenge audiences to think rather than merely empathise, to question rather than passively absorb, led to his theory of 'alienation', a controversial and provocative notion which influenced styles of writing and styles of production and performance. Alienation implies a distancing from the event perceived, so as to stress under-standing and the raising of political consciousness. Whether this of itself precludes empathy, or emotional engagement, is, of course, a contentious issue, since it is undoubtedly true that Brecht's own work is as passionate (and conveys and evokes passion) as much as it provokes thought, even while it fractures the fourth wall convention, where audience and performers collude in the illusion that we are eaves-dropping on something 'real'.

It was not until after 1968 that the full theatrical implications of Brecht's work infused the new generation of theatre groups and writers. With the rediscovery of agitprop during the late 1960s, and the spate of topical political plays after the end of censorship, a critical shift came from the 'private' domestic play to the broader canvas of the 'public' play, setting the individual(s) in clearly recognisable historical and political contexts. Many of these plays were not only 'political' in con-tent – about historical events and ideas – but companies also politicised the theatre space, as it were, by representing public spaces within theatre buildings – the public represented semi-privately within the public. Thus the intermediate space of the stage became a locus where public and private could be symbolically linked through the fictional world of the play. Charting this development, and discussing how it is reflected not only historically but in the work of male and female playwrights is one of the major themes of this book.

Between the two polar theatrical opposites of the West End and Stratford East (paradoxical, because when Littlewood's work hit the headlines of success, plays were then transferred to West End theatres) stood the Royal Court Theatre in Sloane Square. Here George Devine led the English Stage Company, which was responsible for much of the radical new writing and directing during the 1950s and 1960s. Here too, other kinds of European drama appeared during the 1950s: the bleak post-war world of Samuel Beckett (writing in French and English), alongside the absurdist Ionesco, in a melting-pot of styles and chal-lenges to middle-class realism.

My own earlier Littlewood/Shakespeare theatre-going axis was augmented at Cambridge University where undergraduate-run theatre devoured the new playwrights alongside the old: Wesker, N.F. Simpson, Ionesco and Beckett ran alongside Strindberg, Shakespeare and Congreve. Other undergraduates (male, of course) scooped up plays to produce from the Royal Court almost as fast as they were produced there. While I imagine that many of my contemporaries knew they were trawling in new waters, I was largely unaware of how radical this work was at the time; being besotted with the theatre and acting, I had no idea that I was in at the start of something new in theatre. Now I am extremely glad I was there.

Thus already during the 1950s experimentation was underway: absurdism, didacticism, working-class realism – all found voices in the work of British playwrights during this time. All these elements later fed into the mix of agitprop, performance art, theatrical experimentation and the new realism which developed after 1968. The radical drama of the post-1968 period may have had to wait until censorship was abolished, but the cast of ideas and devices was already waiting in the wings.

Public and private

> When this silly war is over
> Oh how happy I shall be
> When I get my civvy clothes on
> No more Land Army for me.
> No more digging up potatoes
> No more threshing out the corn
> We will make that bossy foreman
> Regret the day that he was born.
> (*Land Girls' Song,* quoted by Sheila Rowbotham, ibid.,
> and John Costello, *Love, Sex and War, 1939–1945,*
> Pan Books, 1986, pp. 213–14)

The first part of this book looks at plays written while theatre censorship was still in operation. It is extraordinary (and salutary) to remember that pre-production censorship continued in theatre until 1968. Censorship which controls access to films on the basis of age still operates, but only after the film has been made, post-production and pre-distribution. In the theatre, until 1968, no play could be performed until it was given approval by the office of the Lord Chamberlain. Once approved (often with specific changes stipulated to 'clean up' a script along lines elaborated in the piece by Kenneth Tynan, in Chapter 6), nothing could be changed. Clearly this made topical, spontaneous and improvised drama impossible.

After the abolition of censorship, British theatre not only came of age but literally came into its age. New theatres sprang up virtually over-night, in pub rooms, in tiny converted theatre spaces, and, with subject matter, language and form no longer liable to pre-production scrutiny and censorship, plays could be topical, improvised, and designed to shock. They were, and often they did.

While the end of censorship was the major catalyst for change, many experimental techniques and approaches had already been tested in the theatres of the 1950s and 1960s. Following the new presence of regional, working-class content and the early influences of Brecht came two other important elements: the upsurge in socialist consciousness at the end of the 1960s, and as part of and alongside it, the Women's Liberation Movement (WLM). Just as the Brechtian theatre aesthetic stressed the placing of the individual in social context (private in public), so the WLM generated analyses of the way in which so-called 'private' experiences and emotions were ideologically and culturally shaped. What happened in the bedroom and in the privacy of the home (even in the head and the senses) might be about relationships between individuals, but when those individuals were seen as part of a wider social fabric, then it could be seen that the 'personal' was, in one sense, actually 'political'.

Thus, along with all the other influences came the challenges and insights of feminism to feed into the creative tension between the 'domestic' and the 'public' play, and, by association, with the way the family is (or is not) represented. As soon as the family is addressed, issues of gender come into the foreground. The family is, after all, still the primary form of social unit, whatever we think of its ideologies, its laws and practices. Since the family is also at the centre of the ways women's complex sense of identity and life choices are constructed (Marriage or not? Sexuality in what context? To work or not to work? One job or two? Children or not? When? And so on), the representation (or not) of the family in drama becomes something of an index of the way in which personal and political interact – or do not.

The family is, of course, also the formative influence behind the ways in which male identity is constructed – issues of power and patriarchal authority, the bread-winner, what kind of fathering, etc. Charting the movement from the more domestic to the more public play over the past forty years raises interesting questions about what happens to the 'personal' in the personal–political equation. It also raises the question about whether there are different ways in which male/female playwrights tackle these issues, and if there are differences, what they are. There is a popular belief that women write domestic plays and men write political plays. We shall see whether that is indeed the case.

The function of gender is central to this dance between the public and the private, the personal and the political, the home as the nexus of privacy, and work and politics as the sphere of the public and social – the contradiction between the 'world' of women and the 'world' of men. In part, therefore, this analysis will look at the way the family, real and symbolic, parenthood and authority, real and symbolic, motherhood, real and symbolic, relationships between men and

women, real and symbolic, impact on the growing political consciousness of theatre between 1956 and the 1990s, to chart and discern
trends of development, as well as point to anomalies and gaps. The
book will also examine how notions of politics are themselves defined
by assumptions about gender.

Throughout, there is continuity in the way the imperative of gender
shapes story (plot), and the way it is structured; the nature of the
relationships in each play, with particular reference to the way the
family is represented (is it real, symbolic, whole, fractured? Is it
the site for other struggles to be played out, or is it itself under
scrutiny?). Gender and gender roles inevitably also inform the way
sexuality is represented – both actual relationships, and the function
of sexuality (straight and gay) in the fabric of the play. Between the
family and sexuality nestles the mother – actual and figurative – and
thus, also by implication, the father – actual and figurative. Parent
(mother)–child relationships become important, and therefore
pregnancy (as reality and symbol) itself becomes a significant feature.

Here too are questions about the nature of gender roles themselves –
authority, nurturing, emotional dependence, explicit, implicit. All
these derive from an urgent imaginative need to explore the new
worlds and ideas of the 1950s and 1960s, and to make sense of the
new shakedown of roles: What is it to be a 'man'? What is it to be a
'woman'? Who is asking the questions, and how does their perspective
(male or female) affect the play and its dilemmas?

As the 1950s/1960s 'parent' playwrights of the radical young things of
1968 and after, what stage worlds were created as a legacy for the post-
censorship generation? In the post-war world, who belonged and who
did not – and to what did they belong? If the world was being created
anew, who was part of the creating team and where did the power
lie? As new political and social rules changed, who was making the
rules, and how did the drama suggest ways of living in this new, shifting
world? What do these plays tell us about the relationship between the
present and our history? If all the terms are shifting, is everyone an
outsider, or are some people more outsiders than others? How is the
relationship mediated between the private/personal worlds of sexuality
and the family and the public/social world of nation and state?

All these questions hover behind the analyses of each play. I begin
with the milestone year of 1956, the year John Osborne's *Look Back
in Anger* was produced at the Royal Court Theatre in London.

Part II

Chapter 3

The 1950s

Good causes. Displacement: kitchen sink and psyche

Look Back in Anger *(1956) by John Osborne*

Look Back in Anger is set in Jimmy Porter's one-room flat in a large Midlands town. It is here that the fortunes of a group of people in exile – from London and Wales – are played out. The bed-sitting-room setting is important both realistically and symbolically. It tells us that Jimmy is young and poor, and it shows us (literally) how all the domestic functions (except lavatory and bathroom) co-exist within one space: eating, entertaining and sleeping. In cultural context, it is the antithesis of the 'drawing-room drama', in which the messier functions all happen off stage. Symbolically, as the play unfolds, this cluster of practical functions also represents the hotbed and hothouse of emotions, flung together, displaced upon one another, no longer taboo or neatly compartmentalised.

The school of theatre which this play helped generate became known as 'kitchen-sink theatre', an ironic label if ever there was one. While the kitchen sink may have been either literally or figuratively on stage, it very rarely gave rise to a narrative built round the woman one might expect to see working at it. The relationship between sink and psyche is critical to this play and to many others of the time. At one level it is a very clear class statement about the nature of the world represented on stage – no longer the drawing-room, with invisible servants working at an invisible sink. The more 'ordinary' (i.e. non-gentry) people who are the subjects of these plays shift the class bias of post-war subject matter. At another level, it is the relationship between sink, psyche and gender which is also important. Whose world, dilemmas, emotions, story, is it that we are following?

The opening scene shows us the 'household'. Jimmy and Cliff read the Sunday newspapers (sign of new luxury leisure), while Alison, Jimmy's wife, stands ironing (working). The stage directions (which tend to be fulsome in the social realist plays of the 1950s) state that Alison is ironing one of Jimmy's shirts and wearing another. Immediately she is identified as 'his'; servicing his clothes, wearing 'his' uniform and working on his behalf – ironing his clothes while he is at leisure.

The power of language – the articulacy of the newly educated post-war man (*sic*) – belong to Jimmy throughout the play. Brilliantly, performerly, exhilaratingly, of all the characters, Jimmy is the one who throughout is never lost for words, who can break into soliloquy whenever the meticulously structured play commands, can control his audience (in the play and out). Jimmy is still part of the generation which faced compulsory National Service, and from the beginning his class-based chip on the shoulder shows, as he goads Alison:

> I think I can understand how her Daddy must have felt when he came back from India. . . . The old Edwardian brigade do make their brief little world look pretty tempting. All home-made cakes and croquet, bright ideas, bright uniforms. . . . What a romantic picture. Phoney, too, of course.

Alison's family (and Alison herself) represents all that Jimmy despises in a ruling class which no longer espouses an old-style patriotism, and since that cause is dead, for Jimmy there is longer any good cause to die for. The anguish is ironic, since while Jimmy may despise their cause, he has none of his own. It is worth noting that Jimmy has no links to a broader base of solidarity. He runs a sweet stall in a market, and so is not involved in organised labour. He has no other political allegiances – not with the trade unions, or the newly successful Labour Party, or even with the Communist Party, for example, past or present. Osborne has made him (in Marxist parlance) a 'lumpen' figure, not belonging to any class, and displaced as a result.

Jimmy is, however, a man who needs a cause. Alison describes her first impressions of him:

> He'd come to the party on a bicycle, he told me, and there was oil all over his dinner jacket. It had been such a lovely day, and he'd been in the sun. Everything about him seemed to burn, his face,

the edges of his hair glistened and seemed to spring off his head, and his eyes were so blue and full of the sun . . . Jimmy went into battle with his axe swinging round his head – frail and so full of fire. I had never seen anything like it. The old story of the knight in shining armour – except that his armour didn't really shine very much.

However, displaced as Jimmy is, and with an enemy in his camp (Alison, from a class he despises), he creates his own war zone, and his own targets. His attack on the old class system and its lifestyle focuses on Alison's family, and, since she is their representative and female, on women in general. Gender conflict thus has two functions: it becomes the site for a displaced class conflict which Jimmy cannot – and need not – fight anywhere else – after all, he has the 'enemy' on his own territory. The fact that his mastery is incomplete is demonstrated by the fact that he has to keep asserting it. Second, the 'battle' with Alison is also a fight for sexual identity, for it is through her that Jimmy has the potential to feel like a 'real' man. In order to establish his manhood, he has to attack women:

> Have you ever noticed how noisy women are? . . . The way they kick the floor about simply walking over it? Or have you watched them sitting at their dressing tables, dropping their weapons and banging down their bits of boxes and brushes and lipsticks?

The military metaphor is double-edged; on the one hand it is evocative of her supposed physical roughness. On the other, however, it is part of a series of military metaphors, harking back to her imperialist relatives.

The playing out of their gender battle becomes the central dynamic of the action, with the attacks virtually all (literally) below the belt and one-way. Alison and Jimmy have been married for three years, and she tells Cliff that they did not sleep together before the wedding: 'And, afterwards, he actually taunted me with my virginity. He was quite angry about it, as if I had deceived him in some strange way. He seemed to think an untouched woman would defile him.'

Jimmy's sexual desire, coupled with his emotional vulnerability, links with his feelings about motherhood in a knot of emotional turmoil and violence that is shocking, poignant, honest and repulsive by turns, and sometimes all of these at once. There are very few plays which show masculinity/manhood in crisis with such honesty and violence.

Jimmy's apparent search for a cause even leads him towards a wistful nostalgia for the appeal of a still-taboo homosexuality:

> Sometimes I almost envy old Gide and the Greek Chorus boys. Oh, I'm not saying that it mustn't be hell for them a lot of the time. But at least they do seem to have a cause – not a particularly good one, it's true. But plenty of them do seem to have a revolutionary fire about them, which is more than you can say for the rest of us.

However, most centrally, Jimmy wants and needs Alison, sexually and emotionally. He is not unaware of his vulnerability, confessing in a rare moment of openness to her: 'There's hardly a moment when I'm not – watching or wanting you. I've got to hit out somehow.' Yet vulnerability is weakness (for a man), and Jimmy fights it off whenever it looms, transforming it into aggression. The climax of Act 1, when all Jimmy's feelings about female sexuality and motherhood coalesce, comes after a scene when Alison has told Cliff she is pregnant. The brutal dramatic irony, of which we are aware, is that Jimmy does not yet know, when he flings the following apparently unprovoked polemic at her, knowing that Cliff is listening:

> If only something – something would wake you out of your beauty sleep! (*Coming in close to her.*) If you could have a child and it would die. Let it grow, let a recognisable human face emerge from that little mass of indiarubber and wrinkles. (*She retreats away from him.*) Please, if I could only watch you face that. I wonder if you might become a recognisable human being yourself. But I doubt it. (*She moves away stunned and leans on the gas stove, down left. He stands rather helplessly on his own.*) Do you know, I have never known the great pleasure of lovemaking when I didn't desire it myself. Oh, it's not that she hasn't her own kind of passion. She has the passion of a python. She just devours me whole every time as if I were some over-large rabbit. That's me. That bulge round her navel – if you're wondering what it is – it's me. Me, buried alive down there and going mad, smothered in that peaceful looking coil. Not a sound, not a flicker from her – she doesn't even rumble a little. You'd think that this indigestible mess would stir up some kind of tremor in those distended overfed tripes – but not her!

An attack on the ruling class and discomfort at his own vulnerability are both displaced on to an attack on Alison, her female sexuality and her potential for motherhood. This becomes possible (indeed, imaginatively necessary) because they justify his fear and revulsion of her sexuality, which he experiences (from the violence of his language) as threat. From Jimmy's point of view, nearly all mothers are 'bad' anyway: Jimmy's because she never cared about him, Alison's because she is such an upper-class cow. The only mother who seems half-way decent is Hugh's mother – the person who supplied the money to help Jimmy set up his sweet stall. However, Alison has a gloss on this. When in Act 2 she has a conversation with her friend Helena (who has replaced Alison briefly in Jimmy's life), she comments (resorting again to military metaphor) on the first months of her marriage, when Hugh was still with them: 'I felt as though I'd been dropped in a jungle. . . . Together they were frightening. They both came to regard me as a sort of hostage from those sections of society they had declared war on.'

It is interesting that Jimmy appears to need an audience for his marriage: Hugh, initially, and, during the play, Cliff. Cliff treads a difficult middle way; he is cuddly and fraternally affectionate to Alison, and it is also interesting that he and Jimmy rough-house every so often in an innocent, covertly homo-erotic way. Although Jimmy describes Cliff as a 'sexy little Welshman', as far as we know Cliff has no sexual relationship with anyone, male or female. In this dislocated family, Cliff functions as a surrogate child, old enough to look after himself, asexual enough to be no threat. It is as if friendship and sexuality have to be mutually exclusive, an unresolved conflict, as Jimmy later almost articulates to Cliff, when he says: 'You're worth half a dozen Helenas to me.'

It is not until Act 3 that Jimmy fully articulates the ideological centre of the play:

I suppose people of our generation aren't able to die for good causes any longer. We had all that done for us, in the thirties and the forties, when we were still kids. . . . There aren't any good brave causes left. If the big bang does come and we all get killed off, it won't be in aid of the old-fashioned grand design. It'll just be for the Brave New-nothing-very-much-thank-you. About as pointless and inglorious as stepping in front of a bus. No, there's nothing left for it, me boy, but to let yourself be butchered by the women.

When Alison returns, she and Helena have a scene together, but the dominance of Jimmy's territorial power manifests itself with a vengeance. Just as he did in the scene between the two women earlier in the play, he plays his jazz trumpet throughout, not even allowing them to have an acoustic space of their own.

Helena leaves, refusing to collude in Jimmy's emotional world, while Alison finally capitulates to Jimmy, entirely on his terms. She confesses that she miscarried, but Jimmy has no sympathy, since he asserts that it is not his first loss. In the battle between the sexes, he still bears more scars. She has lost her child, just as he wished she would, and with this also the possibility of having other children, of becoming a real mother. Alone at last, without Cliff, she and Jimmy retrace their steps into an imaginary nursery world of bears and squirrels, in a childlike pre-sexual place where they can find some peace and rapport, and where they may never have to grow up to be parents. Or at any rate, where Jimmy may never have to confront responsibility as a father.

The play ends with Alison comforting Jimmy, her arms around him. From now on, any maternal qualities she has are for him alone. It is as if he has had to destroy (and certainly glory in the destruction of) the possibility of motherhood in her in order to gain her as a mother for himself. Because Jimmy's own mother did not love him properly, perhaps he has to find a surrogate mother rather than an adult, sexual companion. Real adult companionship remains as something only possible between men (Jimmy and Cliff), or in the sibling-like Alison and Cliff affection.

Look Back in Anger is a complex play. The narrated psyche at the centre is structurally male. We never follow Alison off stage. The single set is Jimmy's territory, and the women come and go. We do not follow their stories. We do not see Alison's response to her miscarriage, nor the reason why she comes back. The scenes between Alison and Helena, touching and delicately written, are largely about Jimmy, both because the sound of his trumpet always reminds them (and us) of his dominating presence, and because Osborne does not really 'write' the women from within their own experiences. They are only important for their relationships to Jimmy. Of course, all writing is selective, but within this convention of the individual hero-centred play, inevitably there is no space for other stories. Thus, in this instance, there can be no space for Alison's story. However, this formal limitation does not account for the way the theatrical metaphors work, with Alison as the objective correlative for Jimmy's crisis.

Because Jimmy has every crisis of male identity in the book – class – no place, or 'cause', gender identity, sexual assurance – a need for, and fear of, women – the way the family is represented takes an interesting turn. Because the setting is a home, a facsimile of the family needs to take up residence. We have the surrogate son in Cliff – son, because his life seems to revolve round Alison and Jimmy, without any evident independent dynamic of his own. When necessary, the son becomes a friend to each protagonist, but for the reconciliation at the end, he has to be dismissed. The family has worked itself out; it can only survive with a mixture of infantile sexuality, one-way mothering, and no threat of competition from other children.

This sterile and emotionally confused (and confusing) family is thus, in an emblematic way, symbolic of the uncertainties of post-war life, and the fragmentation of personal and family life; but this is a post-war life defined entirely in terms of a male identity. It is not merely that the play contains a character who has no respect for women (to call Jimmy a misogynist is too simplistic) – that is too easy a dismissal of something which is extremely powerful, both in craft and emotion. Jimmy's dilemmas are real, but they are specifically the dilemmas of a young post-war male. By the very way in which the play is structured, the gender bias of its hero is reinforced. This is a virtue, because of the play's clarity and power, but it cannot in any way be considered as a general statement about post-war angst because of the way in which Alison is imagined: as symbolic of the defeat of the old class, and as realistically defeated in order that Jimmy may survive and acquire some kind of identity.

The imaginative process of inventing Jimmy Porter has necessarily involved inventing a woman who has little stage identity in her own right (even though it may be a 'good part' to play). (In more traditional terms, one might say that Alison does not have a 'fully rounded character' – but character exists only in relationship, which is why I phrase it rather differently.) Alison does, of course, have a kind of strength – not giving up on Jimmy, understanding his needs, able to respond to them – but at the expense of (in terms of the play) her own gendered identity as a mother in her own right, and her own emotional space to express this crisis. Jimmy thus not only controls her class basis (on his territory), but also her sexual being and what she is 'allowed' to feel. He is her author. She can be sexual and motherly, but only to him. If she has any agony or conflict as a result of this, we never know about it; and of course, by implication, the family itself is therefore in crisis, since it can produce no children. This post-war world can see its own end. Peacetime is still a battleground, its site that of the nuclear family.

Men, authority and the state

Waiting for Godot *(1955) by Samuel Beckett*

Samuel Beckett's play was, of course, written before *Look Back in Anger*. *En Attendant Godot* was originally written in French and produced in Paris in 1953, before Beckett himself 'translated' it into English. It was performed in London in 1955. The new realism represented in the post-war working-class novel had its dramatic counterpart in the 1950s in plays such as *Look Back in Anger*. Beckett brings the abstraction of the post-war French avant-garde on to the stage, and, because of his bilingual authorship, signals the importance of continental influences on new writing and production.

Waiting for Godot has generated an enormous amount of debate, central to which is the question of meaning – in simple terms, what it might be 'about', beneath its seemingly abstract nature. As we shall see in Pinter (more realistically delineated than in Beckett), issues about authority, the state and power begin to come into question in post-war drama; in Beckett these questions are at their most abstract, and it is interesting to explore the function of gender within the apparent limbo of his stage world.

Godot's universe is all-male – the cast of five are all referred to by male pronouns. No location is specified. It could be a post-nuclear landscape; it could be the world of the homeless; it could be a symbolic world on to which we each inscribe our own associations. However, there are some carefully stated clues; first, the all-male environment. Second, four of the cast (not the Boy) wear bowler hats. The iconography of these hats (and later where they exchange hats in a ritualistic game) points to an ambience in which the city gent, or the faceless bureaucrat, symbolised by his hat and suit, prevail. Third, the circular, repetitive structure of the play. Everyone is waiting for Godot who never arrives. Characters say they are going to leave and then do not, or cannot. They are caught in this world, fated to continue in a ritualised and bewildering series of 'turns'.

The external rationale for their being there is open to interpretation; I suggest that the context of this stage world is the post-war political state. Is it beneficent? Is it threatening? Are its officials our servants or our masters (*sic*)? The concept of the 'state' is an abstract one, even though it exists in terms of political reality, as a result of a democratic process in which we have all participated. Somewhere between the sense of democratic process which belongs to us all, the procedure of voting and the setting up of the bureaucratic apparatus, the 'men' who run it have become faceless, anonymous, and in the course of this process, the rest of us are mere ciphers, bewildered and dislocated. If we are male, that is. Men speak to men, about men.

What is left? Well, in a sense, everything. What is left is relationship – and *Waiting for Godot* is about men trying to find comradeship, to create a social structure for themselves with meaning. The relationships can only emerge from a culture of which the characters are already a part; thus Estragon and Vladimir mirror some of the symbiotic relationships of marriage. They do not know why they are together, but they do know they cannot live without one another. Pozzo and his servant Lucky exemplify a more traditional master–slave relationship, in which Lucky, because he is treated like an animal, to all intents and purposes becomes one. The play has no consciousness within itself of its own history, and everyone is therefore an outcast, clinging on to the semblances of relationships which come from somewhere else. The 'somewhere else' is the place from which Godot is expected. The mediator between Godot's world and the world on stage (the worlds of home and work?) is a Boy (the son), with an abstract title, rather than a specific, named identity, symbolising development, innocence, potential, insofar as there is any.

In this world there are no women (no wonder there is no future – except that one does wonder where the Boy came from). Associations with women occasionally appear in some of the sexual remarks, but the absence of women, and any heterosexual input, leaves the men in a half-childlike, half pornographic homo-eroticism. There is a section about Vladimir buttoning his fly, and chat about erections (the object of the censor's blue pencil – no *double entendre* intended). Trousers are pulled up and down, and the men hug one another. This elides animal creature comfort with a homo-erotic subtext, too submerged for awareness within the play.

The modern state, it seems, produces a sexless parody of marriage instead of real friendship between men, who are reduced from potent sexual beings to bewildered, displaced children, with no ethical code to control either their world or their violent impulses. In this world, there is no family, only the parody of one. There can also be no mother, literal or figurative. All the men, then, are like J. M. Barrie's

Lost Boys in *Peter Pan*. Only the nameless 'Boy' seems to be free of angst and sins, a child embodying a moment of abstract, symbolic hope. He can only be such a symbol because he has neither friends nor family.

Political causes: Communism and the Jewish family

Chicken Soup with Barley *(1958)*, Roots *(1959)*, I'm Talking about Jerusalem *(1960) by Arnold Wesker*

Like Osborne, Wesker shows personal relationships which deal with the new post-war reality; but unlike Osborne, Wesker homes in on a more complete extended family: mother, father and children. The trilogy takes on an epic overview, spanning a period from the mid-1930s to the 'present'. Both the first and third plays of the trilogy move through the decades (the first from the 1930s to the 1950s, the second beginning in the 1940s), whereas the second is set during a short time in the late 1950s. The first and third plays deal with the relationship between the old and the young Kahn generations, whereas the second looks at the younger generation. Like Osborne, Wesker began his theatrical career as an actor, and in both cases this clearly contributes to their meticulous sense of dramatic structure and stagecraft.

Wesker is particularly careful in his stage directions, giving a lot of detail about the stage furniture and its practical functions. This is not a mere hangover from the novelistic convention of earlier twentieth-century stage directions, but is also part of his political theme – that work, craft, the maintaining of daily life is part of the noble tradition of left-wing attitudes to labour. In theoretical terms, the production and reproduction of labour power becomes part of the social reality represented on stage; by implication, emotions and dilemmas of all kinds are shown to be not merely the product of a leisured lifestyle, and as the performers 'work' on stage they have a dual role: working as actors and actresses, and representing specific labours (cooking, carpentry and so on).

Chicken Soup with Barley is set in the 1930s in a flat in the East End, where the Jewish Kahn family live. The time is one of increasing anti-Semitism in Europe and England, and the Kahn family are staunch members of the Communist Party. From the beginning, it is clear that Sarah is the dominant figure. She is articulate, feisty, full of passion and action – feeding and nurturing the family, going out to work, and urging on the vitality of Communism. Harry, by contrast, is described as 'the antithesis of Sarah. He is amiable but weak'.

The situation of *Look Back* is reversed: the domestic territory is in the charge of a strong woman, with the man here as a secondary figure. Sarah mocks Harry's love of books. In her eyes he is a dreamer who does not value the kind of communication – emotional and verbal – which is a high priority in the Kahn family. Here there is no question of searching for causes – Sarah is a political activist, and Dave, her future son-in-law, joins the International Brigade to fight against fascism in the Spanish Civil War. Sarah is proud of her fiery daughter Ada and her tough son Ronnie.

The play is set before the Second World War, when a cause worth dying for (not, of course, the imperialist cause of the Colonel in *Look Back*) still gripped people. In part the trilogy's political journey travels from this earlier idealism to the late 1950s, when both politics and the family underwent a sea-change, testing the dislocations in new uncertainties; but at this early stage, the first scene in the play bustles round the family as they prepare to go off on a demonstration. For Sarah, being 'political' is expressed in terms which combine the larger aims with the more personal ones of warmth and love: Sarah comments on her sister-in-law Cissy:

> I hate her! Not a bit of warmth, not a bit . . . ! What is the good of being a socialist if you're not warm? People like that can't teach love and brotherhood. . . . Love comes now. You have to start with love. How can you talk about socialism otherwise?

In Act 2 we are in 1946, with the family now in a block of flats and beginning to disperse. Ada and Dave are planning to leave London for life in the country. In contrast to Sarah, still a vigorous Communist Party member, Ada prefigures some of the concerns of the hippy 1960s. She sees the new industrial progress as the enemy, destroying inner equilibrium: 'What right have we to care? How can we care for a world outside ourselves when the world inside is in disorder?'

Sarah is aware of the possibility that the family may disintegrate. She warns Ronnie: 'Remember this, Ronnie: the family should be a unit and your work and your life should be part of one existence, not something hacked about by a bus queue and office hours.' Meanwhile, Harry is still the lesser and the weaker, as tired and evasive as he was a decade earlier. Sarah still maintains the family – cooking and cleaning, going out to work, and urging her principles and ideals. Harry, more silent, less articulate, has a less militant philosophy: 'You can't alter people, Ronnie. You can only give them love and hope they will take it.'

In Act 3, ten years later, Harry is paralysed and slightly senile after two strokes. He is physically frail, unable to control his bowels. Ada has moved away with Dave. They have two children, and Dave makes furniture – from industry, back to craft. Ronnie is working as a cook. As we move towards the end of 1956, Sarah becomes more and more isolated. The flats are lonely, and she has to deal with the rudeness and bureaucracy of the Welfare State. The one relationship which holds is that between Sarah and Ronnie – mother and son. They discuss the Communist invasion of Hungary, and Ronnie attacks Sarah for the way she taught him a Communism which did not allow for any doubt: 'Why do I feel ashamed to use words like democracy and freedom and brotherhood? They don't have meaning any more.'

The parallel journeys of politics and the family are symbiotically entwined in this play. The 1930s, with their passionate solidarity, are also a time of strong family (and therefore community) unity. However, the imaginative trajectory is not quite so linear. Within the family, the centre of power is the woman – Sarah – and it seems to be the very nature of her strength and power which necessitates creating her opposite: the physically weak, frail, intellectual, cinema-loving Harry. He is not a 'real' man; he cannot keep down a job, he cannot maintain his family, he is not a political activist. It is as if the family already carries the seeds of its own disintegration in the 'unnatural' reversal of gender roles. Imaginatively, it appears that a woman can only be strong if the man is weak, and vice versa. The dualism of sexual power is inscribed in the physicalisation of this relationship, and one of the themes which is traced through the play becomes the nature of manhood and the definition of male identity. As Ronnie comments: 'I don't suppose there is anything more terrifying to a man than his own sense of failure.'

Harry's failure is total, literally embodied in his physical disintegration. Sarah's powerful voice seems to take wing almost at Harry's expense, as if (rather in the mode of one strand of the nineteenth-century novel) the damaged male is the necessary corollary of female strength (i.e. as in *Jane Eyre*), just as Alison's capitulation is a necessary condition for Jimmy's survival. By the end of *Chicken Soup*, Sarah too has become Harry's mother, since he needs to be looked after as if he were a baby. Sarah's articulacy is at the expense of his silence.

The mantle of articulacy is (interestingly) passed down through the male – via Ronnie rather than Ada. Ronnie, however, is the custodian of the new uncertainty, attacking Sarah where it will hurt most; this is the tragedy of her situation: 'The family you always wanted has disintegrated and the great ideal you always cherished has exploded in front of your eyes. But you won't face it.' Communism and motherhood (the two poles of Sarah's identity) are being destroyed, and with it the family also begins to go.

Roots takes us to a ramshackle house in Norfolk. It opens with the domestic image of a woman (Jenny) putting her child to bed. Her husband enters, complaining of a pain in his back. The echoes here of the damaged male again establish the domestic territory as under female control. Sure enough, when Beatie, Jennie's sister, arrives home for a visit, female control over the territory is complete. This is reinforced when Beatie's father later arrives with stomach ache. As we have already seen with Sarah, it appears that female strength can only be imagined if male weakness is its corollary, calling on women to provide mothering skills.

However, the core of the play's theme is at odds with this. Beatie has arrived, and the family prepares to welcome her boyfriend Ronnie (from the first play). Beatie is a bridge between the worlds of town and country, bringing with her the world of culture and the arts, yet immediately slotting back in at home, getting stuck into the housework. Beatie is (literally) full of Ronnie. He has encouraged her to talk in the way his mother did. He loves words, speaking of them as 'bridges'. He likes books, paintings and classical music, just as did his father Harry. He is critical of the new popular culture – comics, football and rock and roll. He stands on chairs when he wants to make speeches, and Beatie imitates him, allowing herself a small moment of irony at all this educational overload: 'Once we're married and I got babies I won't need to be interested in half the things I got to be interested in now.'

Beatie brings all these ideas back to her non-Jewish family; in Sarah's words: 'socialism isn't talking all the time, it's living, it's singing, it's dancing, it's being interested in what goes on around you.' And Harry's ideas: 'you can't change people, you can only give them some love and hope they'll take it.' Ronnie dominates the inside of Beatie's head. However, he also intervenes on traditional female territory. He is a chef, and has been teaching Beatie to cook; she uses his recipe for sponge cake.

The denouement comes with a message from Ronnie saying he has decided not to come, and that their relationship is over. As Beatie, surrounded by her family, has to deal with this, she appeals for support:

'Your daughter's been ditched. It's your problem as well, ain't it? I'm part of your family, aren't I? Well, help me then! . . . Talk to me – for God's sake, someone talk to me.'

But no one does. Her mother suggests having tea, her father does not know. Beatie's emergence from chrysalis to butterfly involves a struggle within herself. From being, as it were, a mother giving birth to Ronnie's ideas as she describes them to her family, she has to take responsibility for her own beliefs. This includes being able to mock Ronnie's idealised view of her family 'living in mystic communion with Nature'. She needs to reconcile herself to her own family, non-London and non-Jewish people as they are, and to recognise 'The things that make you proud of yourself – roots'.

By the end, she is still distanced from her own family; she continues to be a restless seeker after her own lifestyle, but she is beginning to find her own voice in the security of her own extended family. The final triumphant statement comes from the stage directions: *As Beatie stands alone, articulate at last, the curtain falls.*

This play continues the theme of female articulacy (i.e. Sarah), but presents it in a different light at a different time. Here we have a young (gentile) woman, who takes charge of her own voice. Articulacy is passed on from Jewish mother (Sarah), via Jewish son (Ronnie) to gentile woman (Beatie). Beatie's family cannot provide the support she needs at a time of crisis, and in any case she has already defected, acquring a new voice: Ronnie's. Her own voice, therefore, must necessarily separate itself both from her natural family and her acquired ideology.

Once free of both, she stands proud and individual – perhaps the new prophetic voice of the 1950s, full of vigour and promise, but (in realistic terms) a transgressor, because female, although as a symbolic figure she becomes a proto-feminist custodian of the unknown new, just as Sarah was of the known old. As the old family disintegrates, the new individual emerges, although such an apocalyptic ending to a realistic play leaves us simultaneously full of hope and without anywhere very specific to direct it.

Beatie has not discovered a political cause, and is paradoxically removed from the very milieu (London and Ronnie) which has given her the power to be articulate. Bringing her articulacy home, as it were, is simultaneously a celebration of her independence and her separation from the relatively non-articulate world of Norfolk. Beatie's optimism and joy at least have realistic sense within her own story, although she also carries the weight of the symbolism of a more abstract sense of hoping. At least Beatie leaves no damaged male in her wake, as do the women in her own family, and as Sarah did. Here it is also worth noting that she is the centre of the play – still within the convention of the single hero(ine), the story follows the twists and turns of her story.

The third play in the trilogy, *I'm Talking about Jerusalem*, returns to a moment from the first play – the late 1940s, after Ada and Dave's move to Norfolk. Another female-centred scene opens the play – Sarah, on a visit, buttering bread. She has brought some bottled chicken soup with her, like a good Jewish mother. Indeed, the whole family is involved in the move – away from the world of the new Labour Party, with its electricity and running water, to a 'utopia' with no proper lavatory.

Ronnie, true to type, stands on a box, conducting the gramophone and shouting his un-Porterish slogans: 'Down with capitalism! Long live the workers' revolution. . . . And long live Ronnie Kahn too!' The political always incorporates the personal. Dave's ideals are set up in very clear relation to the effect of urban life, which has 'emasculated' manhood: 'All their humanity gone. These you call men.'

His solution is a William Morris-style life, based on craft, where work and family are one. These are ideals absolutely in line with Sarah's, but enacted differently (no Communism here, no organised politics), and with the consequence that Sarah is upset that Ada has moved so far away.

In Act 2 an outsider figure arrives – a figure who, as we shall see, represents a device which enables the playwright to bring critical commentary, disruption and challenge into the world of the play. Libby is not Jewish. He is ex-RAF, and he is cynical about the back-to-nature move, accusing Dave and Ada of being individualists. With him he also brings ideas about women which could easily come from Jimmy Porter's world: 'A woman dirties you up as well, you know. She and the world – they change you, they bruise you, they dirty you up – between them, you'll see.'

He describes his ex-wife:

> She marries a man in order to have something to attach to herself, a possession! The man provides a home – bang! She's got another possession. Her furniture, her saucepans, her kitchen – bang, bang, bang! Then she has a baby – bang again. . . . And this is the way she grows. She grows and she grows and she grows and she takes

from a man all the things she once loved him for – so that no-one else can have them . . . I think I hate women because they have no vision.

Although Libby is an outsider to the Jewish family, he is of course from the dominant, gentile culture, and these ideas in themselves carry an implied threat both to the traditional Jewish family with its woman as the strong centre and the more emancipated version in the Kahn household. Although his language is nowhere near as visceral as Jimmy Porter's, Libby carries the same fraught misogyny, and barely concealed anxiety about his own male identity. This is signalled also by the sexual ambiguity of his name.

Dave and Ada's utopia proves to have its own problems. The furniture making does not bring in enough, and in 1956 they decide to return to London, where Dave plans to start a new workshop. By 1959 the popularity of the Labour Party is waning, and with it Ronnie is becoming more wistful about his earlier ideals. Ronnie's role as custodian of both parents' ideals leads him into conflict with Dave and Ada. Where the latter believe in putting ideals into practice, Ronnie has always clung to the magic and power of language, and his doubts crystallise here: 'As soon as I say something, somehow I don't believe it . . . As soon as you pronounce something it doesn't seem true.'

However, in practice, Ronnie also keeps familial devotion alive. He cares for Harry's physical needs lovingly and intimately in a rare demonstration of male closeness, and he is still close to his mother; at the end, he comments with wry reverberation: 'Well, Sarah – your children are coming home now.' Despite everything, he carries the torch of desperate optimism in his last shout: 'We must be bloody mad to cry.'

The Wesker trilogy is unique in post-war British drama both in its epic sweep and the way it seamlessly intersects political vision and family life. It is interesting that it does so through the lives of a Jewish family (relative outsiders), who seem to present themselves as entirely assimilated (no religion or Yiddish anywhere), and yet still carry with them the intensities of a traditional Jewish family lifestyle with a passionate, argumentative vigour.

Yet, as the politics move from the secure anti-fascist Communism of the 1930s to the bewildered and disaffected leftism of the late 1950s, so the family follows a similar path – from strong social unity to fragmentation as generational lifestyles diverge. However, British society, viewed through the eyes of a Jewish family, is something of an anomaly. They are 'outsiders'. Sarah, the custodian of the strongest personal and political values at the outset, is a double outsider – both Jewish and a woman.

This creates a double tension. While the fortunes of the Kahn family are both 'realistic' (dispersion of the family after the war) and symbolic (of the political uncertainties of the 1950s), the function of Sarah is less easily categorised, because her strength and articulacy are symbiotically linked with Harry's frailty. The similarities with the imaginative gender divide in *Look Back* come into play. Just as Jimmy's identity and articulacy can only be strong if Alison is flawed, it appears (imaginatively) to be the case that Sarah's strength and articulacy can only operate if Harry is damaged.

In both cases, differences between husband and wife are not realised through any explicit conflict within the play. There is no partnership, no theatrical collaboration, but sublimated conflict: for Jimmy in the class war, and here in Harry's physical disintegration. This gives both plays great emotional potency – as if it is impossible for the playwrights (in these plays) to imagine any kind of emotional parity between their male/female protagonists.

However, whereas Jimmy seeks Alison's downfall (in the primal sexual chase), Sarah seems not to wish Harry's illness upon him. If anything, she appears to want the opposite. The question which is really interesting is whether the capacity to imagine a strong woman has to be predicated on having to imagine a weak man, since in the battle of the sexes (as we are educated to believe) only one can be the boss. Whatever the conscious intentions of Osborne and Wesker, two very different playwrights, this imaginative pattern applies to both.

This is, of course, fascinatingly ironic, in view of the fact that Wesker also engages with some extraordinary radical and far-sighted issues: with the way in which Jewish traditions and intellectual vitality hover behind Ronnie's influences on Beatie (the Old Testament influencing the New?), and the way in which Beatie herself, in her polemical role, prefigures some of the proto-feminist concerns of a drama which did not come fully into being until the 1970s. It will be interesting to note the difference between this play which follows Beatie's breakthrough to a utopian happy ending based on hope, and the way in which women become emblematic of emotion and hope in the work of some male playwrights in the 1970s.

The outsider at the door

The Birthday Party (1958) by Harold Pinter

This play has a deceptively simple title: domestic, reassuring, suggesting the comfort of childhood and the celebration of an important personal occasion – a ritual shared by intimates.

The setting is a living room, with a hatch through to a separate and invisible kitchen. Just as the domestic functions can be visually separated, so the familial roles here are more clearly defined than in Osborne's play. This play starts with a woman serving a man food – Meg looking after husband Petey, parental figures apparently waiting for their son to come down to breakfast. However, this couple is childless. There is merely a surrogate child (very different from Cliff): Stanley the lodger. Meg teases and flirts, treating him alternately as a little boy and an adult sexual male (possibly the implication here is that Meg and Petey's sexual relationship is wanting).

The world of this strange 'family' is a transitional world, a boarding-house open to outsiders whose arrival is sanctioned; indeed, is a condition of its functioning. The main action of the play takes off with the arrival of two further, sinister outsiders: the Irish McCann and the Jewish Goldberg (outsiders to Britishness in a double sense, even if they do speak English).

McCann and Goldberg control the action in every respect – form and content. They take over Meg's territory in a way which goes beyond the prerogative of lodgers, by deciding to give Stanley a party for his birthday. The confidence with which they assert their power is bolstered by the way Pinter gives them official, bureaucratic language: they refer to their 'job', their 'assignment', their 'mission'. We have another example of the way a woman's minimal territorial power (pace Alison) has to be usurped in order to make way for the action proper – between the men.

Two other gender-determined elements confirm this: at the beginning of Act 1, Petey sits reading a newspaper (pace Look Back), and at the beginning of Act 2, McCann sits tearing a newspaper into strips. Newspapers come from the outside world and belong to men, who either read them (integrating them) or tear them up (symbolising destruction). The other factor is the presence of the only other woman in the play: the dolly-bird bimbo figure of Lulu, who has no real relationship with anyone, and certainly no territorial or emotional control.

Here a fear about the invasion of ethnic diversity (cultural 'otherness'), is enacted. The Irishman and the Jew do indeed bring fear and trembling into this 'home', as if they are angels avenging themselves on an inglorious military past. The irony is that they have to wreak their revenge on someone who is even weaker than they are: Stanley.

Stanley appears to be the ideal scapegoat because he has no history, he belongs to no one and has no family. This makes him fair game both for verbal and physical assault. The 'party' which the two are organising for him entails a violent attempt to force him to integrate with his society. Goldberg says:

> What happened to the love, the bonhomie, the unashamed expression of affection of the day before yesterday, that our Mums taught us in the nursery. . . . We all wander on our tod through this world. It's a lonely pillow to kip on.

McCann and Goldberg finally take Stanley away, after a frightening choric litany of how they are going to help him to 'reintegrate'. Stanley is reduced to gibberish; he has lost all control of his voice, of the language, and can no longer manage anything. Petey tries vainly to stop the process, but when Meg returns he pretends that Stanley is still upstairs in bed, keeping the truth from her.

This reinforces Meg's powerlessness on her own domestic territory. She is completely excluded from the central power struggle between Stanley and his two 'angels'. The 'father' in this family, Petey, witnesses, comprehends and colludes, but Meg, as the 'mother', does not even know what has happened. She is not only materially powerless, but also powerless in terms of how much she is allowed to know about the (her) world. Here, as in *Look Back*, men co-opt domestic territory, since it is their actions, gripping and sinister as they are, which determine the course of the dramatic narrative.

Pinter's political concerns introduce a new factor: the cultural outsiders, intruding on already shifting social and familial conventions. Even the domestic territory is not privately controlled: it is either rented, or semi-public, in the boarding-house, an intermediate place between public and private. Meg's predatory (if theoretical) sexuality takes on additional overtones in relation to Stanley, the surrogate son. Here the actions of a 'mother' overwhelming her son with potentially incestuous advances have to be countered by removing him from the nest – even if it is to the unknown and sinister world of McCann and Goldberg.

Interestingly, while McCann and Goldberg come from cultural backgrounds different from those of Meg, Petey and Stanley, they also embody the language of officialdom – of the new bureaucratic state (see Beckett above). An obscure (male) authority somewhere is controlling everyone's lives, throwing men into disorder, and women into power-lessness. However, while there are small-scale power compensations for men (Goldberg, McCann and Petey), for women there is helpless-ness, ignorance or dolly-bird vapidity.

Voices from the distaff side: mother and daughter

A Taste of Honey (1958) by Shelagh Delaney

The post-war theme of domestic displacement here takes on a new gendered turn. Recently moved into 'a comfortless flat in Manchester', Helen ('a semi-whore') and her daughter Jo establish their love-hate relationship in a home where familial roles are raw and unconventional. There is no father around, and Jo and Helen share the ironic intimacy of a double bed – ironic since their intimacy is fraught, painful and based on a closeness which at the same time is undermined by the needs of each woman to establish her separate identity.

This 'family', then, has no man to head it, no secure, long-term home to house it. The expected norms are reversed: Jo is the more responsible of the two (shades of *Absolutely Fabulous* . . .), Helen more interested in how she looks and in going out to have a good time. Marking the generational changes, Helen comments:

> You bring them up and they turn round and talk to you like that. I would never have dared talk to my mother like that when I was her age. She'd have knocked me into the middle of next week.

Jo wants to leave school, and to get away from Helen. The two are clearly used to their nomadic existence, and Helen's succession of boyfriends. She may be cynical about men, but she cannot do with-out one. Expectations are reversed and taboos broken. Helen refuses to be defined as only a mother. She is an older woman who likes drink-ing, sex and going out. However, there are painful consequences to this:

> *Jo*:   You should prepare my meals like a proper mother.
> *Helen*: Have I ever laid claim to being a proper mother?

A further and striking theatrical taboo is also broken: here is a play, in a domestic setting, which follows the fortunes of the women at its centre. Male characters come and go according to the needs of the female gender-driven story, and we do not follow the men's emotions or dilemmas. This familial 'outsider' paring – single mum and daughter – is joined by the further outsider figure of Jo's boyfriend, described as 'a coloured naval rating', doing his National Service. Unlike Pinter's McCann, this man carries none of the immediately sinister overtones of a feared racial Other, although he is depersonalised in the cast list as 'Boy', his name, Jimmy, only spoken much later on in the play.

When Peter and Helen decide to get married and go on honeymoon, Boy stays with Jo over Christmas. Helen is a woman who seems very sure of her sexuality; by contrast, Jo, still very young, is less sure. On Helen's wedding day, Jo questions her about her father, to learn that she was the outcome of a one-night stand. Helen, despite her insistence on living her life exactly as she wants, still hankers after conventions, challenging Jo: 'Why don't you learn from my mistakes?'

In Act 2, Boy has gone and Jo is pregnant – from another one-night stand. Geof, a gay man, moves in with Jo, the two of them just good friends. Here the subversion of conventional gender roles goes even further. Jo is deeply ambiguous about her pregnancy, unsure about motherhood: 'I hate babies.' When she talks about breastfeeding, she is even more fearful: 'I'm not having a little animal nibbling away at me, it's cannibalistic. Like being eaten alive.'

When Geof buys her a doll on which to practise, she bursts out: 'I'll bash its brains out. I'll kill it. I don't want his baby, Geof. I don't want to be a mother. I don't want to be a woman.'

Geof, on the other hand, becomes a dual substitute mother, looking after Jo, and preparing cot and clothes for the baby. He has all the feelings which, according to conventional gender expectation, Jo should have. She says: 'It comes natural to you . . . you'd make someone a wonderful wife.'

Despite a bit of effort, both Jo and Geof appear to be primarily asexual. Geof admits that he has never kissed a girl, and when they try, Jo reacts angrily, saying she does not 'enjoy all this panting and grunting'. The struggle to make sense of the complexities of sex, affection and love lead Jo to come down on the side of an undemanding friendship and affection: 'I always want to have you with me because I know you'll never ask anything from me.'

Jo is afraid of becoming a mother because she has not herself been properly mothered: 'I used to try and hold my mother's hands, but she always used to pull them away from me. . . . She had so much love for everyone else, but none for me.' However, the prospect of an unconventional alternative family – single mother, gay father-figure and illegitimate baby – is diverted when Helen comes back, her marriage having broken down. Traditional motherhood imperatives return, and Helen behaves so appallingly towards Geof that he leaves. As soon as he has gone, Helen and Jo revert to their old sniping love-hate relationship, exacerbated when Jo tells Helen that the baby may be black. There is a moment when it appears that Helen might be too shocked to stay – indeed, she is impelled to go out to get a drink – but it is clear from the very end that she is coming back, that Jo wants her to come back. The play concludes with Jo reciting an old-fashioned folk rhyme – a reference, perhaps, to the possible friendship with Geof which, on the basis of everything we have seen, has to be impossible now that Helen is back.

In this shifting family combination, Geof is a good, kind 'brother' throughout, concerned for Jo's best interests, even when he has been thrown out. Imaginatively, this seems to be made possible by the fact that although everything in his manner and speech tells us he is gay, we know nothing about his history, and he has no sexual relationships within the world of the play. Thus, like Cliff, he is an asexual male, who is therefore available for friendship with a woman.

The emotional language of the play is raw and vibrant – these characters have no problems expressing real, nitty-gritty feelings and conflicts about fundamental emotional issues; perhaps this is because of their working-class roots, although each is socially displaced from the conventional norms: single mother and part-time whore, illegitimate teenage mother, gay white man, black sailor boy; a series of 'outsiders' to British culture (of whatever class), in which the hierarchy descends from the biological mother–daughter relationship which wins out over all others, however abrasive it is.

Sexuality is problematic for everyone – even for Helen, whose relationship breaks down. Interestingly, although all kinds of socially unconventional bondings look possible, in the end the biological, socially validated triumphs: the mother and daughter relationship overrides all the taboos. The issues and dilemmas are radical: motherhood is thrust on many women; nurturing is not necessarily an automatic maternal instinct, whereas a man may well feel 'maternal', yet be prevented from being able to express himself. The values of the mother–daughter blood relationship prevail as the strongest, and thus the women, while they may not be in total control of their emotional relationships, do manage the domestic space, and the gender dynamic of the plot is (unusually) female. Motherhood – even though in two kinds of crisis – takes centre stage, by implication raising questions about what kinds of families audiences of the time live in, and what kinds of alternative families they might set up.

Women and myth

The Sport of My Mad Mother (1958) by Ann Jellicoe

In a preface to the published play, written in 1964, Jellicoe says it was:

> . . . not written intellectually according to a pre-arranged plan. It was shaped bit by bit until the bits felt right in relation to each other and to the whole. It is an anti-intellect play, not only because it is about irrational forces and urges, but because one hopes it will reach the audience directly through rhythm, noise and music and their reaction to basic stimuli.

Using the concept of ritual to encompass both the stage world and the language within it, she comments:

> We create rituals when we want to strengthen, celebrate or define our common life or common values, or when we want to give ourselves confidence to undertake a common course of action.

It is a short step from the concept of ritual to the espousement of myth:

> The Sport of My Mad Mother is concerned with fear and rage at being rejected from the womb or tribe. It uses a very old myth in which a man, rejected by his mother, castrates himself with a stone knife.

Jellicoe spells out her gender concerns in a surprisingly explicit and self-conscious way for the time. The stage world, in which her version of the myth is played out, is explicitly theatrical, playing with the form within which it is contained. At the beginning, Steve arrives with percussion instruments, and he remains on stage throughout, including the interval. This works as a dual device: to bridge the gap between the audience and the hermetic ritualistic world of the characters, and as an 'alienation' tactic – to remind us all the time that what we are seeing is illusion – a part of the ritual which is theatre. It has an additional gender-based function, similar to that of Jimmy Porter's trumpet – to assert, both visually and aurally, the dominance of the male. Steve personifies the unconscious, expressed through the emotion in music, and also functions as a non-verbal repository of gender-based power.

In the play three young women and four young men hang out. Patty is described as 'a pretty little cockney girl with a lot of make-up round her eyes'. The male characters have strange, abstract names – Fak, Cone – which deliberately depersonalise them, enhancing the symbolic quality of the play. There is a conventional cast to the different toys with which they all play: the boys have guns, posturing with macho threats of violence, while Patty has curlers and a home perm kit. The ritual of chatting up is full of repetition, satirising the ritual. Patty keeps having to be reminded by the others of where she has been and what she has done, as if she has no memory, cannot contain her own sense of herself, and has no identity until others give it to her. An awaited outsider figure is in this play too (as in *Godot* and *Roots*), Greta, in a gender reversal. Patty describes Greta's power, in contrast with her own helplessness: 'I wish I was Greta. . . . Like spit on a hot plate, that's her . . . anyone'll do anything for her.'

A strange figure arrives: Dodo, 'either very young or very old', a woman wearing a man's overcoat and making animal noises. In this one figure is encapsulated a clutch of ideas about the relativity of gender roles, identification according to age, and the nature of that which divides human beings from the animal world. By conflating all of these, Jellicoe effectively subverts rigid notions of social roles. However, this has a linguistic corollary: Dodo has no real recognisable 'language', being outside any clear social system. S/he speaks either single words or single syllables.

The mix of social roles and behaviours continues into Act 2. Everyone rushes around with sparklers, and Dean, an American, tries to perm Patty's hair, accompanied by confusing instructions from everyone. Greta finally appears, dressed like the others in old coats and blankets, like Dodo. She speaks with an Australian accent. Dean tries to get hold of her – the two ex-colonial outsiders (parental figures?) trying to get together.

The stage directions ask that whenever Greta moves away from the others, 'the focus of action seems to go with her'. She inspires fear and respect in everyone: when they all fall on Dean, Greta stops them with a word, and then smashes a mug. She beats Cone up, and he loves every minute of it. Although the play is full of sudden outbreaks of violence, Greta's authority is always clear.

It is only at the end of Act 2 that Greta is 'seen to be pregnant'. Her role as holder of both surrogate and actual maternal power is shown first by her authority over others' actions and emotions, and second by her biological capacity to reproduce. At the same time her relationships with the men have strong sexual, sado-masochistic overtones.

Act 3 begins with everyone again waiting for Greta. Dean makes a long, moral speech about human violence:

> Why be angry . . . I'm part of the human race and this waste – this violence – this degradation – it betrays humanity. . . . If people will only have patience and intelligence and will power there's nothing we can't master and control.

His attempt at rationality is countered by the way Greta embodies the elemental, the irrational, the primitive: 'I was reared in a cave by a female wallaby. Until I was seven I ran about on all fours and barked.'

Her pregnancy becomes the centre of attention. Cone is jealous, fearful that Greta will reject him in favour of the new baby. When Greta is in pain (perhaps already in labour), Dean turns on her: 'You're not fit to have a child. . . . You gross thing. Man/woman, cruel. Unstable. Frigid.' Greta counters with references to rational organisation (the state?):

> Rails, rules, laws, guides, promises, terms . . . into the pot with the whole bloody lot. Birth. Birth. That's the thing. Oh, I shall have hundreds of children, millions of hundreds, and hundreds of millions.

Concealed behind a sheet, she gives birth to a small white bundle. Cone bashes himself to death with a brick, unable to take the competition, while Steve, the musical mediator, the reassuring male authority figure, clears up.

Thematically, as in Osborne's play, the relationship between female sexuality and motherhood is explored. However, the dilemma for the men is played out rather differently. Cone, feeling rejected, follows the myth which Jellicoe describes, and destroys himself. Dean, on the other hand, tries to destroy Greta verbally. However, the end leaves Greta as a (literal) mother, having given birth on stage, with the innocent white bundle as a possible symbol of hope (cf. the Boy in *Godot*). Her symbolic power as an archetypal mother is there in her assertions about having millions of children (a reference also to the myth of Lilith, Adam's first wife, who also gave birth to millions of children every day, but was condemned to devour them – a very different gloss on the power of motherhood). There is no father in Greta's world – a further assertion of the abstract power of motherhood, as well as a vigorously subversive notion of the implications of immaculate conception.

In contrast to Greta, Patty (cf. Lulu in *The Birthday Party*) exists as the feminine social role player: vapid, pretty, powerless. The conflict between Dean and Greta, two non-British English speakers, is for territory, with Greta as the elemental, irrational, and Dean, the thinker, the moralist (another stereotyped division between feminine and masculine ideologies). Greta's power at the end is implicitly confirmed by an ironic combination in Steve (the male) of the irrational (music) and the orderly (he clears up the mess).

Here the representation and function of gender operates via an absurdist, ritualised stage world, which works precisely because of its use of referents we know to be 'real': ideas associated with maleness and femaleness, the fear of the mother who (unlike Osborne and Wesker) triumphs, the crisis of manhood (in relation to the mother, but also to the notion of morality and causes – *pace* Osborne). Dean refuses to see the point of being angry (perhaps an implied comment on the school of writers of the 1950s labelled the Angry Young Men), but he also cannot come to terms with the power of a sexually active, maternal woman: Greta.

Here the 'outsider' figure actually arrives, and threatens the men both on the count of gender as such, and the count of conventional gender-based ideology – women supposedly as the irrational, men as the rational, etc. Jellicoe resolves these oppositions finally in (and this is significant) the male figure of Steve, so that despite the threat of 'revolution', the status quo has once more been restored via the agency of a male figure. The 'family' is fragmented – a collection of young people without clear parental figures: Steve, the silent father substitute, restores order, while Greta promises more progeny, without mothering those already in the world.

Women and emancipation

Each His Own Wilderness (1958) by Doris Lessing

The play opens after 'an H bomb explosion'. Tony Bolton has just finished his National Service. He is described as sexually ambiguous: 'an adolescent girl who makes herself attractive as a form of self assertion, but is afraid when the attention she draws is more than gently chivalrous.'

At the core of the play is a volatile mother–son relationship between Tony and his articulate, politically active mother, Myra. There are small subversive touches, such as the fact that Myra wears trousers, still a little naughty in the late 1950s.

Tony craves his mother's affection, but Myra, in trying to control her own life and her relations with men and socialist politics, seems to have to do so at the expense of her relationship with him. Tony is jealous of Myra's young secretary Sandy, and is cynical about the many 'uncles' he has had. He sneers at 'the glorious battle for socialism inside the Labour party', commenting: 'We need a new form of – inner emigration. Drugs, drink, anything. I want to opt out. I don't want any part of it.'

Tony is a young man without a cause, a pre-hippy, and, as in Wesker, it is the mother who is sure of her cause, however much it is under strain.

As Philip, a former boyfriend of Myra's, now engaged to Rosemary, comments: 'Everyone's fed up with politics. It's not the time.' Even Myra remarks on the change in people's sense of their political responsibilities:

> Half the people I know, people who have spent all their lives fight-ing and trying to change things, they've gone inside their homes, shut their front doors and gone domestic and comfortable – and safe.

Domesticity is used as a retreat from the political, and this provides a springboard for personal and political conflicts and arguments. Myra and Tony are passionately commited to arguing with each other, the emotional buzz they thus gain being necessary to both – an echo of the Sarah/Ronnie relationship.

Tony may have a lot of Jimmy Porter in him, but the dynamic of this play operates on Myra's territory; she is the activist with experience and a historical perspective. Tony is the outsider, the alienated youth, disillusioned with the Welfare State:

> Do you know what you've created, you and your lot? What a vision it is. A house for every family. Just imagine – two hundred million families – or is it four hundred million families? To every family a front door. Behind every front door, a family. A house full of clean, well-fed people, and not one of them ever understands one word anyone else says. Everybody a kind of wilderness surrounded by barbed wire shouting across the defences into the other wildernesses and never getting an answer back. That's socialism, I suppose it's progress. Why not? To every man his wife and two children and a chicken in the pot on Sundays. A beautiful picture – I'd die for it. To every man his own front door key. To each his own wilderness.

There is irony in the use of the male pronoun here, because Tony's attack is also on a family which fails to provide values for him. The embodiment of these socialist values is a woman, Myra, and he is talking about *her* wilderness.

In Act 2 Tony becomes more and more childlike, 'making machine-gun noises like a small boy', in a scene where Myra has been joined by Sandy's mother, Milly. In the face of the two grown-up women having a conversation, he behaves like a rather noisy little boy trying to get his mother's attention.

It is extraordinary to have a scene where two older women have a heartfelt conversation, talking seriously about men, but also about their own lives. They are witty, independent, older women for whom sexuality is as much a current reality as is motherhood. It is the same theme which Jellicoe has used – that of the man who feels rejected by his mother – but employed in a very different kind of play. Here are strong and articulate older women who feel that the world's concerns impinge on their personal lives, but who test the mother–son relationship by breaking with convention in order to achieve 'independence'.

The relationship between Tony and Myra is further complicated when Tony and Milly have a vague sexual encounter. This can only be an odd, displaced, Oedipal experience – certainly not sex between equals. Myra finally acknowledges her unwitting devotion to her son: 'It occurs to me that for the last twenty-two years my life has been governed by yours – by your needs.' Thus although Tony feels

neglected, in fact his mother believes her emotional life has been dominated by him. It is an anguished conflict of interests and emotions
between generations, and the play ends with Tony being comforted
by Rosemary, a member of his own generation. The stage direction
'They crouch down with each other' provides a more innocent image
than the bears and squirrels at the end of Look Back in Anger. Where
that image was full of fraught and unresolved violent sexuality, this
image is non-sexual. Tony's call in the end is not for a new kind of
cause for which to fight but for something quite different:

> Rosemary, listen – never in the whole history of the world have
> people made a battle cry out of being ordinary. Never. Supposing
> we all said that to the politicians – we refuse to be heroic. . . . We
> are bored with all the noble gestures.

His plea is for the value of the ordinary, domestic life in contrast to the
traumatic, if exciting, world of wars and political causes, and it is the
mother who believes in politics and social action. The separation of
the political from the personal is carried also through Myra, who may
own her house and run it, has a genuine friendship with another
woman, but a shaky family base and no currently satisfying sexual
relationship.

Play with a Tiger (1958) by Doris Lessing

Here the woman/social outsider themes are brought together more
explicitly. Lessing writes in her introduction:

> Now this play is about rootless de-classed people who live in bed-
> sitting rooms or small flats or the cheaper hotel rooms, and such
> people are usually presented on the stage in a detailed squalor of
> realism which to my mind distracts attention from what is interest-
> ing about them.

Anna Freeman is an Australian writer with a room in Mary Jackson's
house, a bed-sitter where she sleeps and works, a rare representation on
stage of a professional woman. Like Myra, she wears trousers. Although
Anna does not own her home, she establishes her territorial rights
through her friendship with Mary, who is similarly independent. However, this female friendship, although strong and secure, exists in a
world where relationships with men take up a lot of time and attention.

Anna has been having an affair with Dave, a travelling American. Janet Stephens, also American, soon arrives, with conventionally feminine views: 'I believe that marriage and the family is the most rewarding career of all a woman can have.'

Anna guesses that Janet has turned up because she is pregnant by Dave, who subsequently arrives himself, complete with crew-cut and duffle bag. He is charming and articulate, but he argues with Anna, admitting to a fear of the 'mother-figure':

> I'm not going to stand for you either – mother of the world, the great womb, the eternal conscience. I like women, but I'm going to like them my way and not according to the rules laid down by the incorporated mothers of the universe.

Towards the end of Act I the room itself fades and 'seems part of the street', and with this metamorphosis goes the control Anna has had over her own room, and by extension, her own life. It is Dave who 'externalises' Anna, taking her out of the present, back to her childhood in a semi-psychoanalytic role. When Dave considers the 'session' over, he switches on the light, returning us to the room and the present.

Interestingly, it is in the public place (i.e. when the domestic setting gives way to the city) that the psyche comes through most strongly. This territory is also where the man controls the woman's access to her inner life. When she is displaced from her territory the man seizes power, both materially and psychically.

Marriage and family, according to Dave, are no longer adequate compensation for the alienation of America: 'You look at us and you see prosperity – and loneliness. Prosperity and men and women in trouble with each other. Prosperity and people wondering what life is for.'

Anna identifies Dave's disillusion as embodied in a fear of female sexuality:

> She's that terrible woman in your comic papers – a great masculine broad-shouldered, narrow-hipped black-booted blonde beastess, with a whip in one hand and a revolver in the other. And that's why you're running, she's after you . . . as she's after every male American I've ever met. I bet you even see the Statue of Liberty with great black thigh-boots and a pencilled moustache – the frigid tyrant, the frigid goddess.

Anna contends that the war between the sexes: 'is the only clean war left. It's the only war that won't destroy us all. That's why we are fighting it.'

In these speeches there are echoes of Jimmy Porter's substitution of the sex war for the class war, but the ideas are articulated here by a woman. Towards the end, Anna comments with a semi-ironic echo of Sarah's comment in *Chicken Soup with Barley*, 'We must love one another or die. Something new like that.' The end is unresolved. Janet phones, Dave goes out, Anna is upset, Mary comes in. Finally Anna goes towards the bed and 'the city comes up around her'.

It is telling that both Dave and Anna are foreigners – here the outsiders are socially marginal as in Delaney's play, but the middle-class, English-speaking foreigners pass comment on British society, as if those who 'belong' are unable to see it.

In Lessing's two plays women manifest a control over their immediate material environment (their homes), and their ideas and work. Men are both a continuing need and a potential threat – exemplified by Dave's control over the outside world, and the intimacy of Anna's memory. The outcome in both plays is a moment of suspension in which the personal/political conflicts between the men and women may remain unresolved, but the women still inhabit their own spaces – physical and psychological. Realism in the domestic setting is ruptured in an attempt to place the psyche in the city.

Men and the military

Serjeant Musgrave's Dance *(1959) by John Arden*

The final play from the 1950s to be discussed addresses the theme of militarism in the modern world. The play combines a realism of theme with a setting in a representative, 'typical' mining town. There is a strike, and four soldiers arrive to recruit. Led by Serjeant Musgrave, they are subject to his ideology, sanctioned by officialdom: 'We have our duty. A soldier's duty is a soldier's life.'

Even though we learn later on that the soldiers are all deserters, and that Musgrave has stolen money, the power of the military presence still prevails. As Musgrave puts it: 'My power is the power of God.' The play anatomises social authority; just as Musgrave represents (and implements) state order in the community, via his soldiers, so the local parson, who is also a magistrate, controls religious and secular law and order in the town. The local mayor also owns the colliery. Social and political power is thus concentrated in the hands of a small group of men.

The soldiers have come back to the town because of Billy Hicks, a local boy who was killed in the army. His best friend Sparky has his own personal reason for the pilgrimage. Musgrave, however, sees the need to vindicate Billy's death as a crusade, linked to the crisis in the town: 'their rights and our war are the same one corruption.'

There is no domestic setting in the play; it is not totally abstract, in the way that Beckett and Jellicoe create a no-person's-land limbo, where the space is defined by its very home-lessness; a place where people in search of personal identities and relationships have to construct a home. Arden places his characters in a series of public or temporary spaces: streets, a stables, the market place, where people belong only temporarily.

The exception to this is the public house, relatively neutral territory where the men can meet, and where the women have their primary, realistic function. Mrs Hitchcock runs the pub, and Annie is her barmaid. Annie sleeps with soldiers, and Billy and she have had a relationship in the past. She gave birth to a deformed child, who died. Annie is cynical about the life prospects of the military: 'What good's a bloody soldier, except to be dropped into a slit in the ground like a letter in a box' and of her own social role: 'I'm a whore to the soldiers – it's a class by itself.' Mrs Hitchcock, on the other hand, is slightly more detached about the current realities in the town: 'No work in the colliery, the owner calls it a strike, the men call it a lock-out, we call it starvation.'

In the pub, the women serve the men with food and drink, a working extension of women's domestic role. Annie also provides sexual services, while Mrs Hitchcock is the mother-figure, without either a husband or any children of her own. Musgrave, in keeping with his puritan, pocket-Bible morality, his hostility to drunkenness and fornication, is very clear about the social and sexual division of labour: 'There's work for women and there's work for men: and let the two get mixed, you've anarchy.' Samson-like, he warns Annie to keep away from the men: 'You will not stand between them and their strength.'

Annie comes to the stables where the men are billeted, and there is some argument about who she is going to sleep with. One, Hurst, fears sexual contact with her: 'You want me to lose my life inside of you.' Another, Attercliffe, grabs her crudely, kisses her and then tells a

bitter story of how his wife slept with the greengrocer. It is finally
Sparky, Billy's friend, to whom Annie is drawn, both feeling the same
sad passion at Billy's loss. Later there is a brawl among the men, leaving
Sparky dead. Attercliffe holds the bayonet which killed him. After
Sparky's death, in shock, with blood (literally) on her hands, Annie
collapses, and Musgrave tells Mrs Hitchcock to take her away and
lock her up. Mrs Hitchcock accepts his authority without question.

In Act 3, Musgrave reveals his true colours: after a speech in the
market square about the beauty of the gun and its power to kill, he
argues for a holy revenge, in which twenty-five people must die in
return for the accidental and violent death of Billy Hicks. For
Attercliffe this is itself a betrayal, since he believed that Musgrave
was in favour of stopping all killing. Revenge in kind is not the cause
he believed he was supporting. Annie returns, with a sad and simple
speech about the loss of her love. While Musgrave dances with a skeleton which he claims is that of Billy Hicks, Annie cradles the skeleton as
a symbol of her dead lover, echoing the loss of her own dead baby.

At the end of the play, Mrs Hitchcock visits Musgrave and Attercliffe
in prison, comforting them with port and lemon, and telling Musgrave
he has got it all wrong.

In his introduction to the play, John Arden says: 'I would suggest that
a study of the roles of the women and of Private Attercliffe should be
sufficient to remove any doubts as to where the "moral" of the play lies.'

It is certainly clear, from its setting, the way the themes and character
relationships are interwoven and the Brechtian use of songs, that part of
the drive of this extraordinarily powerful play is to expose moral questions about the nature of militarism and violence. However, tracing the
gender dynamic in the play reveals some very interesting ways in which
this moral question is enacted and realised.

Only two of the fifteen characters in the play are women. Fair
enough, this is a man's world. These two women, however, are in the
service of the men – both realistic, in terms of their servicing role
(housekeeping and sexual), and emotional and symbolic. There are
some overlaps between the real and symbolic. Mrs Hitchcock is
relatively straightforward. She is a 'Mrs', but a woman taken out of
the sexual arena. No husband, no children. Boss in her own pub,
but obedient when orders come from outside (i.e. from Musgrave in
relation to Annie). At the end, she comforts Musgrave and Attercliffe
and advises on wrong thinking. She is there as ballast to the story, and
as someone to take Annie out of the main action until she is needed
again.

Annie, on the other hand, is more complex. She has no background or family (nor has anyone else in the play, it is true), and simply falls into bed with soldiers for comfort. Her relationship with Sparky, linked as it is with the absent Billy (another offstage key figure in a play), is moving, touching and genuine as a contact between real people with real emotions. It is interesting that the play's dramatic crisis is precipitated after this one real emotional rapport, as if real emotion cannot be allowed to continue, but becomes a catalyst for more violence and tragedy.

Annie has her own personal tragedies: the loss of Billy, her child, and then later, Sparky. She represents, movingly, it is true, the victims of war, who lose all that is closest to them. She becomes symbolic of the cruelty of war, and her dead child becomes emblematic of all the deformities which militarism produces. Annie is an outsider: she does not belong to the army, nor to the local community. She is vulnerable to the stronger outsiders – the soldiers who come to disrupt the community – and she becomes the community's sacrifice, sexually, in terms of her motherhood, and later her 'madness' after Sparky's death. She is a sacrificial victim (a tart-turned-Ophelia), whose immolation punishes female sexuality and motherhood in order to convey the message about militarism. Her very femaleness becomes symbolic, in a way which does not (and cannot in this imaginative context) apply to any of the men.

This is structurally reinforced in the way the play is built up. The action follows the dictates of the plot as it affects the male characters. Annie is further isolated by her relationship with Mrs Hitchcock; the latter is both her boss and her gaoler. The two women have no scenes together. There is a sense in which they could be written out of the play and the main messages would not need to be fundamentally altered. What would need to happen is the invention of some sort of imaginative corollary to the power of Annie-the-symbol. Given the gender divide, Arden's comment about where the 'moral' of the play lies is certainly borne out, but the moral power of the symbolism works only at the expense of the stage reality of the female characters. Annie becomes a cipher, and therefore has to be destroyed as a 'character', who never significantly acts upon anyone else and has no power over her own destiny. Even her relationship with Billy happened in the past, not in the present world of the play.

Politics and moral issues are thus clearly represented by implication as the concerns of men. The isolation of women from these concerns is shown in their servicing roles, and in the way that, at the moments of greatest emotional power in the play, they are removed from realistic representation, and transported into the symbolic. The family-less mother, Mrs Hitchcock, looks after Annie and services the men, all at Musgrave's behest. He 'rules' over this dispersed, unwieldy family, a patriarch still trying to unite a tribe with an outdated and destructive morality.

Chapter 4

The 1960s

The form and content of the drama of the 1950s demonstrate the legacies of surrealism and the absurd as well as a new realism. The juxtaposition of these speaks of the combination of ideas which drew on psychoanalysis and its notion of the unconscious (Lessing), as well as defiantly asserting that the experiences of more ordinary people had a place on stage. In a curious paradox, the new emphasis on the recognisably 'real' experience by implication pointed up the artifice of theatre, the fictive nature of dramatic art.

In many ways, the Method school of acting, which was so influential in American theatre and cinema work during the 1950s, was predicated on a seamless link between the 'real' and the 'artificial', enhancing the illusion of eavesdropping which is inherent in the identification of the 'fourth wall' – the invisible division between audience and stage. It is interesting that this ultra-naturalistic trend (making scripted work sound and look totally spontaneous) was running parallel with the creation of surreal, sometimes non-linear, absurdist styles of writing and performing.

Sometimes the absurd was incorporated into the domestic setting (for example, the work of N. F. Simpson in Britain); sometimes the refusal to represent the 'real' world on stage ruptured the domestic setting (as we have seen in Beckett and Jellicoe). This shift between domestic and public space is not simply a matter of playing around with form for its own sake. Rather, it also indicates that the relationship between these two spheres is itself beginning to lay claim to attention as subject matter.

Here, of course, Brecht's writings about theatre are explicitly important. His influence is strongly seen in Arden's play, where the individual is let loose into the public world of common spaces which represent common ideologies and the relationships of individual characters to those ideologies.

In addition, the cultural developments in Britain during the 1960s, which culminated in the tag of 'swinging London' as the place with new musical, fashion and media trends, lent a great boost of reinforcement to British culture. This sense of Britain as a rehabilitated cultural force after the war, with influences beyond its shores (no longer totally controlled by American cultural images, as was so common during the 1950s), gave many people a sense of the culture's public importance, and this contributed (alongside the specifically theatrical influences briefly delineated above) to a greater confidence in representing more public worlds on stage.

Military homosexuality

A Patriot for Me (1965) by John Osborne

A *Patriot For Me* is an early post-war example of the British public, 'epic' history play. Osborne's play demands a flexible stage space which changes to accommodate all kinds of settings. The scenes are of very varied lengths and the dialogue formal, belying the intimate aspects of the play's central theme.

The play is set in Eastern Europe in 1890. The central figure, Redl, a bright young officer in the Austro-Hungarian army, is a reserved workaholic, earmarked for promotion. He conforms with all that is expected of a fine soldier – at the start he is a second for a duel in which a friend dies in his arms. This conflation of manly behaviour with the principles of individual loyalty and honour demonstrate military and personal values as synonymous with being male: 'A good soldier always knows another one. That's what comradeship is. It's not an empty thing, not an empty thing at all. It's knowing the *value* of other men. And cherishing it.'

Redl is seen as 'dignified and strikes everyone as the type of a gentleman and distinguished officer of the Royal and Imperial Army', the stuff of which leaders and officers are made. His superiors decide that he needs a socially advantageous marriage, and a Countess is opportunistically enlisted: 'He's steadfast, sober, industrious, orderly, he likes orderly things, hates chaos. That's why marriage would suit him so well.' However, we have learned from a scene in Madame Anna's nightclub that in response to a remark made by a waiter about a 'beautiful' girl, Redl has revealed his opinion of female beauty: 'Garbage often is.'

The relationship which develops between Redl and the Countess, despite its sexual nature, is more that of a mutually prostituted opportunism. She is set up to spy on Redl, and he never kisses her when they are in bed together. She matches Redl's misogyny in her opinions about men:

> But then, when you think of the men one knows who are married and who they're married *to*, and what their real snotty little longings are underneath their proud watch and chains, their constant broken, sidelong glances.

She also has contempt for military comradeship: 'I'm afraid I simply can't understand the army or why any man is ever in it.'

While the Countess seems cool, emotionally impervious to her relations with Redl, he, on the other hand, is deeply disturbed by them: 'Do you know: the only time I drink heavily is when I'm with you? No, I didn't mean that. But when you're badgering me and sitting on my head, and, and, I can't breathe.' The tensions he feels may partly be due to the Porterish cadences, a semi-jeering misogyny, and a simultaneous fear of, and magnetism towards, female sexuality, but in the context of this play, Redl's homsexuality provides a more potent rationale.

Redl's Achilles' heel is revealed when he picks up a young soldier (possibly a decoy). There is a short scene between the men in bed, after which Redl is beaten up by some other soldiers. This scene, together with the drag ball scene which opens Act 2, was targeted by the censor. Without these scenes, the ideological centre of the play would have been excised: it is here that the most direct set of challenges to conflations of militarism with manhood are posed. Because these concepts are based on a macho heterosexuality, the realities of these men's desires and emotions are embodied through the theatrical device of cross-dressing. With a double irony, Redl is punished for what is actually an open secret within the army.

Given the harsh opportunism of the Countess, and the general air of misogyny in the play, the ball scene introduces yet another level of irony. It is through dressing as women (the hated opposite sex), who pose a threat to military camaraderie, that the men can find a route to personal and sexual liberation. It is as if they can only come to terms with women by co-opting them (cross-dressing), and actually 'becoming' women. This gives the men ultimate control over the nature of both manhood and womanhood, while excluding 'real' women from

their world. The Baron comments that the drag ball is 'a celebration of
the individual against the rest'. Another character, Kunz, comments:
'You see, this is a place for people to come together. People who are
very often in their everyday lives, rather lonely and even miserable
and feel hunted.'

For 'People' read 'men'. This all-male society is self-contained and
self-perpetuating. The flaw is Redl, who, while he is part of this
world, refuses to be hypocritical about it. His crime is not that he is
homosexual, but that he refuses to play by the army's rules. He does
not mind if his love letters and presents become public. He never
compromises in his work, but the military machine will not tolerate
public efficiency without acceptance of its private codes of behaviour.
This makes him a dispensable scapegoat.

Throughout he never compromises on the primary (heterosexual)
codes of honour and manhood. This includes seeing women as a
threat to male camaraderie – it is telling that the critical change in
his behaviour happens after he has slept with the Countess – as if he
has been violated by the outside world, represented in his bed by a
woman. (Compare the twists of plot in Arden.)

Like Arden, Osborne addresses the nature of militarism and manhood, but he also explores the consequences for the relationship
between public and private conduct, of a camaraderie and ideology
which of necessity is all-male. The army here becomes a community
which substitutes for the family, and taking this metaphor to its conclusion also entails addressing what was then still legally taboo: homosexuality. The moral message is about the relationship between desire,
hypocrisy and dominant social codes of conduct, and what happens
when someone transgresses.

The explicitly all-male world rationalises the fact that the Countess
is never given her own stage space – we never follow her story. The
relationship between public and personal invests the rapid change of
locales and scenes (rather like an army on the move) with a new
stage freedom, in which the space itself becomes one of epic possibility
– have space, will travel anywhere. We can begin to see some of the
ways in which these plays prefigure issues and styles which settle into
the drama after 1968, and which here are radical in terms of both subject matter (homosexuality) and staging. In plays such as these the
family is usurped by the army hierarchy, and the domestic has no
place, as the dominant expectations of what it is to be a man (i.e.
male) are held up for scrutiny. The values of male comradeship can
only emerge in an all-male environment.

The crisis here is still the crisis of post-war manhood, but it is interesting that, by not (in this instance) displacing the crisis of social identity on to relationships with women, the way is opened to address male–male relationships more fully. It is also interesting that Osborne displaces the action on to another country and another time – the end of the nineteenth century, and in another part of Europe. Even so, *A Patriot For Me* stands out with a kind of theatrical and thematic daring similar to that of *Look Back in Anger*.

Behind the lace curtains

Entertaining Mr Sloane *(1964) by Joe Orton*

The family, however, is still with us, along with the spirit of Harold Pinter. Sloane arrives to rent a room with Kath, who is in no doubt about her territory: 'This is my lounge.' The two become intimate fairly quickly; she invites Sloane: 'You'll live with us, then, as one of the family?' For Sloane this is a welcome comfort: 'I never had no family of my own . . . I was brought up in an orphanage.'

Kath fuses maternity, sexuality and possessiveness in her relationship with Sloane, which is shaken when Sloane meets Kath's father, Kemp, and the two men take a dislike to one another. Language and action are brutal and explicit. Kemp lunges at Sloane with a toasting fork. Kath gets Sloane to remove his trousers so she can bandage his leg: 'You've a skin on you like a princess . . . I like a lad with a smooth body.' She teases Sloane, mixing up the maternal and the sexual: 'I'll be your mamma, I need to be loved. Gently. Oh, I shall be so ashamed in the morning. . . . What a big heavy baby you are.'

When Kath's brother Ed arrives, the power relations shift. Ed is gay, obsessed with physical fitness, his conversation peppered with anti-women comments: 'She's like a sow. Though she is my sister.' There are hints that Kath is dependent on Ed, and that she had a baby by a friend of his. Because his world is built round men, women – even his sister – pose a threat to male bonding: 'She got him to put her in the family way, that's what I always maintain. Nothing was the same after. Not ever. A typical story.'

As soon as Ed arrives, he takes over control of the home. Sloane becomes his chauffeur, and Ed decides he wants Sloane to come and live with him. He is furious when he discovers that Sloane and Kath have been sleeping together.

In Act 3, Sloane attacks Kemp and kills him. After this the plot does its final dance: since both Kath and Ed want Sloane, they reach an agreement that he will spend six months with each of them. This sinister inversion of the Persephone myth clinches Sloane's security, since if Kath marries him she cannot be asked to testify against him in court about Kemp's murder.

The play turns all the family conventions upside-down, ending with an incestuous parody of a family. At one level, Kath and Ed are the brother-and-sister parents, with Sloane as their incestuous child. At another, Sloane has murdered a father to sleep with Kath (the mother, who herself cannot tell the difference between mothering and sexual desire). The semblance of a familial lifestyle continues, but behind the lace curtains nothing is what it should be. The codes of private conduct are anarchic, but because they are secret, they are dangerous, redolent with violence and power play, sexualities which seem based on need and greed rather than love and affection. The outward conventions of family life are observed, while behind the lace curtains the taboos are a source of unconventional expression.

Suburbia fights back

Loot (1966) by Joe Orton

As in the previous play, this has only one woman, Fay, in the cast. One living woman, that is. The centre of the stage is dominated throughout by the presence of McLeavy's dead wife in her coffin. Fay is both nurse (a kind of mother) and sexual predator. She has had seven husbands: '. . . one a year on average since I was sixteen. I'm extravagant, you see.'

In this play, there is a gay couple: McLeavy's son Harold and his friend Dennis. They have stolen some money, which they hide in the coffin (no respect for mother, alive or dead), and there is an absurdist element introduced in the figure of Truscott, a policeman pretending to be from the Water Board, who has information about Fay's murky past and the fates of her husbands.

During the course of the play, Fay continually dresses herself and other people, carrying not only the titillatory connotations of a strip-tease, but also the suggestion of constantly shifting identities and relationships. This is reinforced by the fact that every time someone looks at the dead woman in the coffin, she never quite resembles the mother they remembered.

At the end, Truscott forces Fay to admit that she killed Mrs McLeavy, but because all the men fall for her, they see her as a heroine. Suburban lace curtain values have again been vindicated, and this travesty of a family continues to maintain the outward forms expected of them. As Fay says: 'We must keep up appearances.'

Orton's imaginative daring implodes the family within its domestic setting. Every taboo is broken, almost every stereotype invoked: incest, sadistic homosexuality (between men), and at the core, a frightening, voracious female sexuality which triumphs over the men in its orbit. In *Loot*, the core of the family is there before us: the mother, brutally murdered (by a woman who is jealous of her). The power roles in the plays are divided according to gender. The women, deprived of real motherhood, are left with only sexual violence; the men also wield the power of sexuality for their own greed and gain. Yet the woman at the centre of both plays survives only because the men allow her to, so, in a sense, the men still retain power over their stage worlds. In addition, Truscott, as the representative of the outside world, with access to law and order, is revealed as a comic figure with no real bite. Authority can have no hold on the personal.

The domestic setting has been invaded from within by the socially taboo desires of its members, and every single relationship norm has been subverted. This is coruscating satire trying to burst out of its own containment with a vengeance.

Respectable lesbians

The Killing of Sister George (1965) by Frank Marcus

In all the domestic settings thus far, alternatives to the middle-class drawing-room have predominated: suburban, seaside, socially displaced homes. Here we return, on the surface, at least, to a traditional pre- and immediately post-war drawing-room drama: the living room of a West End flat. Doors lead to the bathroom and kitchen; the messier aspects of life all decently removed off stage.

> *The furniture, an incongruous mixture of antique 1930-ish and modern, looks expensive but ill-assorted.*

The latter phrase in this stage direction hints at what we are about to witness with the relationships on stage. This menage consists of two women, June and Alice, who call each other by substitute names: George and Childie. June is an actress who plays the nurse in an Archers-style BBC radio soap opera. The domestic gender roles are conventionally divided: George, the 'man', smokes a cheroot, throws Childie's dolls out of her way, drinks, and generally bangs around in imitation of the traditional husbandly role. Childie clears up after George, loving her dolls in her dual role of 'wife' and 'mother'.

The kind of flat in which the two live asserts their place in the world. There is no direct subtext here, and the cultural world they relate to literally overlooks their flat. They can see Broadcasting House from their window. Work and home are cheek by jowl. George speaks of the way the radio serial 'stands for the traditional values of English life – common sense – tenacity – our rural heritage'.

George is a good actress, and defends her role, both as an acting part and, by extension, as an essential 'real' social role, eliding the distinction between real life and fiction: 'Applehurst needs a District Nurse. Who'd deliver the babies, who'd look after the old folks, I'd like to know.' However, below the surface, she and Childie have a very different real life from the cosy soap model. Their life is based on layers of illusion. Emotionally, their relationship is turbulent, hedged in by rituals. After a row between them, Childie goes through the ritual of pretending to eat the butt of George's cigar (obvious symbolism here . . .), but, despite these sado-masochistic overtones, the relationship between them is one of great vitality. They control and enjoy their own rituals, by comparison with members of Orton's family, who often seem gripped by events outside their control.

The disjuncture between the two worlds – the community codes put out by the soap, and the women's covert gay reality – is revealed with the arrival of George's boss Mrs Mercy (a misnomer if ever there was one). George and Mercy both served in the army during the war, affording a brief glimpse into the distaff side of the service, and linking its conventions with the English public school:

Mercy: Oh dear, just like a dormitory feast – all this girlish banter.
George: I was captain of the hockey team and a keen disciplinarian
        – God help the girl I caught making me an apple pie bed.

Mercy has come to reprimand George for her 'bad' behaviour, getting drunk and having 'proceeded to assault two nuns'. As with Redl, her colleagues know the truth about her private life, but cannot condone it when it threatens to become public knowledge. George is told off because she has behaved publicly like a man, not as either her stage 'character' or her female social role dictate as 'proper'. While George reacts to this, Childie and Mercy flirt, colluding in 'feminine' behaviour.

As the play proceeds into Act 2, the tensions from the outside world enter the relationship. George learns that she is to be written out of an episode, and she is sure that this is the beginning of the end. There are echoes of the Helen/Jo relationship in A *Taste of Honey*, where two women in a close relationship can only bicker and snipe at one another. The bickering spills over into the rituals which enable the relationship to find an acceptable form, almost like a kind of repeated marriage ceremonial which is used to constantly re-invent the relationship. The moments of ritual also provide a space within which the women can harmonise – such as when they dress as Laurel and Hardy, creating a 'camp' space where they can be safe. When they are in these 'fictional' roles their real relationship is at its most secure. As George shows, there is real attraction between them, as she describes the first time she met Childie: 'There was a smell of talcum powder and bath crystals – it was like an enchanted wood.'

The final crisis comes when Mercy brings them the bad news that George is to be killed off: 'We live in a violent world, Miss Buckridge, surrounded by death and destruction. It's the policy of the BBC to face up to reality.' Although this is a blow, George comes to terms with her fate with some relief: 'George and I have parted company. And do you know, I'm glad to be free of the silly bitch . . . I am saying that my name is June. June Buckridge. I'm endeavouring to memorise it.'

However, this is not the end. Mercy offers June a job playing Clarabelle Cow in a children's programme, but since for June the dividing line between fantasy and reality is blurred, she takes this as the insult it is clearly meant to be. Mrs Mercy, as the 'outsider' figure, is of course the catalyst Greek messenger bringing the bad news, but she also invades June's private life, joining Childie in talking childishly to the dolls, as if the two of them are ganging up against the adult 'male' persona of George.

The revelations are not over. As the tension between George and Childie mounts, another secret is out. Childie too is not what she appears to be. She is actually 34, having had an illegitimate child at 18. There are roles within roles, all acquired for the sake of conformity with the dominant ideology. Mercy comments on George's soap fate with a backhanded compliment:

Remember: Sister George was killed not because she was hated, but because she was loved. . . . If you study anthropology you'll discover that in primitive societies it was always the best loved member of the community who was selected as the sacrificial victim. They felt that by killing him (*sic*) the goodness and strength of the victim would pass into them. It was both a purge and a rededication.

For George, of course, this is double-edged; she has lost her job, and her respectable public identity. It is also an ironic comment on her private life, since as a lesbian she would be far from loved; prevailing prejudice would see her as a freak. Because the 'actress' has transgressed in her public behaviour (behaving like a man), the (private) lesbian is punished by losing her job.

In this all-female play, Mercy mediates between the personal and professional worlds. She represents the power of the BBC, controlled by faceless men lurking behind the walls of the theatre. Although we know nothing of her sexuality for sure, she can function in both business power play and in the sado-masochistic world of George and Childie. We are left at the end with the re-establishment of the status quo: the serial will continue, Alice will never grow up, but continue to prance around wearing baby doll pyjamas. June agrees to take the job of Clarabelle, mooing a 'heart-rending' sound. She will continue to work, and ironically, though she has rehabilitated her own name, she has in the process lost her professional voice – she has only the language of a cow.

The theatrical strand in the plot helps to highlight the theatrical need of the couple to play roles which are different from their real selves, in a world where their sexual reality is taboo. The unacceptable must remain contained within the domestic; June and Alice can no more 'come out' into this world than George can get away with being drunk in public. Given these restrictions, the only model they have is to play the part of yet another perverse and subversive family: Childie as both wife and child (she too has had to have her motherhood imaginatively and poignantly destroyed), George as the man, with private rituals to replace the social rituals which more 'conventional' couples can enjoy. However, the relationship does survive, even though it has taken a bashing and has to remain secret, because it has to find a *modus vivendi* within the delineation of the conventional.

Beginning to come out

Staircase (1966) by Charles Dyer

Set in a barber's shop after hours, we are on neutral territory, neither fully public nor fully private. Harry has just finished shaving Charlie, in a comfortable image of one man caring for another (cf. Wesker). The dialogue is camp and intimate, and homes straight in on a discussion about sex and reproduction:

> I believe half Man's trouble is due to Nature's reproductive systems. I do . . . it should be nicer, cleaner, *prettier*. It shouldn't be so folded up and sort of underneath. . . . What's wrong with having, say, a couple of antennas. Males. Females. The lot. Nothing different or sniggery. Pleasant smile; raise your hat; shake antennas; good laugh in the bargain.

The irony, poignancy and honesty of this is far removed from the tortured displacement of Jimmy Porter's bewilderment about male gender identity. Because in the world of male homosexuality (twilight though it still is), sexual identity is seen straightforwardly for what it is, paternity enters as an issue. Charlie has been married and has a child, to the envy of Harry. Charlie has received a summons from the police for behaving, in police jargon: 'in a manner likely to cause a serious breach of the peace and did parade in female attire . . . and did importune in a manner calculated to bring – depravity.' Charlie's defence is that he was (1) married with a baby and that this makes him normal, and (2) simply doing his old panto act.

The play includes overt references to the possibilities of a new law legalising homosexuality for consenting males over 21, but Charlie comments: 'I need no laws, need no laws.' The men play on their need for fantasy; Charlie says, 'I need excitement, Harry. Haven't your guts to be ordinary, Harry. Hate being ordinary.' There is the added irony that the author uses his own name for one of the characters:

> By hell, if ever I finish me great play I'll name the villain after meself, to prove I've a spot of faith in humanity. . . . To prove I've enough humility to travel under any label . . . without shame.

Their relationship, like that between George and Childie, has to be sustained by private ritual, by ways of speaking and behaving which constitute a private replacement for a real social milieu in which they can be themselves. However, here there is no external metaphor, and the camp wit is more intimate and theatrically creative than in *Sister George*, which gives a greater security to Charlie and Harry, despite the latter's sad comment: 'Trouble with our sort, you're never left with anyone.' Homosexuality is approached more confrontationally and realistically, allowing the vulnerabilities of the characters: two men who are trying to recognise each other and themselves as having a sexual identity which is socially problematical and therefore cannot be clearly defined or named with comfort – yet.

Urban violence

Saved (1965) by Edward Bond

The final play in this section is one in which the family, the domestic setting and the public space encounter one another in a collision which spells danger for urban life and personal relationships. At its centre is a startling and shocking image of violence against the innocent: a baby stoned to death in its pram.

Three generations of the same family share a house. Harry and Mary, their daughter Pam, and her baby. The play opens in a living room, where Pam has brought back Len, whom she has picked up. They have sex and he feeds her sweets until she almost chokes. Sexuality, violence, pleasure and sado-masochism are all part of this nexus of young relationships. Len moves in (lodger, outsider figure), and, in the context of a not very good relationship between Harry and Mary, Len and Pam cling together – there is a running gag about her knitting him a jumper which she never quite finishes.

The action shifts to a park. Four men draw Len into their group, with a series of choral jokes about women and sex. The group banter is a kind of male bonding, but it is one based on bewilderment about, and fear of, women. At home, Mary serves food while everyone silently watches television. Upstairs, Pam's baby is crying, ignored by everyone, even when it chokes. Pam is too lazy, and even though Len expresses some concern, he does not actually do anything, lending an irony to his comment that 'Kids need proper 'omes'.

Later (cf. Geof, in *A Taste of Honey*), Len looks after the baby, and he also 'mothers' Pam, telling her she does not know how to look after herself. When they argue about the baby, they both call it 'it'; later, it is only Len who calls the baby 'he', the only one to ascribe it any identity at all.

Even in the lead-up to the stoning, goaded on by the other young people, Len still tries to protect the baby, telling Pam she has left the brake off the pram. However, Pam has already gone off with another man, Fred, and although Fred starts by defending the baby when the lads make cruel jokes, he is finally goaded into throwing the first stone. When Pam comes back, she wheels the pram away without even looking into it, in a final closing statement about her heartlessness as a mother. The fact that she is taken off stage also prevents us from seeing how she responds when she discovers that her baby is dead.

The act of stoning the baby to death operates at a number of different levels. It is a symptom of an urban lawlessness and (male) disaffection which results in a murderous lack of any 'natural' tender feeling. The 'baby' represents all that is helpless and innocent, and therefore becomes an easy scapegoat for the undirected social aggression of the (male) gang. This cipherisation of the baby thus removes it (it realises its 'itness', as it were) from associations with the 'real' – and thus Pam cannot be allowed to be imagined as a 'real' mother who, despite her earlier neglect, might show grief and anger at what has happened to her child. Social aggression, as well as gender crisis – the gang's descent into violence because of a lack of manhood role (no good causes left?), and Pam and Mary's detachment from the tenderness of motherhood – are both 'taken out' on the baby.

Later, Fred is in prison, an almost unwilling victim, carried along by the others. Len does nothing. Throughout there is a strong sense that the young men have to close ranks against Pam, unable to face the fact that she is a mother; they have to screen out the concept of 'mother', and effectively destroy it by killing the baby. Conversely, they cannot kill the baby without denying Pam's motherhood.

The remainder of the play witnesses a further disintegration of the family, and a subversion of gender roles: Len takes on more and more of the conventionally female roles: cleaning shoes, sewing buttons on his shirt, darning Mary's stockings. There is some sexual by-play between Len and Mary (reminiscent of Orton), with Harry (*pace* Wesker) as an asexual older husband. Later, Mary hits Harry and scalds him with the teapot – she is continually wounding him throughout the play; the male here is actively damaged by his wife. If one were to add a Freudian dimension to this analysis, one could say that Mary is symbolically castrating Harry, as well as castigating him for his lack of manliness, his 'masculinity'. The social anarchy also disrupts gender roles. *Pace* Osborne, Harry harks back nostalgically to the war: 'Most I remember the peace and quiet . . . everything still. You don't get it that quiet now.'

The implication here (ironic, given the thunder and blood of war) is that even war is peaceful, compared with the thunder of domestic battles. At the end, they are all back on domestic territory, in the living room, each attending quietly to their own business; the only sound is Len banging as he repairs a chair. Even at the end, when all efforts at verbal communication have broken down, he is still the only one trying to mend something.

The play balances and interweaves the inner and outer worlds of the domestic/private with the social/public. This is exemplified in the way the staging moves from living room to public space, and in the plotted comparative breakdowns of domestic and social order. Although there is no explicit cause and effect spelled out (does the breakdown of the family cause social violence, or vice versa?) there is an implied causal hierarchy in the gender dynamics of the plot. The action follows the fortunes (largely) of the men. Both in the public and private worlds, Pam and Mary are doubly atomised and isolated. There is no significant relationship between the two of them; compared with Delaney, there is no space here to play out the mother–daughter relationship. There is also no female 'gang' equivalent, no female bonding, no social nexus for femaleness, only the vulnerable, precarious locus of a domestic life in which female sexuality and motherhood are skewed and destroyed.

The figure of Len becomes significant here. As an 'outsider' both from public and private groupings he is free to move between the two, and he is the linking device around which the two worlds of the play pivot. Interestingly, he is something of a gender chameleon; when he is with the gang he is accepted by them as a 'man', and when he is in the house he can take on (and effectively usurp!) the domestic functions of mothering and nurturing (cf. Steve in *The Sport of my Mad Mother*). He becomes an almost utopian anti-hero, embodying the 'positive' qualities of masculinity and femininity, marginally rising above his fellow men, but actually usurping the emotional territories of the women. The women never engage with the moral questions; the men literally speak for them.

Of course, the play shocks and challenges with the strength of its moral questioning about the ease, function and dangers of violence. This is a 'political' issue attached, not as in Arden, to the army, an arm of the state, but to the ethics of everyday life and interpersonal relationships. These questions are, of course, relevant to both men and women (general), but the theatrical force is repositioned because of the gender imbalance and point of view. In everything we have seen, Pam and Mary have little to redeem them. They are excluded from public life (no place in the gang) and they are shown as heartless and violent within the family, enabling their functions to be taken over by Len, a man. The only emergent hope is in a male figure, who also literally keeps the home going.

However anarchic this world, women have no place in it. Because Len is a man, and triumphs at the end (insofar as anyone does), he functions as both a real and symbolic carrier of hope. He can run the family, and perhaps, if his sensibilities prevail, even gangland could be affected. The moral message thus carries a contradictory subtext: only men can engage in both social reality and moral questioning; women fail before they even start.

Chapter 5

The Lady Macbeth syndrome

The 1950s and 1960s: conclusions

It may appear to be a long journey from Jimmy Porter's disaffected cries in the new world of 1956 to Edward Bond's dead baby (the term 'stoned' here carries a chilling *double entendre*) in 1965. In one sense, of course, it is a long journey. Where Jimmy and Alison retreat to a cocoon-like game of bears and squirrels, at least with some form of comfort in the storm of gender role uncertainty, Bond's family maintains the outer form, but has imploded from within to self-destruct into social and personal violence.

The model of the family, real and symbolic, is central to all the plays of these two decades. All the relationships and actions in the plays take place within the conventions of a 'family' model (parent couple and child/children, however distorted), and so inevitably the plays become about what has happened or is perceived as happening to the family itself – real and symbolic. The limitations on what is permitted within family life, the codes of repression, the imagery, are themselves represented in ways indirectly produced by censorship.

The biological family appears in Wesker; the depleted family in crisis in Osborne, Lessing, Bond and Delaney, the family manifesting symptoms of the taboo in Orton, Pinter and Marcus. The memory of family–community bonding is there in Arden, and in its painful absence in the displaced, orphaned worlds of Beckett and Jellicoe.

Thus Orton's mix of the emotional realities behind the lace curtains includes tortured same-sex relations, death, voracious sexuality and greed as virtually coterminous. Osborne, Wesker and Lessing give us families just about hanging on by their fingernails, and Orton's and Pinter's families are helpless travesties. In Osborne's case, the family is reduced to a childless, defensive coupledom; in Wesker's, political idealism, however bruised, remains a binding element in familial relationships. Of all the families, Wesker's retains the most conventional signs – an extended family – and perhaps this is because for this family there is a meeting point between public and private, between political engagement and personal emotion. In his plays, significantly, the characters are most aware of the outside, political world, in relation to which they take on conscious positions. The fact that the family is Jewish (in however secular a fashion) is significant: as Jews, they are culturally marginal, and the family is an important grounding focus. By comparison, Bond's family – also extended – is disintegrating from within, as social order breaks down outside. Here too the links between public and private are symbiotic, with a far bleaker vision on offer.

New, alternative families are offered by Delaney and Marcus. In the first, the biological mother–daughter relationship, fractured and unhappy as it is, remains more powerful than the unconventional (and socially challenging) bonding of single mother and gay father-figure. This carries a certain poignant irony: the biological relationship is full of abrasive struggle, while the socially unconventional at least appears to offer something like happiness. The play may breach taboos, but it does not have the imaginative courage to follow the convictions, and in the end a semblance of family unity, however bitter, triumphs.

Similarly, Sister George and Childie are contained by social role models, conventions. Almost 'outed', in the end they take the crumbs offered to them, and retreat (*pace* Osborne) into their private rituals and games – bolstered with a private and still secret affection. They also cannot free themselves from the model of the familial roles – a curious cross-over, in which Childie is both 'wife' and child, and where both she and George conform to the male/female-based gay role models of butch and femme.

In the worlds of Arden and Osborne (*A Patriot for Me*), larger social organisations are at the centre of the action: the all-male world of the army, past and present, its ethos and its codes. Here familial organisation is replaced by social community; the closest we come to any home in Arden is the pub, and in Osborne domestic rooms are merely the places where sex (hetero and homo) takes place.

The worlds of Beckett and Jellicoe share a formal similarity; a fragmented social language, which mixes poetic ritual with the vernacular, which fragments any conventional notions of character and recognisable relationship. They also share a limbo-like setting, where the signs of domestic and/or public life are absent. Neither settings nor the conventions of dialogue use the surface trappings of realism – of the externals which signal realistic representation of the domestic.

Beckett uses this limbo to suggest state authority in relation to the individual, where Jellicoe uses limbo to call on myth to interrogate gender roles. There are homo-erotic undertones in Beckett's all-male world, and Delaney's mythic and symbolic subject matter centres around heterosexual tension, with, as its focus, the figure of the mother.

The moral questions, or questions of personal identity and meaningfulness, either revolve around a specifically male figure: Osborne (*Look Back in Anger* and *A Patriot for Me*), Arden, or are clustered round male groupings: Beckett, Arden, Osborne (*A Patriot for Me*); or, where they involve mixed family groupings, always where the women are in a minority, centre round the concerns of the male majority: Pinter, Orton, Bond. Where there is a stronger female presence – Wesker, Marcus, and (oddly) Jellicoe – the authority of the male is ultimately invoked; in the first, by the fact that although Sarah is a person of amazing strength and distinction, and Beatie finds her voice, the real mantle of personal and political questing has been passed on to Ronnie. In the case of Marcus, the dominating presence of the male-powered BBC controls the worlds of all three women. The 'voice' of the BBC thus also represents the institutional voice of the dominant culture and its ethos.

Even in the surreal world of Jellicoe, where the sexual and maternal power of Greta is total, in the end the status quo – calm, security – is restored via the agency of the (non-verbal) male musician who controls the stage world, symbolising wider male power, with no need to incorporate the male into the plot, or give him language/culture. In one sense, even though each play treats them slightly differently, the issues addressed in all these plays are ones concerning male identity: what it is to be male, what it is for men to hold and live by certain values ('causes', *pace* Jimmy Porter) in the second half of the twentieth century. The male, present or absent, verbal or silent, controls the dramatic structure of these worlds.

Delaney and Lessing do not fall into quite such a clear category. Of course Delaney's partial family still ascribes to conventions which ultimately derive from a male-dominant political system, but within the stage world the women are shown to have choices, and in part they choose a solidarity based on gender, as well as biological relationship. Helen need not return, Jo could have insisted on Geof staying. This is enabled by the idiomatic and gritty realism of the mother–daughter relationship and the matching language (eat your heart out, *Eastenders*!), but more significantly because this, together with Lessing's plays, is a rare piece in which the women are not only centre stage –

the dramatic structure is driven by what happens to Jo – but in which the mother–daughter (or mother–son) relationship, and indeed maternity/motherhood itself – are at the centre of the play's actions, emotions and dilemmas.

This brings me to the heart of the family, and to the key symbolic feature of the drama of the 1950s and 1960s: the mother. At the physical and domestic centre of the family is the mother. In Marxist terms, she is in charge of the reproduction of labour power in two senses. She gives birth to the next generation, and thus she can come to represent not only procreation and the link between generations, but also hope and power. She does the housework (Osborne, Wesker, Pinter, etc.). Her maternal being clinches the definition of the 'family'; before there are children there is only the couple, adult peers. With children come inter-generational relationships, the extended family (aunts, uncles, cousins, etc.), a whole nexus of biological and socially linked relationships. Motherhood is more obviously visible than fatherhood in its early stages – pregnancy, birth, early childcare – even though both are crucial biological, social and emotional roles.

It thus becomes fascinating to see how, in the plays of the 1950s and 1960s, the mother (actual and figurative) appears again and again, attracting to her presence so much of the emotional symbolism accruing to the dilemmas (social and personal) which are explored in the dramas. In Osborne (*Look Back in Anger*), for Jimmy to flourish and become a 'man', Alison must lose her capacity to bear children – she is subjected to a kind of imaginative female castration. There is room here for only one child: Jimmy. In Wesker, powerful, multi-faceted as she is, Sarah and the women in *Roots* can only have as their counterparts damaged or absent males, fulfilling the mirror image of the Alison–Jimmy axis. Only one sex can be strong, and, for it to be so, the other has to be conceptually and actually weakened or deprived. Since women, by social tradition, are already the 'weaker' sex, where a strong woman has been imagined, the otherwise strong male must be seen to be damaged. This damage is visited upon the male body – he is ill, dying, incapacitated.

Pinter's Meg has no biological children, only a conflated maternal/sexual attraction to Stanley. She loses this surrogate child, and is left with the sterile relationship with Petey to nurture. Beckett's lost boys (old and young) have no mother to help them tie their shoe-laces or keep their hats clean. Arden's Annie, like Alison and Meg, has to lose her child (and she has the added bonus of briefly going 'mad' – traditionally signalled by the woman character, *à la* Ophelia, starting to sing, an interesting conflation of Brechtian device with traditional sexist representation), while Mrs Hitchcock becomes the army's 'mother', just as Annie has become the army's whore.

Orton lays the dead mother full-frontally before us on stage throughout the evening. Fay becomes the substitute – with a defiant (liberated?) sexuality which has no moral boundaries – money or people, it's all the same to her if she wants it. (Here we have a suggestive prefiguring of the way Caryl Churchill dovetails the sexual/economic in *Owners*.) Marcus' Childie is presented as a sad woman who can never have children, and is doomed to play with dolls (and thus pretend to be a child) forever. Bond's mothers, both Mary and Pam, seem to have been emotionally lobotomised in their inability to respond to the needs of a helpless baby.

Interestingly, the three women playwrights take a slightly different imaginative tack. In Delaney, active, living, life-choice motherhood is contrasted across generations. Helen, with her desire for independence, has chosen to deny any softer emotions towards Jo (guilt?). Jo, on the other hand, despite her fears and doubts (and despite the fact that, like Bond's Len, Geof is a 'maternal' male), is going to have the baby. Delaney allows her women to be mothers, to take motherhood seriously, to question its expectations, explore its norms and fears and to prepare to give birth. Jellicoe turns Orton's image upside-down, and we have a live birth on stage (the bundle discreetly hidden behind screens). Greta celebrates mythic motherhood with a desire to give birth to millions more (à la Lilith). Greta's defiance is explicit in response to men's fear of her sexual and maternal being. In this version the mother survives, albeit with no father, a formidable virgin birth. Lessing shows us mothers whose lives are divided between nurturing and intellectual activities.

Here then, in the two contrasting theatrical forms of the period – realism and abstract absurdism – we have an example of a clear gender divide. Whereas for the male-gendered imaginations motherhood has to be denied or destroyed for men to develop a sense of self, and female strength is therefore hedged around, for the female-gendered imaginations female articulacy, dominance in the stage structure and actual motherhood can be explored, although within other imaginative limits, defined by social taboos and theatrical censorship.

In many of these plays a social 'outsider' has a catalytic function: Pinter, Arden, Orton, Marcus, Delaney, Beckett, Lessing and Bond all use outsider or marginal figures to trigger the central action. The use of such a figure has a long history in drama, and in one sense it is quite logical; the arrival of someone, or something, out of the ordinary will always highlight existing structures, and/or reveal hidden dilemmas. The exceptional catalyst generally proves the rule, but alongside this actual outsider figure it is as if, symbolically speaking, the mother must be made into an outsider, has to be expelled from a world in order for men (sic) to face their real angsts and dilemmas. Male identity and independence can only exist if the mother is destroyed. The very being of the mother herself is at stake. Put simply, for men motherhood must become symbolic, for women it may be symbolic, but it is also more likely to be real.

In terms of the gender dynamic, structurally, and in terms of the weight of meaning, one of the implications of the above analysis is that in the plays of the period by men, powerful and effective as they all are, women are not only *not* the subjects in male-authored plays, but they become ossified into symbols, ciphers, symbolic objects for the male-centred dilemmas. Even in Wesker, where Sarah carries the historic anguish and commitment from the 1930s through to the late 1950s, and where Beatie discovers her (more symbolic than real) voice, there are costs in terms of male identity.

From Osborne through to Bond we have the foundations for what I call the Lady Macbeth Syndrome; an approach to the defining of male identity in a way that is predicated on the imaginative annihilation of motherhood. Further, since it is only women who are mothers, this means that of necessity femaleness itself has to be delimited at best, destroyed at worst, or transformed into a metaphor. Mother becomes metaphor. In the plays by women, on the other hand, women and some of their concerns are more clearly the subjects of the plays; literally in Delaney, realistically in the world of ideas in Lessing, more hedged in and symbolically in Jellicoe.

A word about form here: I have described somewhat simplistically the two arenas of form in these plays, but I hope it is clear that in the end it is not the form itself which either transcends or determines the meaning. Clearly form is vital (form and style are what enable us to distinguish the language of one play from another), but there is no necessary value judgement to be attached to form in this context. Realism is no worse and no better than absurdism/abstraction in terms of the gender divide or the gender dynamic. Form itself carries no meaning in the abstract, but only as a consequence of how it affects and refracts content, argument or message. This is relevant, as will be seen later, when I confront some of the well-meaning but cul-de-sac attempts to define aesthetics itself as in some way 'gendered', and to ascribe certain kinds of form to male- or female-gendered imaginations.

It therefore follows that in an imaginative sense, form 'follows' from, is a by-product of, content; and it means that form is not, in and of itself, either 'reactionary' or 'progressive', as some radical critics and academics, eager to annex the signs of radicalism, assert.

Beckett and Jellicoe achieve a mesh of form and content which has enabled their plays to herald coherences of meaning and theatrical effectiveness, even if we may discuss what they are 'about' and what they 'mean', even if their impetus comes from different points on the gender divide. Less able writers playing around with limbo and mythic language might just produce jumbled rubbish. Similarly, a care-fully spelled out social realist play can be radical, amazingly powerful and moving, or pedantic and pedestrian. In terms of value judgements, the aesthetic yardsticks depend not simply on the presence of certain elements but on the way these elements are organised, structured and built into their particular narrative textual patterns.

This becomes particularly important when we address the relation-ship between gender and the post-censorship theatre world, where taboos were ostensibly removed, where realpolitik and ideological debate became part of sections of the theatre industry itself. The voice which follows comes from 1965, a moment when the campaign to abolish theatre censorship was gathering momentum. Kenneth Tynan unwittingly announces the arrival of new writing which proved his case.

Chapter 6

The Royal Smut-Hound by Kenneth Tynan (1965)

For 'wind from a duck's behind', substitute 'wind from Mount Zion'.
Omit 'crap', substitute 'jazz'.
Omit 'balls of the Medici': 'testicles of the Medici' would be acceptable.
Delete 'postcoital', substitute 'late evening'.
For 'the Vicar's got the clappers', substitute 'the Vicar's dropped a clanger'.
Omit 'piss off, piss off, piss off', substitute 'shut your steaming gob'.

These staccato commands are authentic and typical extracts from letters dispatched in recent years from the office of the Lord Chamberlain of Great Britain, second ranking dignitary of Her Majesty's Court. He is the official in charge of the royal household, responsible for receiving visiting potentates and for arranging all state ceremonies from christenings to coronations. He also appoints the Keeper of the Royal Swans. On no account must he be confused with the Lord *Great* Chamberlain – a lowly sixth in the dignitary ratings – who supervises royal openings of Parliament and helps the monarch (if the latter is male) to dress on coronation mornings.

Among the other duties of the Lord Small Chamberlain, as we may call him in passing, is that of censoring all plays presented for public performance in the United Kingdom; and it is this which explains the obscene correspondence that issues from his headquarters in St James' Palace. On royally embossed notepaper, producers all over the country are gravely informed that 'fart', 'tits', 'sod', 'sperm', 'arse', 'Jesus!', etc. are illicit expressions, and that 'the Lord Chamberlain cannot accept the word "screwed" in place of the word "shagged"'. It is something of a wonder that no one has lodged a complaint against His Lordship for corrupting and depraving the innocent secretaries to whom this spicy stuff is dictated; at the very least, the Post Office might intervene to prevent what looks to me like a flagrant misuse of the mail.

At the moment there is nothing we can do about it. The Lord Chamberlain's role as legal censor dates back to 1737, when Sir Robert Walpole's administration – probably the most venal in British history – rushed an Act through Parliament to protect itself from criticism in the theatre. Ever since Tudor times, the Chamberlain (or his subordinate, the Master of the Revels) had been empowered by royal proclamation to regulate dramatic entertainments, but he had mainly confined his cuts to matters of heresy or sedition that might offend the monarch. It was Walpole's panicky vengefulness that gave statutory recognition and legislative force to the Chamberlain's powers, and established a Court official as the sole dictator of the British theatre. Henceforth, no new plays or additions to old ones could be staged without his approval.

This authority was toughened and extended by the Theatres Act of 1843, a repellent piece of legislation that is still in force. Under its provisions, anything previously unperformed must be submitted to 'the Malvolio of St James' Palace' (Bernard Shaw's phrase) at least a week before opening night; a reading fee of two guineas is charged, so that you pay for the privilege of being banned; licences already granted may be revoked if the Chamberlain changes his mind (or if there is a change of Chamberlain); and any theatre presenting an unlicensed work to a paying audience will be summarily closed down. His Lordship can impose a ban 'whenever he shall be of opinion that it is fitting for the Preservation of Good Manners, Decorum, or of the Public Peace'. He need give no reason for his decisions, from which there is no appeal. Since he is appointed directly by the sovereign, he is not responsible to the House of Commons. He inhabits a limbo aloof from democracy, answerable only to his own hunches. The rules by which he judges plays are nowhere defined in law; to quote Shaw again and not for the last time, 'they simply codify the present and most of the past prejudices of the class he represents'.

Since he is always recruited from the peerage, he naturally tends to forbid attacks on institutions like the Church and the Crown. He never permits plays about eminent British subjects, living or recently dead, no matter how harmless the content and despite the fact that Britain's libel laws are about the strictest on earth. Above all, he feels a paternal need to protect his flock from exposure to words or gestures relating to bodily functions below the navel and above the upper thigh.

This – the bedding-*cum*-liquid-and-solid-eliminating area – is what preoccupies him most, and involves the writers and producers who have to deal with him in the largest amount of wasted time.

The normal procedure is as follows: enclosing the two-guinea fee, you submit your script, which is then read by one of three 'Examiners' – anonymous part-time workers, occasionally with some theatrical background. The Examiner passes it on with his comments to the Chamberlain's two Comptrollers – army officers in early middle age – who add their own observations before referring it to the boss himself. Then begins the salty correspondence, which may go on for months. The Comptroller lists the required cuts and changes; the producer replies, agreeing, protesting or proposing alternatives. (A fine recent protest was penned by the director of John Osborne's *Inadmissible Evidence*: 'We find that the cutting of the words "menstrual periods" is blocking the flow of the scene.')

If postal deadlock is reached, the next stage is a chat with the Comptroller, who usually comes over as a breezy man of the world who knows as much about four-letter words as the next man but somehow feels that the next man should be prevented from hearing them. Insane bargaining takes place: the Comptroller may permit you a 'pee' in Act 1 so long as you delete a 'Christ!' in Act 3. Discussing a one-line gag about the hero's mother-in-law in Osborne's *Look Back in Anger* ('She's as rough as a night in a Bombay brothel'), the Comptroller roared with laugher and said: 'That's a splendid phrase, and I shall use it in the Guards' Club, but it won't do for the theatre, where people don't know one another.' If the author still declines to be slashed and rewritten by strangers, he can apply for an interview with the Chamberlain himself; but unless he has a pretty powerful management behind him he is unlikely to get one; and it has seldom been known to do any good.

Chamberlains are rarely garrulous. Shaw said of the one who held office in his youth that he made only two recorded pronouncements: 'I am not an agricultural labourer', and 'Who is Tolstoy?' The present incumbent is more of a loose-mouth. In the spring of 1965 he gave an interview to the London *Sunday Times*, in the course of which he said: 'You'd be surprised to see the number of four-letter words and I think I can say obscenities, that are sometimes included in scripts by the most reputable people.' (He meant, of course, 'piss', 'arse' and 'shit' as well as the obvious venereal monosyllables.) 'We normally cut certain expletives, for example, "Christ" and "Jesus",' he went on, 'which are admittedly used in common parlance . . . but still do give offence to a great number of people.' When asked by the interviewer which subject – sex, religion or politics – raised the most problems, he replied that in terms of quantity, sex was the most troublesome, although: 'I have personally found the religious ones most difficult of all.' He admitted that, if faced with a play that satirised Christianity, 'I would start with a bias against it'. In the six months immediately preceding this colloquy, his office had received 441 scripts, of which sixty-three had been returned for cutting and changing. In eighteen cases the proposed alterations were radical. One of the latter group was John Osborne's *A Patriot For Me*, a play factually based on the career of a homosexual colonel in the Austro-Hungarian army who was black-mailed into spying for the Russians and finally committed suicide. The Chamberlain demanded the excision of five whole scenes. The author refused, and the producers had to turn their theatre into a private club in order to present a major new work by one of Britain's leading dramatists.

Who is the Lord Chamberlain? As I write, he is Cameron Fromanteel, first Baron Cobbold, educated at Eton and Cambridge, and a former Governor of the Bank of England; a cheerful, toothy, soothing chap in his early sixties. His predecessor, who retired in 1963, was the 11th Earl of Scarbrough, educated at Eton and Oxford, and a former Governor of Bombay. Unlike Lord Cobbold, he could boast firsthand experience of artistic endeavour, having written, in 1936, *The History of the Eleventh Hussars*.

These are the men who have exercised absolute power over British drama for the past fourteen years. As a highly respected director once put it: 'Why should a colonial administrator be allowed to put fig leaves on statues? Or a banker to paint out the bits of pictures that he doesn't like?' He is not alone in his bewilderment, which history amply supports. Around the turn of the century, the poet Swinburne declared that the Lord Chamberlain had exposed the English stage 'to the contempt and compassion of civilised Europe'. To cite a few other spokesmen from the same period:

> All I can say is that something or other – which probably is consciousness of the Censor – appears to deter men of letters who have other channels for communicating with the public, from writing for the stage.
>
> (Thomas Hardy)

The censorship, with its quite wanton power of suppression, has always been one of the reasons why I haven't ventured into play-writing.

(H.G. Wells)

I am certain that a dramatic author may be shamefully hindered, and that such a situation is intolerable; a disgrace to the tone, to the character, of this country's civilization.

(Joseph Conrad)

There is not perhaps another field so fine in the England of today for a man or woman of letters, but all the other literary fields are free. This one alone has a blind bull in it.
(From a protest signed by many writers, including Henry James, J. M. Barrie, Galsworthy, Conan Doyle and Shaw)

All this suggests that Shaw was right when he argued that the dearth of good English plays between the early eighteenth century and his own début in the late nineteenth century was entirely due to the existence of the Lord Chamberlain, a baleful deterrent lurking on the threshold of creativity. After all, why should a first-rate writer venture into a theatre where Sophocles' *Oedipus Rex* was banned? Just before the First World War, Sir Herbert Beerbohm Tree wanted to stage this great tragedy of incest; the censor brusquely turned him down, a decision which moved the popular playwright Henry Arthur Jones to publish a suave letter of complaint. It read in part:

Now, of course, if any considerable body of Englishmen are arranging to marry their mothers, whether by accident or design, it must be stopped at once. But it is not a frequent occurrence in any class of English society. Throughout the course of my life I have not met more than six men who were anxious to do it.

We know very little about the qualities the sovereign looks for when he or she appoints a Chamberlain. According to the current holder of the office, whose opinion may not be wholly disinterested, they include 'wide experience, a knowledge of what is going on in the contemporary world, and the habit of sifting advice, reaching decisions and taking responsibility'. Of the methods employed by the Chamberlain to select an Examiner of plays, we know nothing at all. Shaw wrote in 1899:

It will be inferred that no pains are spared to secure the services of a very highly qualified and distinguished person to wield this astonishing power – say the holder of a University chair of Literature and Dramaturgy. The inference is erroneous. You are not allowed to sell stamps in an English post office without previously passing an examination; but you may become Examiner of plays without necessarily knowing how to read or write.

This is not to say that a fully qualified Examiner would be an improvement. Rather the contrary: a censor with a first-rate mind, capable of penetrating the elaborate disguises under which contraband ideas are smuggled to the public, and shrewd enough to detect potential non-conformity in the foetal stage, could castrate the drama far more effectively than the present posse of numskulls. All censors are bad, but clever ones are the worst.

In Elizabethan times and throughout the seventeenth century, when censorship was largely carried out by the Master of the Revels, the chief qualification for the job was greed. The fee for reading a script rose during this period from five shillings to one pound, and in the 1660s a particularly corrupt Master attempted to raise his income by claiming authority over such public pleasures as cockfights, billiards and ninepins. But although the censor was grasping, he was relatively harmless; he did not see himself as the nation's moral guardian, and as long as authors refrained from advocating the overthrow of the monarchy and the established Church, their freedom – especially in sexual matters – was virtually complete.

The rot that still plagues the British theatre set in with Walpole, who began to get worried in 1728 when John Gay pilloried the ruling classes with tremendous popular success in *The Beggar's Opera*. Detailed and specific attacks on Walpole's premiership followed in the plays of Henry Fielding; and the result was the crippling, muzzling Censorship Act of 1737. Thereafter Fielding gave up the theatre in favour of the novel: English literature gained the author of *Tom Jones*, but English drama lost the services of a man who might well have developed into the greatest playwright since Shakespeare.

Britain did not at first take kindly to Walpole's encroachment on freedom of speech. Lord Chesterfield argued vainly against it in a majestic and permanently valid speech to the House of Lords:

If Poets and Players are to be restrained, let them be restrained as other Subjects are, by the known Laws of their Country; if they offend, let them be tried as every Englishman ought to be, by God and their Country. Do not let us subject them to the arbitrary Will and Pleasure of any one Man. A Power lodged in the hands of one single Man, to judge and determine, without any Limitation, without any Control or Appeal, is a sort of Power unknown to our Laws, inconsistent with our Constitution. It is a higher, a more absolute Power than we trust even to the King himself; and therefore I must think we ought not to vest any such Power in His Majesty's Lord Chamberlain.

Samuel Johnson wrote an essay ironically defending the censorship against a playwright who objected that the Chamberlain had banned one of his works without giving a reason:

Is it for a Poet to demand a Licenser's reason for his proceedings? Is he not rather to acquiesce in the decision of Authority and conclude that there are reasons he cannot comprehend? Unhappy would it be for men in power were they always obliged to publish the motives of their conduct. What is power but the liberty of acting without being accountable?

Johnson went on to propose that the censor's power should be extended to the press, and that it should be made a felony for a citizen to *read* without the Chamberlain's licence.

However, idiocy triumphed and swiftly entrenched itself. The nineteenth century was the censor's paradise and playground. In 1832 the Examiner of plays was quizzed by a royal commission. He said it was indecent for a dramatic hero to call his mistress an 'angel' because angels were characters in Scripture, and Scripture was 'much too sacred for the stage'. When asked why he forbade oaths like 'Damme', he replied: 'I think it is immoral and improper, to say nothing of the vulgarity of it in assemblies where high characters and females congregate.'

The same Examiner had lately banned a meek little play about Charles I, whom the British people had decapitated two centuries earlier. He realised (he said) that its intentions were harmless, 'but mischief may be unconsciously done, as a house may be set on fire by a little innocent in the nursery'. This tone of lofty condescension resounded through the rest of the century. *La Dame aux Camélias* was condemned because it might inflame the public to commit acts of sexual riot. A stage version of Disraeli's novel *Coningsby* was banned on the eve of its opening. 'You see,' the Chamberlain explained to the baffled adapter, 'you are writing a kind of quasi-political piece, and here you are exhibiting a sort of contrast between the manufacturing people and the lower classes. Don't you think, now, that that would be a pity?' When Henry Irving sought to appear in a poetic play about the life of Mohammed, he was tetchily informed that Queen Victoria's subjects included millions of Mohammedans who would be outraged if the Prophet were represented on stage. The Chamberlain's nervousness about holy metaphysics is notorious; as late as 1912, an extremely godly play was rejected because it contained such blasphemous lines as 'Christ comfort you' and 'The real Good Friday would be that which brought the cure for cancer'.

The arch-fiends, however, were Ibsen and Shaw – social critics who brutally exposed the hypocrisies of official morality and their destructive effect on personal relationships. Both suffered from the censor's gag. 'I have studied Ibsen's plays pretty carefully,' said the Chamberlain's Examiner in 1891, 'and all the characters appear to me morally deranged.' Two years later he ambushed Shaw by banning *Mrs Warren's Profession*; and when the Examiner died in 1895, Shaw wrote a cruel and classic obituary:

> The late Mr Piggot is declared on all hands to have been the best reader of plays we have ever had; and yet he was a walking compendium of vulgar insular prejudice. . . . He had French immorality on the brain; he had American indecency on the brain; he had the womanly woman on the brain; he had the divorce court on the brain; he had 'not before a mixed audience' on the brain; his official career in relation to the higher drama was one long folly and panic. . . . It is a frightening thing to see the great thinkers, poets and authors of modern Europe – men like Ibsen, Wagner, Tolstoy and the leaders of our own literature – delivered into the vulgar hands of such a noodle as this amiable old gentleman – this despised, incapable old official – most notoriously was.

Seventy years have passed since then, but appallingly little has changed. Under a decade ago, the Chamberlain stamped on Arthur Miller's *A View From the Bridge* and Tennessee Williams' *Cat on a Hot Tin Roof* because he believed them to be tainted with homosexuality. These ludicrous bans have not been lifted, but the censor still forbids all theatrical representations of queer characters who follow their sexual leanings without being tragically punished or revealing any sense of guilt. Everything remotely anal, no matter how far removed from sensual enjoyment, is automatically prohibited. In 1964 the Royal Shakespeare Company (Patron: the Queen) put on a French surrealist play of the 1920s in which a stately Edwardian beauty, symbolising death, was required to break wind at regular intervals. The stage directions indicated that the effect could be made by a bass trombone in the wings, but this was not precise enough for the Chamberlain. He passed the script only when the director agreed to let the trombonist play the Destiny Theme from Beethoven's Fifth Symphony. This apparently made farting respectable.

John Osborne, probably the most important British dramatist since Shaw, has naturally been singled out for the censor's special attention. His first play, an assault on McCarthyism, was presented by a provincial repertory company in 1951; it contained a scene in which one of the characters was falsely smeared as a homosexual. The Chamberlain cut the imputation of queerness and thus crippled the play. 'It's the sheer humiliation that's bad for the artist,' Osborne said to me not long ago. 'I know playwrights who almost seem to be *living* with the Lord Chamberlain – it's like an affair. There's a virgin period when you aren't aware of him, but eventually you can't avoid thinking of him while you're writing. He sits on your shoulder, like a terrible nanny.'

In 1959 Osborne wrote and directed a musical called *The World of Paul Slickey*. Before it opened on tour, the usual exchange of letters with the censor had taken place, including the following concession from Osborne's lawyer:

> My client is prepared to substitute for:
> 'Leaping from the bridal bed,
> He preferred his youthful squire instead'
> the line:
> 'He preferred the *companionship* of his youthful squire instead.'

However, while the show was on its way to London, the Chamberlain received one or two complaints that prompted him to demand new cuts and revisions. Among several offending lines, there was a lyric that ran:

> And before I make a pass,
> I'll tell her that the sun shines out of her – face.

On this the censor's comment was curt and final. 'If the pause before "face" is retained, this couplet will be unacceptable.' Osborne sat down in fury to register a general protest:

Your office seems intent on treating me as if I were the producer of a third-rate nude revue. What I find most bewildering is the lack of moral consistency and objectivity which seems to characterise your recent decisions – decisions which seem to be reversed and changed because of the whim of any twisted neurotic who cares to write to you and exploit his own particular sexual frustration or moral oddity. In paying attention to what is without question an infinitesimal and lunatic minority, you are doing a grave injustice not only to myself but to the general public and your own office.

I sympathise with Osborne's rage, while regretting that he let it trap him into implying that special privileges should be granted to serious drama and withheld from 'third-rate nude revues'. Erotic stimulation is a perfectly legitimate function of bad art as well as good, and a censor who bans a stripper is behaving just as illiberally and indefensibly as one who eviscerates a masterpiece.

Osborne returned to the attack in 1960, when the Chamberlain blue-pencilled eighteen passages – many of them entire speeches – from his chronicle play *Luther*, in which Albert Finney was to conquer the West End and Broadway. Osborne stated his terms in a white-hot letter to the London producer:

I cannot agree to any of the cuts demanded, *under any circumstances*. Nor will I agree to any possible substitutions. I don't write plays to have them rewritten by someone else. I intend to make a clear unequivocal stand on this because (a) I think it is high time that someone did so, and (b) . . . the suggested cuts or alternatives would result in such damage to the psychological structure, meaning and depth of the play that the result would be a travesty. . . . I will not even contemplate any compromise . . . I am quite prepared to withdraw the play from production altogether and wait for the day when Lord Scarbrough [at that time the Lord Chamberlain] is no more. . . . I have made up my mind and, in fact, did so long ago.

This blast had its effect. For once the censor crumpled, and *Luther* went on with only five small verbal changes, three of them involving the substitution of 'urine' or 'kidney juice' for 'piss'. Osborne wrote to the producer congratulating him on an 'astonishing victory'. His present belief, shared by most of his contemporaries in the British theatre, is that censorship is not only offensive but superfluous: the existing laws relating to libel and obscenity are already ferocious enough to warm any bigot's heart, and constitute, in themselves, quite a sizeable deterrent to freedom of speech. Would Osborne allow a Black Muslim play to be performed in a community of white supremacists? 'Yes – anything that creates energy and vitality is good for the theatre.' When I posed the ultimate question – would he permit sexual intercourse on stage – Osborne replied: 'It might make me ill, and I'd like to know beforehand what I was in for. But I'm prepared to be exposed to it – although I might want a seat on the aisle.'

Improvisation – the utterance of words unfiltered by the authorised sin-sieve – is one of the Chamberlain's abiding hates. A few years ago, when the off-Broadway revue called *The Premise* came to London, he forbade the cast to improvise, despite the fact that at least half of the show (according to its publicity) was made up on the moment's spur. On this occasion, mindful perhaps of Anglo–American relations, he took no legal action; but in 1958 there were convictions and fines when the producers of a play entitled *You Won't Always Be On Top* enhanced the text with an unlicensed impersonation of Sir Winston Churchill opening a public lavatory.

With these anomalies in mind, consider an antic sequence of events which unfolded in April 1965. The management of an Australian revue called *Guarding the Change* was instructed by the Chamberlain, three hours before the curtain was due to rise at the New Lyric Theatre in London, that two sketches would have to be omitted. One concerned Scott of the Antarctic, who died half a century ago, and the other was a parody of a characteristically radiant royal address which ended with the words:

> Our thoughts/good wishes/carpet salesmen/aircraft carriers are on their way toward you. And so, on this beautiful morning/afternoon/evening, what is there for us to say but hello/how-do-you-do/goodbye/well done/arise, Sir Robert Menzies.

This, like the passage about Scott, was expunged on the grounds of good taste. The management at once telephoned to ask whether they could fill the gap left in their programme by reading to the audience the letter in which the Chamberlain imposed his ban. The request was refused. 'Without fear or favour,' as a wag later remarked, 'the Lord Chamberlain also banned his own letter.'

That same evening, however, members of the royal family were rocking with laughter at an inspired Irish clown called Spike Milligan, most of whose gags are famously impromptu. To quote at length the wag cited above (Michael Frayn of the *Observer*):

> They were at the Comedy Theatre, watching *Son of Oblomov*, with Spike Milligan departing from the script to make jokes in which he mentioned their names, like 'Why does Prince Philip wear red, white and blue braces?' (Answer: 'To keep his trousers up.') . . . But the point is, what is the Lord Chamberlain going to do about Mr Milligan? Mentioning Prince Philip or his braces on the West End stage is not allowed. . . . And what will he do about the royal family? If the reporters saw correctly through their night glasses in the darkness, the whole party seem to have aided and abetted Mr Milligan by providing sensible evidence of appreciation. In other words, they are all accessories after the fact. Will the Lord Chamberlain revoke *their* licences?

Mr Milligan has in his files what may well be the strangest single document in the history of theatre censorship. In 1962 he collaborated with John Antrobus on a clearly deranged but maniacally funny comedy called *The Bed-Sitting Room*. In January 1963, the joint authors received a communication from the Lord Chamberlain, from which I quote:

> This Licence is issued on the understanding that the following alterations are made to the script.
>
> ACT I
>
> Page 1:   Omit the name of the Prime Minister; no representation of his voice is allowed.
>
> Page 16:   Omit '. . . clockwork Virgin Mary made in Hong Kong, whistles the Twist.' Omit references to the Royal Family, the Queen's Christmas Message, and the Duke's shooting. . . .
>
> Page 21:   The detergent song. Omit 'You get all the dirt off the tail of your shirt.' Substitute 'You get all the dirt off the front of your shirt.'
>
> ACT II
>
> Page 8:   The mock priest must not wear a crucifix on his snorkel. It must be immediately made clear that the book the priest handles is not the Bible.

Page 10:	Omit from 'We've just consummated our marriage' to and inclusive of 'a steaming hot summer's night'.
Page 13:	Omit from 'In return they are willing . . . to and inclusive of 'the Duke of Edinburgh is a wow with Greek dishes.' Substitute 'Hark ye! Hark ye! The Day of Judgement is at hand.'

ACT III

Pages 12–13:	Omit the song 'Plastic Mac Man' and substitute 'Oh you dirty young devil, how dare you presume to wet the bed when the po's in the room. I'll wallop your bum with a dirty great broom when I get up in the morning.'
Page 14:	Omit 'the perversions of the rubber'. Substitute 'the kreurpels and blinges of the rubber'. Omit the chamber pot under the bed.

No argument I have yet heard in favour of dramatic censorship is strong enough to withstand the armour-plated case against it, which I can sum up in three quotations:

> To purchase freedom of thought with human blood and then delegate its exercise to a censor at £400 a year is a proceeding which must make the gods laugh.
>
> (Frank Fowell and Frank Palmer, authors of
> *Censorship in England*, 1912)

> What, then, is to be done with the Censorship? Nothing can be simpler. Abolish it, root and branch, throwing the whole legal responsibility for plays on the author and manager, precisely as the legal responsibility for a book is thrown on the author, the printer and the publisher. The managers will not like this; their present slavery is safer and easier; but it will be good for them, and good for the Drama.
>
> (Bernard Shaw, 1909)

> The Stage, my Lords, and the Press are two of our Out-sentries; if we remove them − if we hoodwink them − if we throw them in Fetters − the Enemy may surprise us. Therefore I must look upon the Bill now before us as a Step, and a most necessary Step too, for introducing arbitrary Power into this Kingdom. It is a

Step so necessary, that if ever any future ambitious King, or guilty Minister, should form to himself so wicked a Design, he will have reason to thank us for having done so much of the work to his Hand; but such Thanks I am convinced every one of your Lordships would blush to receive – and scorn to deserve.

(Lord Chesterfield to the House of Lords, 1737)

Chesterfield was right when he carried the case against the Lord Chamberlain beyond the boundaries of dramatic art into the broader domain of civil liberties and democratic rights. The fundamental objection to censorship is not that it is exercised against artists, but that it is exercised at all.

Sixty-odd years ago, Shaw was alarmed to hear a rumour that the United States was proposing to censor the theatre. 'O my friends across the sea,' he wrote with a passion I echo today, 'remember how the censorship works in England, and DON'T.' From *A View of the English Stage* by Kenneth Tynan (Paladin, 1976).

Part III

Chapter 7

New contexts

Sexual politics

Kenneth Tynan's acerbic protests helped generate an energy which brought new cultural practices into theatre after the abolition of censorship in 1968. Politics, art, street culture, music and community- or constituency-based activities created new spaces, some improvised, some custom-built, expanded ideas of what an audience could or should be, and laid the foundations of the theatre we have now.

This theatre came about at a time when there was an upsurge in working-class industrial unrest, a radical student movement which engaged with world politics (the war in Vietnam, the Chinese Cultural Revolution in the 1960s, the Soviet invasion of Czechoslovakia), culminating in political demonstrations and upheavals in the late 1960s. The consumerist youth culture which had been expanding since the 1950s became securely established during the 1960s in Britain: new musics, alternative entertainments, a blurring of old categories and the creation of new ones in art, tested the boundaries of convention.

Theatre and performance skills have always played a role during periods of social and political change in Britain, and radical ideas have in turn influenced those already 'there', the establishment as well as the avant-garde. During the 1840s, plays were performed in support of the Chartists, and during the course of the nineteenth century, various attempts were made in London to establish theatres to produce plays for 'worker-audiences'.

Towards the end of the nineteenth century, with the founding of the Independent Labour Party and the Co-operative Movement, the influence of socially conscious playwrights such as Ibsen and Shaw provided sustenance as well as entertainment, and helped re-establish the British theatre. Eleanor Marx (one of Karl Marx's daughters) translated the first

English version of Ibsen's play *An Enemy of the People* in 1888 (it was published in 1890). In 1895 she took part in a reading of *The Doll's House*, together with Edward Aveling and George Bernard Shaw.

The Worker's Theatre Movement (WTM) (1928–36), responding to the rapidly changing situation after the First World War, and influenced by left-wing theatre in Germany and the Soviet Union, introduced the agitprop montage form into British theatre, drawing also on indigenous British forms such as music-hall and variety. The WTM was essentially an amateur project. In 1936, Unity Theatre was founded, and while it too involved a number of enthusiastic amateurs, it also included professional theatre workers who were drawn to the anti-fascist politics of the 1930s. In 1937, the Left Book Club (founded by publisher Victor Gollancz) created a Theatre Guild, which by 1938 consisted of some 250 groups all over the country.

The growing agitation for female suffrage helped draw women into radical theatre work too. At the turn of the century, many actresses welcomed Ibsen's plays, both because of the way he took on debates about women and independence, and because it gave them chances to play challenging, contemporary roles: 'What you won't be able to imagine . . . is the joy of having in our hands . . . such glorious actable stuff. . . . Ibsen taught us something we were never to unlearn' (actress Elizabeth Robins, quoted in Julie Holledge, *Innocent Flowers*, Virago, 1981).

In December 1908, the Actresses' Franchise League was formed, dedicated to supporting the struggle for female suffrage. At first they just provided poems and monologues to entertain at political meetings, but they soon began writing and producing short plays, satirical and naturalistic sketches, showing up anti-suffrage feeling among the upper and working classes, expressing (albeit sometimes patronisingly) sympathy with the plight of working-class women.

Around 1913 the actresses turned their attention to conditions for women within the acting profession, campaigning against prejudice. An Independent Women's Theatre Company flourished briefly, but with the advent of the First World War, and the muffling of suffragette militancy, this early campaigning theatre work by women faded from the public eye. During the 1920s and 1930s, organised political feminism was less evident, although organisations continued to campaign for changes in contraception and childcare, and the Co-operative Guild, for example, still represented working-class feminism. The final granting of the vote in 1928 to women on the same terms as men heralded the culmination of much of the impetus of early twentieth-century feminism.

The extraordinary spread of new cultural and political promise at the end of the 1960s inevitably contained its own contradictions, and it was from some of these that a new wave of feminism emerged. When women faced the implications of the slogan that 'the personal is political', which emerged as part of the vivid student protests in Paris and America around 1968, it was soon evident that a degree of hypocrisy was still around:

> Glance at any left theoretical journal or go to any large meeting, you won't find many articles either by or about women, and you won't see many women speaking. Think of the way women relate to the left groups. Very largely, we complement the men: we hold small groups together, we send out reminders, we type the leaflets, we administer rather than initiate. . . . Revolutionary students are quite capable of wolf-whistling and cat-calling when a girl speaks; more common though is tolerant humour, patronising derision or that silence after which everyone continues as if nobody had spoken.
>
> (Sheila Rowbotham, 'Women's liberation and the new politics', in The Body Politic, compiled by M. Wandor, 1972, p. 22)

The relatively privileged, highly articulate world of students, calling for increased democratic participation, was still male-dominated, with women seen as secondary. A fierce response to this led to a weekend conference, initially organised to discuss women in history, at Ruskin College, Oxford, in the spring of 1970. This effectively launched the Women's Liberation Movement in Britain. Over 500 women came from all over the country, and by the end of the weekend four basic 'demands' had been formulated, in the style of left-wing practice of the time:

1   Equal pay.
2   Equal education and opportunity.
3   Twenty-four-hour nurseries.
4   Free contraception and abortion on demand.

The demands were expressions of the basic changes needed to give women a more equal and radical relationship to training and education, the workplace, the family, to individual sexual choice. The term 'sexism', already in active use in America, by analogy with the term 'racism', was used to refer to the socially systemic ways in which men and women are brought up with a dualistic view of the value and roles of the sexes. Men, so the argument goes, are superior to women. Where women may do something that is specifically a female action (from having babies to doing particular jobs), that function will be valued as lesser, generally paid less or not at all. Men in general (whatever the virtues of individual exceptions) both exploit and oppress women.

Fierce debates ensued for over a decade. Causes were argued, solutions proposed, coherent ideologies developed and propounded. Pamphlets, articles, books emerged. New histories, new ways of looking at history, evolved. New art and fiction, films and theatre were generated. In the political sphere(s) of feminism, there were three distinct tendencies, each implying an analysis of causes and a programme of solutions. These will be elaborated in the next chapter – where they are harnessed for the purpose of identifying the nature of the feminist (or otherwise) dynamic in particular plays. The broad outlines are, however, as follows.

Radical feminism argued that sexism pre-dated all other kinds of social oppression (class and race), and therefore was *the* fundamental political struggle. Socialist feminists argued that the class system exploited and oppressed both men and women, but that, within and alongside that, women experienced particular kinds of exploitation specific to them, and that the individual oppression of women by individual men was part of that same pattern. The struggle for women, therefore, was to combat an internalised belief in their own inferiority, to be both socially and personally independent. The third tendency, bourgeois feminism, took slightly longer to emerge, but put simply, it meant arguing for more power for women at the top, an 'equalling up' with men, without questioning any of the foundations of the current system.

Whichever of these forms of feminism one adopted, there were certain shared assumptions between feminists: (1) that wherever it is found, collectively and/or individually, assumptions of male superiority should be challenged; (2) that women needed to organise separately, to take charge of their own activities, and (3) that the social/sexual division of labour is not a 'natural' or a biological given, but socially constructed and learned, and that therefore inequalities, lifestyles and roles can be changed, and that society itself can be modified to accord with this. The personal, in other, simpler, terms, is political.

Although the Ruskin conference was dominated by educated, probably mostly middle-class women, there were also women involved in
some of the industrial struggles of the time (at Ford and other factories).
There were also women who were 'just' housewives, and, like the
women in Friedan and Gavron's earlier surveys, were responding with
frustration to their isolation.

The conference was followed by national and regional marches and
demonstrations, and by 1972 the Women's Liberation Movement had
established its own communications and cultural networks. I edited
The Body Politic (Stage 1, 1972), a collection of papers given at the
conference, and other specially written pieces. There were political
journals produced by women, including (also in 1972) *Red Rag*,
produced by a mixture of unaligned socialist-feminists and women
members of the Communist Party, and *Spare Rib*, set up after a meeting
I organised for women working on the alternative, 'underground'
papers, including *Time Out*, where I was currently working part-time,
editing the Poetry section, and writing theatre and other reviews.

In the mid-1970s, Virago and The Women's Press were the most
visible tip of the iceberg to reclaim forgotten work by women, and to
re-evaluate contributions 'hidden from history'. There were also
groups which addressed themselves specifically to the place of women
in media – covering publishing, television and film.

Alongside the emergence of the Women's Liberation Movement
came the Gay Liberation Front. Because sexuality in general had
become 'politicised' – changes in the law, developments in contraception which gave women greater choice – homosexuality came out
of the closet of relative secrecy. The history of legislation on homosexual issues goes back most recently to 1885, when a law was passed
making homosexuality illegal for men. In one sense (apart from the
earlier anecdote about Queen Victoria) this was itself a sexist measure,
assuming, with Victorian correctness, that since women were supposed
to relate to the world via men and the family, they were no real threat.
Virile, procreative sexuality, on the other hand, had to be 'protected',
for any other kind of male sexuality would threaten the very idea of
the paterfamilias upon which both the home front and the empire
turned. Challenges to such conservatism followed:

> from the 1880s to the 1920s the most sympathetic supporters for
> sex reform in general and homosexual reform in particular had
> come from the left; and, as a corollary, most of the reformers
> were clearly men and women of the left. But the theoretical and

practical problems that this connection raised had never been clearly explored. . . . One of the problems was that there was no fully worked-out theoretical position on women and sexuality in the socialist tradition.

(Jeff Weeks, *Coming Out*, Quartet, 1977, p. 144)

In addition to the fact that during the 1920s and 1930s feminist and sexual reform issues lost impetus, the Soviet ideology of the 1930s was heavily anti-homosexual, arguing that it was at best a symptom of bourgeois decadence, at worst of fascism. Thus it was not until the 1950s and 1960s that changes in the cultural climate because of the reorganising of family life, and the liberalising of laws on personal life, resulted in a partial decriminalising of homosexuality in 1967.

Changing the law was one thing, changing attitudes and behaviour, another. In the autumn of 1970, the Gay Liberation Front (GLF) was formed in Britain. The GLF encouraged the proud demonstration of homosexual relationships in reaction against the shadowy, ghetto-like culture of pre-1967 lifestyles:

In the GLF this change revolved around three basic concepts: first, the idea of 'coming out', of being open about one's homosexuality, of rejecting the shame and guilt and the enforced 'double life', of asserting 'gay pride' and 'gay anger' around the cry 'out of the closets, into the streets'. Secondly, the idea of 'coming together', of solidarity and strength coming through collective endeavour, and of the mass confrontation of oppression. And thirdly, and centrally, the identification of the roots of oppression in the concept of sexism and of exploring the means to extirpate it.

(Weeks, ibid., p. 191)

The connection between the oppression of women and gays was clearly made, but within the GLF the contradictions between men and women were also played out, so that while they shared a general social oppression, women felt that men still dominated. The movement thus divided along gender lines, although this was not necessarily always a hostile development, but more one which the women felt was enabling. Like the WLM, the GLF produced its own manifesto. This included an interesting claim:

. . . in some ways [we] are already more advanced than straight people. We are already outside the family, and we have already,

in part, at least, rejected the 'masculine' and 'feminine' roles
society has designed for us. . . . Gay men don't need to oppress
women in order to fulfil their own psycho-sexual needs, and gay
women don't have to relate sexually to the male oppressor, so
that at this moment in time the freest and most equal relationships
are likely to be between homosexuals.

(GLF Manifesto, 1970)

For rather different reasons, both feminists and gay activists necessarily focused on the family, either by demanding changes in the way
it worked, or by arguing for alternative ways of living. Central to
these discussions was an analysis of family relations, with their
economic imbalance and division of labour; women's dependence on
men, men's exclusion from childcare, women's isolation at the centre
of the family, the implications for the experiences of children – all
these combined standard Marxist analyses of economic relations
between men and women with the newer libertarian possibilities.

Given the significance of the way that the family and gender roles
within it are represented in this analysis of post-war British drama,
the new, critical, radical, and very varied input by some women and
gay people (male and female) inevitably involved a more self-conscious
approach to the function of gender in society in general, and also to
gender roles in theatre – in the broadest sense. I am not, of course,
suggesting that all the playwrights were fully fledged Marxists in any
sense, but the strength of the prevailing (largely urban) cultural climate
created a situation in which 'lifestyle politics' became as important as
public, political protest. The site of theatre reflected its own versions
of what was happening elsewhere.

Alternative theatres

From the late 1960s, people working in the variously styled alternative,
fringe and/or political theatre developed an enormous variety of
approaches to style, form, content, performance practice and audiences.
Arts labs 'happenings', the growth of lunchtime and pub theatre, avant-
garde and experimental work which crossed media boundaries (many
art school graduates evolved performance art-based theatre work)
jostled alongside the self-conscious socialist companies, whose plays
were largely built around immediate political issues and events, such
as tenants on a housing estate protesting against rent rises. Many
groups toured the country with mobile, easily transportable plays,

agitprop both in style and intention, and often following performances with audience discussion about the ideas and politics involved – so that the theatre group was not only engaging with theatricality, but acting as a 'consciousness-raiser'. The 'fourth wall' convention was being blurred, as lines of communication between performers and audience continued to be open after the performances.

For a few years, into the early 1970s, this theatre had a strongly militant edge, in the context of general industrial militancy in Britain following anti-working-class measures introduced by the Conservative government of 1970 to 1974. After the return of a Labour government in 1974, some of the militant edge abated, more theatre went 'indoors', given a more solid underpinning by state subsidy via the Arts Council, which had itself been influenced by a younger generation of more activist, politically self-conscious theatre workers. Subsidy increased dramatically between 1971 and 1978, from £7000 to £1,500,000, and alongside this outreach consciousness-raising, grew a militancy within the theatre industry itself.

In 1972 an Association of Lunchtime Theatres was formed 'to promote lunchtime theatre, to present principally new and neglected plays and playwrights, to provide alternative venues for actors, directors and designers, to encourage audiences by making them more accessible'.

In 1974 The Association of Community Theatre (TACT) held its first conference; one of its aims was to put pressure on the Arts Council for subsidy to enable it to pay Equity minimum wages. Shortly after this the Independent Theatres Council (ITC) organised individuals and theatres not covered by TACT, and the two organisations merged. In October 1975 they held a joint conference at the Oval House community centre in South London, to which a number of playwrights were invited. Out of this came the Theatre Writers' Group, which a year later changed its name to the Theatre Writers' Union, to campaign for better contracts, terms and conditions for writers in the subsidised theatre. Within a couple of years TWU was co-operating with the older writers' union, the Writers' Guild, although the two organisations remained separate for a long time.

Early street and public theatre disrupted public spectacles with alternative displays. A leaflet distributed by a group of women demonstrators at the November 1970 Miss World contest at the Royal Albert Hall in London declared: 'We're not beautiful, we're not ugly, we're angry.' At a prearranged signal, the women interrupted Bob Hope's compère banter in full view of millions of television viewers. They threw flour, smoke and stink bombs, blew whistles, waved rattles. The women were arrested, Bob Hope ad libbed a few jokes and the show continued. Writing later about the event, the protestors described it as 'a blow against passivity, not only the enforced passivity of the girls on stage, but the passivity that we all felt in ourselves' ('Miss World', in *The Body Politic*, compiled by M. Wandor, Stage 1, 1972, p. 252).

The following year there was another demonstration, led this time by the Women's Street Theatre Group who were joined by the all-male Gay Street Theatre Group. The women parodied the contest in 'The Flashing Nipple Show', dressed in dark trousers and tops, each woman with flashing lights fixed at crotch and breasts. A simple, satirical imagery brought sexual politics into street theatre, identifying the particular focus for women:

> . . . it's in the home, around sexuality, that our oppression bites deepest, holds hardest. The 'left' has always said that the economy, our exploitation, has to be changed first, before our lives, our oppression. We say both have to be changed at once – the struggle against internalised oppression, against how we live our lives, is where we begin, where we've been put. . . . Women's oppression cuts across class, but our roles serve capitalism and are caused and dictated by it.
>
> ('Miss World', in ibid., p. 260)

The Women's Street Theatre Group had already performed in the demonstration to celebrate International Women's Day on 6 March 1971. They danced along with the marchers through a spring snow shower in London, while a gramophone in a pram played 'Keep Young and Beautiful'. In Trafalgar Square they performed their first 'play', *Sugar and Spice*, satirising the way women are trapped as sex objects and within the family. The imagery included an enormous deodorant, a huge sanitary towel and a gigantic red, white and blue penis (artificial!). Various other events were also staged in public places: in the ladies' lavatory in Selfridges, feminists pretended to shave their faces in front of the mirrors in an attempt to get other women to think about their own mirror images, and on the London underground, where various female 'types' were auctioned off to the crowd – dolly-bird, academic and housewife.

In September 1971 the women and men took part in a demonstration organised by the Christian Festival of Light. Overblown, mobile visual imagery was again a central part of the show – a placard with the word 'Holy Family' on one side and 'Fuck the Family' on the other, with asterisks in 'Family' but not in 'fuck'. There were also two large stuffed white hands, inscribed with the words 'Church' and State', and attached with chains to a 'typical' hierarchical human family: the husband beat his wife, the wife beat the child, and the child beat up a teddy bear.

After these initial responses to public events, the WTG went inside, as it were, still collectively researching, devising, scripting and, in effect, directing and performing, themselves. This was very much in tune with the political theatre group practice of the time (with some exceptions, such as the group 7:84, which performed plays written by one of its founders, writer John McGrath), where the concept of 'collective' work represented a number of political principles. First, it reacted against traditional hierarchies, both social and theatrical. By doing away with the specialist skills of writer, director, designer, the assertion was made that everyone's input was equally valuable. (This of course, is, not to say that the principle was always perfectly translated into practice. Different people had different skills, talents and ambitions; some people were more dominating than others, some quieter, people had different political ideas as well as aesthetic desires; but generally speaking, the enterprise at this stage was whole-hearted, exhilarating and in many cases entertaining and productive.) Second, it made an assertion by analogy with the political, for the *democratisation* of social institutions to give everyone a voice, and to make people accountable to one another.

The socialist agitprop groups developed a formula: short, naturalistic 'real' life scenes, along the lines of television naturalism, punctuated by music, or cartoon-like 'types' to represent the baddies and/or the goodies of capitalism, or whatever the oppressive system was. *The Amazing Equal Pay Show*, performed by the Women's Street Theatre Group (who had now changed their name to the Punching Judies) was inspired by the Equal Pay Act of 1970, both welcomed in principle and criticised for its loopholes. The play followed a group of women workers, based on a strike for equal pay by women machinists at Ford in 1968, beginning to organise out from the bottom of the capitalist heap, and confronting both their bosses and their husbands. The naturalistic story of the women was punctuated by the capitalist magician, Mr Marvo, wearing a huge cloak lined with money, accompanied by his obedient and sexy female sidekick, Poodle. Members of Parliament did deals with each other and with the unions using oversized playing cards. The all-women group thus got a chance to reverse the theatrical convention – here women cross-dressed to play the male characters. Interestingly, the appearance of this group, as well as the various all-women groups which formed during the 1970s, were constantly challenged by critics on the basis of their 'separatism' – a charge which is never laid against either all-male or male-dominated groups, who are the norm.

Many of the already existing touring socialist theatre groups, because they were mixed, and because sexual politics was in the air, began to respond through their own work and their own working practices. Red Ladder, one of the earliest of the companies, founded in 1968, planned to do a short play about women as part of a sequence of 10–15-minute 'units' which could be taken out to different audiences on different occasions. However, in 1972 the company decided the play merited longer treatment, and over the next two years it worked on a play which was finally called A Woman's Work is Never Done, and performed in 1974.

The play follows moments in the life of a working-class woman through marriage, children, jobs, trade union consciousness, and finally a new equality and independence both at home and at work. Although the focus centres on Helen, the 'message' operates a gender balance: paralleling the 'lessons' Helen learns about work, trade unions and organised struggle, Dave also learns 'lessons' about doing housework and looking after the children. Again, the stylistic mixtures were of naturalistic scenes contrasted with cartoon-like visual metaphor: a time-and-motion man wore huge clock faces as spectacles, a discussion about the relationship between concepts of parity and equal pay was illustrated in a scene in a pub, where the men ordered pints of beer and the women half-pints. At the end of the scene, Helen wraps up the discussion when asked what she wants to drink by saying that she will have a pint.

In these – and other – plays of the first half of the 1970s, where the experiences of women provided much of the starting point and perspective, home and family relationships were shown as one of the sites of political struggle, integrally linked to the political struggle at work. The family in these plays is highlighted, first, as a form of social institution which contains within it exploitative and oppressive aspects, and second, as an area where politics has a place, even though the two 'sides' are also closely and personally (and sexually) involved with each other. The family is implicitly reinforced as a politicised social unit. Its relations are questioned, but from within, in order to be transformed into better social relations At the same time, the relationship between domestic and public life, family and work is constantly stressed, since women's lives and their destinies are bound up with both spheres, and part of the lesson is to show that the same is/has to be true for men as well. It is shown that men are as much part of the family as are women, just as women have their own productive role to play in the world of work and politics.

The importance of this period of essentially group-authored and group-sponsored theatre work cannot be overestimated, even though standards of performance were often mixed (some performers were clearly more competent or talented than others), even though imagery was often bold and crude, and the writing did not have the stylistic distinctiveness of individually authored plays. However, the enterprise had an energy and an impact which emphasised content, message, and a shared urgency between performers and audience. Of course there was a drive which stressed message and idea, but there was also a genuine commitment to working collaboratively in an unalienated way. Many now established playwrights, whose work is linguistically more sophisticated, owed an enormous amount to the climate of participation and debate generated by these groups.

In 1973 a Women's Theatre Festival took place at the Almost Free Theatre in London, a venue run by an American, Ed Berman, who had spearheaded a community arts organisation called Inter-Action. The Festival was written, directed, designed and stage-managed by women, with some discreet male support backstage and as actors in some of the plays. The concluding paragraph in the press release indirectly referred to the fact that the women involved in the festival were a mix of professional theatre workers, and women for whom theatre, exciting as it was to be involved in, was perhaps mainly a medium through which to express political ideas:

> The Festival is designed to display the viability, competence and capability of women as a vital and necessary force within theatre. The WTG hopes to provide not only a platform but also an atmosphere of creative understanding and impetus. The Group is dependent on the responsible participation and mutual support of all its members and the expertise each can contribute. In this way we hope to exchange skills and acquire new talents while developing a group of interchangeable *people* to work together at a high level of professionalism.

There were four lunchtime programmes; interestingly, they consisted of individually authored plays, not the collective-style work of the political fringe. Pam Gems and I both had short plays put on during the season. I had only recently begun writing plays and poetry, and had already had some plays put on in small theatres and London pub theatres. The festival attracted a varied amount of press response, from predictable support in *Time Out* through to the timorous John Barber in the *Daily Telegraph* – 'I went along expecting an aggressively feminist point of view and rather dreading it' – to the prejudiced relief of an anonymous critic in the *Kensington Post*: 'Women's Theatre Festival did the valuable service of showing a mixed audience that females can laugh at themselves and are capable of amusement as well as awareness.'

The season sparked off various other events combining feminism and theatre, and involving women working in theatre. I self-published a pamphlet of short plays (1975), half written by myself, half by another woman writer, Dinah Brooke, who had also had a play on during the festival. There was, for example, a notably ambitious Women's Theatre Festival at the Haymarket Theatre in Leicester in the autumn of 1975, during which (as I discovered many years later) a young actor called Alan Rickman appeared in one of my plays.

After the Almost Free season, two groups emerged in London: one continued with the name the Women's Theatre Group, in the collective style of the street theatre group of the same name, on issue-based subjects seen from the point of view of women and feminism. The WTG later commissioned women writers to write plays for them, although they always kept a strong drive to have a say in the content and form of the play.

The second group called itself the Women's Company, and some of its members were involved in setting up Monstrous Regiment during 1975 to 1976. The politics of this group was slightly differently formulated from the all-woman WTG:

> The company ensures that women form the majority and take on decisive roles, and also commissions work by women writers [they did also commission work by men] dealing with themes throwing light on the position of society. . . . We see ourselves as part of the growing and lively movement to improve the status of women. Our work explores the experience of women past and present, and we want to place that experience in the centre of the stage, instead of in the wings.

Following the success of the Women's Theatre Festival at the Almost Free, Ed Berman invited gay theatre workers to organise a similar season. All the plays were by men (a play about coming out as a lesbian,

Any Woman Can by Jill Posener, had been turned down by Ed Berman on the grounds that it was not 'theatrical' enough), and a higher proportion of those taking part were already seasoned professionals. Tellingly (demonstrating the point I made earlier about the greater visibility in theatre of male gays), Inter-Action published this collection of plays by gay men (they did not publish the plays from the women's festival), and in Roger Baker's introduction he throws down a gauntlet to the profession:

> No sense of gay identification has emerged from the theatre, be it mainstream, fringe or experimental. Yet, traditionally the theatre is supposed to employ a higher percentage of homosexuals than any other profession. Members of Gay Sweatshop who have approached professional actors and directors have met with responses ranging from guarded interest to downright terror. . . . Audiences are invited to deride gays. But audiences include homosexuals as well, and they too will willingly enter into the complicity and go armoured to withstand the barbs and grotesque parodies of themselves.

The name Gay Sweatshop evolved during the season, and the group continued after the festival. The company included women, and during 1976 they staged a season of plays at the Institute of Contemporary Arts (where Jill Posener's play was produced), but although the men and women did work on a number of shows together, in 1977 they decided to divide into two groups, each with artistic autonomy. This was, interestingly, for two reasons, one explicitly political, the other explicitly aesthetic: patterns of male dominance over women were still being experienced, even within this radical gay set-up, and there was also an aesthetic divide. Whereas the men drew on an already established camp and drag tradition developed in the gay subculture, the women were drawn more towards the newer agitprop, documentary-based styles as a way of showing hitherto suppressed or denied experience 'as it really is'. In part because of the exigencies of touring, in part because of the nature of the content, virtually all these plays used the stage area fluidly, to suggest locations with single props ('signs' of a room, a public place), minimalist indicators of geographical or social location, allowing the story to move between public and private spheres.

These three companies represented the shop-front, as it were, of the way the new sexual politics and theatre informed each other. There were many other small, energetic groups, script and/or performance based, and a Feminist Theatre Study Group met regularly in London during the latter part of the 1970s. In October 1978 members organised a week of action, picketing five West End shows, handing out leaflets, challenging the stereotypical representations of women on stage:

> Did the characters in this play imply that:
> Blondes are dumb?
> Wives nag?
> Feminists are frustrated?
> Whores have hearts of gold?
> Mothers-in-law interfere?
> Lesbians are aggressive?
> Intellectual women are frigid?
> Women who enjoy sex are nymphomaniacs?
> Older women are sexless?

A more specifically oriented group called the Standing Conference of Women Theatre Directors and Administrators (I never quite understood why they had to be standing) formed in 1980, and, in their collection of conference papers from 1979 to 1981, defined their professional aims:

1   Conference is committed to achieving equal rights and opportunities for women theatre directors and administrators and will adopt a radical campaigning policy to achieve those aims.
2   Conference will act as a pressure group in pursuance of the acceptance of feminist perspectives in the profession, whilst creating more job opportunities and a better working climate for women in all areas of theatre.
3   Conference will provide a forum for the definition of these perspectives and develop a debate on the inherent values of our work as women, through a constant exchange of ideas and experience.

In 1983, the group undertook a survey of the employment of women directors, administrators and playwrights, concentrating on subsidised theatres and companies, and concluded that:

> . . . the more money and more prestige a theatre has, the less (sic) women will be employed in decision making positions and the less (sic) women will be on the board. Hence women are the least

subsidised artists in the theatre and have least influence in determining policy and programme.

In a 1985 leaflet, a concrete programme of action was outlined:

FUNDING BODIES
Equal opportunity policies, including no discrimination against
women, should be a condition of public subsidy for theatres.
INDIVIDUALS WORKING IN THE THEATRE
Commitment for all theatre workers to break down attitudinal
barriers and to establish equal access to employment for women.
THEATRES
All theatres should apply an active equal opportunities policy and
monitor its operation. Theatres' staffing committees, advisory
bodies and boards of directors should reflect the breadth of society
that the theatre serves and have a healthy male/female balance.

This approach to parity of employment between the sexes in the theatre
industry has a particular reverberation for playwrights. A brief look at
the social and sexual division of labour in the contemporary theatre
will yield some insight into why women playwrights are still in such a
minority.

Who works where: writers and the rest

In the division of labour in theatre, and the status which accrues from it,
'creative' and artistic roles (those of director and writer) traditionally
have the highest status (not necessarily always with the greatest
power). Two surveys, in 1987 and 1994 (see *The Routledge Reader in
Gender and Performance*) of the gender divide show that there is still a
fairly bleak landscape as far as parity goes. The latter study showed
that about one-third of senior posts in British theatres are filled by
women, that women controlled only 8 per cent of allocated Arts
Council funding, and that new plays written or dramatised by women
playwrights formed only about one-fifth of all produced plays.

   The sexual division of labour operates on the basis of a pyramid-
shaped structure, where men dominate at the top of the hierarchy,
and also at the other end of the scale, in the technological and
manual areas of backstage production. Women working in theatre
(apart from actresses) tend to cluster in the middle. Although since
the nineteenth century there has been a strong tradition of women

designers, the top professional designers are almost all male. Apart from that, women tend to work in areas which reflect 'servicing' roles similar to those in other industries and in the domestic division of labour – the 'housekeeping' parts of theatre: secretarial, administration, assisting, personnel, casting, wardrobe, publicity. All are vital and highly skilled jobs, but also jobs which are largely invisible, not particularly well paid, and rarely given as much credit as they deserve.

As far as playwrights go, the figures are dauntingly revealing. In 1977 the St James' Press published a compendious volume, *Contemporary Dramatists*. The advisory board consisted of thirty-two men and one woman. The book listed 321 playwrights working in English throughout the world. Of these, fewer than 10 per cent were women. *The British Alternative Theatre Directory* (1980), in which anyone who wanted could be listed, showed women to represent slightly over 10 per cent, and in the edition of 1983 women rose to just under 20 per cent, including playwrights who also wrote for television and radio – the latter has a higher proportion of women writers than either of the former.

In their 1985 catalogue, Methuen, the main drama publisher in this country, listed eighty twentieth-century writers, of whom seven were women. Information given for the male–female ratio of characters in their published plays was 2212 male characters and 908 female characters. One can immediately see the knock-on effect in terms of the relative employment available for actors and actresses. More work for the boys, because more male characters in more plays by male playwrights.

In the 1999 Methuen catalogue there was little improvement. The percentage of published contemporary women playwrights has, indeed, increased to something like 15 per cent, and while this is an important step in the right direction it is scandalously low as a percentage. In the 1999 catalogue of playscripts published by Nick Hern Books, the percentage of plays by women writers was about 12 per cent.

When it comes to publishing plays for the amateur drama market the picture is a little different. Of course, amateur productions also include successful mainstream plays as well as specially written work. Samuel French's catalogues of plays for the amateur market reveal an interesting fact: they publish plays for different categories of performer – for mixed casts, for all-female and for all-male casts. In their 1984 catalogue, women constituted on average about 15 per cent of the writers, except for the category of all-female one-act plays, where just under half are by women. Moreover, the list of dramatic pieces for all-female casts ran to forty-six pages, while the list for all-male performers ran to twenty pages. In their 1997 to 1999 catalogue, in Samuel French's full-length play section, just over 10 per cent of the playwrights are women. In the short plays and revue sketches the percentage increases to just below 25 per cent.

It is clear from this that there is a decisive amateur/professional divide. At amateur level there are more actresses than actors. At professional level the opposite is true. More women write plays for the amateur market, especially when they have all-female casts, but male writers dominate in both spheres. Why?

Gender and playwriting

Women writers were formative in the development of the novel as a literary genre. With the rise of a leisured class in the eighteenth century, the occupation of novel-writing (and the more private form of diary- and letter-writing) was taken up by these new ladies of leisure. Their contemporary reading public also consisted largely of such women, writing and reading in private, while the public world of book publishing and distribution was controlled by men.

As attitudes to women crystallised in the Victorian period, women novelists faced a contradictory situation. On the one hand, their work was widely published and acclaimed (novelists such as Jane Austen and George Eliot (sic) have become part of our literary canon); on the other hand, the Victorian ideology which claimed that womanhood should be a passive vocation in itself asserted that it was not 'natural' for women to use their brains in this way. It was widely thought that over-use of the brain adversely affected the womb, and, however ridiculous this may sound now, it touches on the assumption that women who wrote – who effectively took on a public voice – were transgressing their natural role. The widespread use of the male pseudonym is one strategy adopted by women which points up this attitude.

In the twentieth century the woman novelist and poet has become less of an anomaly. This has coincided with higher education being made available to women, and in changes in the professions, especially teaching, in which women have a significant role. As playwrights, however, women scarcely figure on the literary map. The figures quoted earlier still show that women playwrights are in a very small minority, and it is worth giving some attention to what is distinctive about the act of writing drama which makes it such a special, and indeed difficult, field for women writers.

First of all, there is a clear link between the fact that men dominate the economic and artistic decisions in theatre, and the way women are represented in the plays themselves, as well as which writers are commissioned. In this sense the content of plays is ideologically 'policed' far more explicitly than the content of novels, because a play is only published once it has achieved some interest and/or success in performance. The plays which survive, and which become the history of theatre to a very large extent, are plays which have been through a complex and exciting testing process, in which the gender dynamic of play, production process, critical response and audience attendance are all under scrutiny at different stages. Talk about overdetermined judgements!

It is often said that theatre is a 'collaborative' art. This term needs to be understood, and then gainsaid. Of course, all the performance arts are dependent on ensemble work of one kind or another, but it is important not to romanticise theatre as special. What is important is to understand the nature of the particular division of labour which operates in theatre, as opposed to, say, dance or concert music.

In the vast majority of theatres, the written script comes about because it is either 'discovered' in an unsolicited submission, or it is commissioned by the artistic director(s). Either way, the executive choice is not made by the writer. For most playwrights, however much research, discussion, etc. is carried out, the actual process of writing is as solitary an activity as is writing anything else. It means that, whatever the edifice of collective cultural input, the creating mind combines the various elements (which might include devising with the company, for example) in its own particular way.

A director co-ordinates and guides the rehearsal and production process, in which many different people with different skills participate. Rarely is the writer fully involved at this stage. (They may or may not want to be, but they do not make the final decisions.) The finished product looks like (on a good night) a smooth-running, ensemble piece of magic. That is one of its illusory joys. The reality of a play's run might be that members of the cast hate the director, fight with each other, do not have a high opinion of the play, but can still turn out a brilliant theatrical experience. This is the skill of ensemble work. This description is, of course, the worst possible gloss, but it is only a hypothetical example. It is pointless to simply assert that theatre is a collaborative art, since, like all production, it has specific relations of production based on a complex hierarchical structure of individual skill and labour.

The shop-front looks rather different. The playwright's name will appear outside a theatre, on leaflets, posters. The profile is high for the duration of the play's run (in lights, even). Writers are often around in rehearsal for at least some of the time, and the writer therefore has a more public profile than the relatively private editorial relationship between, say, a novelist and a publisher's editor. During the process of production, the odds are that the novelist only needs to have contact with the editor, whereas the playwright may well come into contact with the cast.

The playwright thus needs to be prepared to 'come out'; he or she cannot hide behind the finiteness of a published text. Rehearsals may involve changes, modifications, explanation, justification. The playwright may word process alone in a garret, but after that others engage with vested interest in his or her text. With the tradition that theatre (ironically enhanced during the years of censorship) is seen as a potentially subversive medium (the gathering of many in a small space to share an experience), the critical establishment seems to look specifically to its 'leading' playwrights to give public voice to social criticism, to original, moral voice.

For a woman writer to take on this kind of public, authoritative voice means that in some way, consciously or not, she will be challenging the dominant image of the male as moral and literary arbiter. However conservative and anti-feminist she may be, a woman playwright will always therefore appear more radical than her work may bear out. Theatre lags far behind the novel and poetry in being prepared to accept women giving voice, for reasons that are related to long-standing gender taboos on public speaking which relate back to the strictures on women in politics and religion, described earlier:

> The taboo, it is stronger than prejudice, against women's entry into public discourse as speakers or writers, was in grave danger of being definitively broken in the mid-nineteenth century as more and more educated, literate women entered the arena as imaginative writers, social critics and reformers. . . . Public writing and public speech, closely allied, were both real and symbolic acts of self-determination for women.
>
> (Cora Kaplan, Introduction to reprint of *Aurora Leigh*, by Elizabeth Barrett Browning, The Women's Press, 1978, p. 9)

A woman playwright, therefore, is still reacted to as a woman as much or sometimes more than she is as a writer, and a woman playwright has more to overcome than a man before she can be accepted as an artistic 'equal' in the theatre. This means that artistic directors who run theatres, even sometimes female artistic directors, are operating a hidden agenda in which the norms of important subject matter, as well as literary capacity, are still determined by men.

The other reason why it is probably harder for women to 'choose' to write plays relates to another aspect of its 'public' form. Writing a play involves not only finding a voice in the characteristic literary sense and developing craft skills. It also entails writing in dialogue, which even at its most introverted moments is creating a social activity: interaction. At the same time there is an openness between any two speeches, where the meaning is carried subtextually. A monologue or a soliloquy, even while it appears to connote an individual talking to him- or herself, is in fact a performance, someone talking in public before a crowd of people who are listening attentively. If you did this in the street you would probably be arrested, but in a theatre the formal structure sanctions the activity, and gives us a privileged eavesdrop on the inner voice. The playwright makes inner, private voices become public utterances, as well as building a world through dialogue and action.

In addition, even the most apparently static play involves tension, conflict, resolved or not, and the traditional divide of characteristics along gender lines says that women are not meant to engage in conflict and debate (even though we patently do). Conflict and tension are as much the stuff of women's lives as they are of men's, but since they do not appear in public displays as much as men do (institutional power), women generally deal with conflict in the privacy of home, relationships, and even institutionalised conciliation in female-dominated jobs, such as the caring and servicing industries. This explains to some extent why, even though the site of action in many of the plays discussed in the early part of this book is in the home, it is not the conflicts and dilemmas which women experience that are at the centre of the action. Conflict for women still remains a hidden, concealed force in our lives.

A woman playwright is still potentially in a very powerful position. She animates a stage world in which there are multiple voices, engaging with each other, inventing and creating an imagined world and its history, revealing its unconscious impulses, creating imagery, and embodying herself and others. She is quite literally controlling the voices of others as well as using her own. Such transgression. She is controlling other people's voices, making them speak publicly, while also expressing her own.

No wonder, then, that the woman playwright is seen as at best an anomaly, at worst a threat. The reclaimed histories of women playwrights reveal how many have always gravitated towards theatre, but at any given historical time (including our own) it seems to be the case that only a very few token women playwrights ever emerge to stand alongside men. Who knows what the woman playwright might make other people say or do? Such power.

Cross-dressing and gender

> The queen who's grotesquely obscene
> Or the dyke who is out for a fight,
> Butch or fem, he-women, she-men:
> That's entertainment?
>
> The crowd's guaranteed to laugh loud
> When it hears any jokes about queers,
> Yes, we're good – good targets for mud,
> That's entertainment.
> It may be you've seen how we're shown on the screen,
> A dyke's sister George and she's a has-been.
> Ev'ry Boy in the Band is a queen; did you see Sebastiane?
> It's all cock and blarney.
>
> And so, now where do we go?
> Do we take this image, this fake?
> Or do we say it's good to be gay!
> It's we who have to pay, so let's all shout for gay,
> Gay Entertainment.
> (From *Jingle Ball*, Gay Sweatshop, 1976; lyrics by Drew Griffiths)

The presence of women in theatre and drama, as has been shown, has always had a problematic aspect to it. Similarly, although gay people have always worked in theatre (as in other industries), their position has been at times contradictory. The phenomenon of cross-dressing, which has had different functions in theatre across the centuries, is the place where the representations of gender touch the margins of what is proper, what is accepted as 'normal', and what is transgression or subversion.

As we know, before women were officially accepted as actresses in Britain in 1660 (although travelling groups of players who did not perform in the licensed theatres did include women), the accepted practice was that boys or young men played the female roles. This was certainly the convention during Shakespeare's time, and while it was a functional necessity (someone had to play the parts if the dramas were to include women in the stories), it also provoked a great deal of moral concern: '. . . the taking of female parts by boy players actually occasioned a good deal of contemporary comment, and created considerable moral uneasiness, even amongst those who patronised and supported the theatres' (Lisa Jardine, *Still Harping on Daughters*, p. 9).

The theatre as an institution was a constant puzzle as a place of public gathering. The history of theatre censorship is closely related to the possibility that where large groups of people are gathered together, danger to public order might ensue, even when the purpose was 'entertainment'. However, the issue of cross-dressing had a special force, involved as it was with the complex erotic response to the performance of boys in the female roles, recalling the prohibition in Deuteronomy, 'The woman shall not wear that which pertaineth unto a man, neither shall a man put on a woman's garment: for all that do so are abomination unto the Lord their God' (22:5). Some Elizabethans saw such activities as almost blasphemous, leading to immoral behaviour: 'Sexuality, misdirected towards the boy masquerading in female dress, is "stirred" by attire and gesture; male prostitution and perverted sexual activity is the inevitable accompaniment of female impersonation' (Jardine, ibid., p. 9).

The erotic implications become even more complex when it is a boy masquerading as a woman who is disguised as a boy. The levels of illusion are multiple, multi-gendered and multi-sexualised. The puns about cross-dressing used by Shakespeare, the use of dramatic irony – the audience knows that there is a double level of deception – all combine to produce an erotic charge which combines the associations of sexual attraction towards men and women:

> . . . the dependent role of the boy player doubles for the dependency which is woman's lot, creating a sensuality which is independent of the desired figure, and which is particularly erotic where the sex is confused (when boy player represents woman, disguised as dependent boy).
>
> (Jardine, ibid., p. 24)

These complex erotic meanings doubtless had (and still have today) different impacts on the men and women in the audience. Although most of the theoretical work on the 'gendered gaze' has been done in terms of cinema, it is clearly something which pertains to reception theory for art in general. In theatre, the complexity of response is compounded by the immediate, collective experience in performance. This is highlighted in the analysis later of *Trafford Tanzi*. It is intriguing to speculate on the possible impacts of this for Elizabethan theatre. As well as the *frisson* of 'seeing' – knowing – that androgyny or bisexuality are implied in the fusion of gender characteristics, there is also the subtext of homo-eroticism for men, for women perhaps a displaced narcissism, as they see 'their' gender 'played' by a boy who can simultaneously represent innocence (ie, the symbol of femaleness) and virility.

These strictures on women appearing on stage go very deep, back to the gender biases (sexism) of religion, where the public appearance of women is hedged around with extraordinary strictures involving their literal silencing:

> Women were not allowed to speak in church even for the praiseworthy purposes of exhortation and prayer; how much less would they be tolerated as performers in its sacred mysteries. In a woodcut dating from the twelfth century a group of women are shown suffering extreme torment in a flamy hell for the nefarious sin of having raised their voices in church . . . there was no possibility of women taking part in religious plays, except when they were performed in the seclusion of their own world of the convents.
>
> (Rosamond Gilder, *Enter the Actress*, p. 18)

The taboo on women participating in religious ceremonies is still a matter of contention, not just in the Christian religion but in other major world religions, such as Judaism and Islam. Even when the doors seemed to be opened after the Restoration of Charles II in 1660, the royal patents granted to two theatres included cautionary words about decency and women:

> And forasmuch as many plays formerly acted do contain several profane, obscene, and scurrilous passages, and the women's parts therein have been acted by men in the habits of women, at which some have taken offence; for the preventing of these abuses for the future we do strictly charge, command and enjoin that from henceforth no new play shall be acted by either of the

said companies containing any passage offensive to piety and good manner. . . . And we do likewise permit and give leave that all the women's parts to be acted in either of the said two companies from this time to come may be performed by women, so long as these recreations, which by reason of the abuses aforesaid were scandalous and offensive, may by such reformation be esteemed not only harmless delights, but useful and instructive representations of human life, by such of our good subjects as shall resort to see the same.

The admission of women to the stage, then, was, as much as anything, in order to do away with the 'offensive' business of men playing women's parts. From being seen as potentially little more than a whore, the actress was now viewed as the potential shining light of decency. Since one cannot keep sex away from gender, a reverse convention soon developed – a different kind of cross-dressing, with women in men's clothes – in 'breeches parts', which showed off their legs, and which had a later parallel in the pantomime principal boy, traditionally played by a woman.

This aspect of British theatre developed in the nineteenth century, and was especially prominent in music-hall where male and female impersonation were rife, with Vesta Tilley, perhaps the most successful male impersonator of them all, aware of some of the sexual ambiguities in her audience:

It may be because I generally appeared onstage as a young man that a big percentage of my admirers were women. Girls of all ages would wait in crowds to see me enter or leave the theatre, and each post brought me piles of letters varying from impassioned declarations of undying love to a request for an autograph, or photograph, or a simple flower, or a piece of ribbon I had worn.
(Quoted in Julie Holledge, *Innocent Flowers*, p. 21)

Cross-dressing is enormously complex, but at one level it is a response precisely to the signs of gender which already appear on our stages; performers 'dress' as well as perform their gender, and cross-dressing, in its different manifestations, is both a symptom of this fact and a response to the tension involved in establishing gendered identity. It can reinforce those gender stereotypes (the mother-in-law jokes from the pantomime dame) or it can, more consciously as we will see, function as an act of subversive rebellion, demonstrating absurdities as it purloins the characteristics of the opposite sex.

This has particular reverberations for the traditions of camp and drag in modern theatre. The artistic professions, engaged as they are with creating illusion and artifice, have long been a space within which gay men can operate, expressing characteristics seen as a mixture of the conventionally 'masculine' and the conventionally 'feminine', combining sensitivity and emotional self-expression with ambition and ruthlessness:

> The artistic sphere has long been claimed by gay men as legitimate territory; in this area the male homosexual has found the means to pass by identifying himself as artistic/romantic rather than simply gay. So the social rejection on the basis of sexuality is refocussed by the justification of art.
>
> (Caroline Sheldon, *Gays and Film*, p. 10)

Since all gay people have to 'put on an act' to be accepted in the world, the dividing line between life and art is blurred: 'The art of passing (for straight) is an acting part: to pass is to be 'on stage', to impersonate heterosexual citizenry, to pretend to be a real (ie, straight) man or woman' (Jack Babuscio, ibid., p. 45). However, partly because of the general convention of male dominance, male homosexuals (especially in the twentieth century) have been able to find more sanctioned places than have gay women. Many gay men have worked as playwrights, in dance as choreographers and directors. This means that 'out' or not, male gay theatre workers have been able to find camaraderie and self-expression in a way which has had to be more covert for women. The links between the social division of labour in theatre and the nature of the product – the drama, the imagery, the symbolism, what it is possible to imagine – are thus crucially connected.

Feminist dynamics: radical, bourgeois and socialist feminism

The new questions being asked within and about theatre and gender acted as the backdrop to the work of many writers in the 1970s and 1980s. In the analysis of plays from the 1950s and 1960s, a period of turmoil and change, my approach largely focused on the way the gender dynamic in each play determined the gender bias within it. The representation of the family (real and symbolic) was a site for much of the radical and questioning responses to post-war Britain. These responses can be seen to be about the nature of community, manhood, the place (belonging) and the identity of men. Without an activist politics to espouse, the family becomes the site of the dilemma of male identity and sexuality.

The changing social composition of British society lends an authenticity to the figure of the outsider who appears in so many of the plays, but the outsider figure (black, gay, Jewish) is also a symbol of the displacement of the white English male, as is the figure of the mother who has to be destroyed in order for any kind of male identity to survive. In addition, women characters in the plays, because of the gender bias, themselves become 'outsiders', corralled as symbols for the male dilemmas. In the plays by women, the issues are more precisely and consciously gendered in their own right, since the images of displacement (onto the mother in particular) do not work in the same way. Here, in a small number of plays, the experience of being female begins to move centre stage, and motherhood, while it may be seen as a site for struggle as well as symbol, is acknowledged rather than denied or destroyed, even in stage worlds which ultimately capitulate to the dominant ideology, or to male control.

In the case of post-1968 drama, the new ideas about women's place in the world, about sexism, feminism, homosexuality, the relationship between the 'personal' and the 'political' came out from beneath. Inevitably critical discussion, then and since, consists partly of trying to trace the links between these explicitly argued ideas, and the more slippery imaginative forms which they influenced. It is in this context that the following three feminist dynamics are useful. It must be stressed that this discussion has no bearing on the writer's intentions (where we know them), or on what might be polemically desirable. It is not prescriptive in any way, functioning as an analytic method for plays already written. Neither does it add up to a programme or plan which tells anyone how to write the 'right' kind of play.

It should also be borne in mind that while there are many individual feminists around, and all sorts of activism on behalf of women, we do not have either the groundswell of feminist energy of the 1970s or a formal political feminist movement. However, precisely because the position of women has not substantially changed, these ideas still have relevance and potential bite, and they certainly help clarify some of the muddle induced by trying to establish hard and fast categories pertaining to something called 'feminist' theatre. Many women who think of themselves as feminists work in theatre, and feminism informs various aspects of some people's theatre work, but that is not the same as an understanding of the gender dynamic, and the feminist dynamic in the play itself.

Feminism is not, and never has been, a simple homogeneous idea or political organisation. Thank goodness. At the most inclusive level, whatever the flavour of the specifics, all feminism shares certain aims: (1) To challenge a biological determinism which says that men are superior to women. Feminists generally take issue with various aspects of the realpolitik of male dominance in social, political, cultural and emotional spheres. In other words, power is not genetic. (2) To change the position of women in some way. (3) To assert the importance of self-determination for women, individually and/or collectively.

Two things follow from this: first, that feminism is always likely to be nascent in any society where the social and sexual division of labour results in an ideology where what men are and what they do is valued and rewarded over and above whatever it is that women are and do. Second, it should be clear that men cannot be feminists. They can develop ways of understanding their experiences as specifically male. They can, of course, support feminism, participate in gender-based analyses, they can explore what it means to be male, its advantages and drawbacks, they can, as it were, 'demand' some of the emotional rights which appear to be only privileged for women – emotional self-expression, looking after children, house-husbandry – and in this way they too can challenge the dominant ideology. However, the key issues of a gender-based self-determination, allied with an excision of internally absorbed notions of inferiority, do not belong to the ideology of masculinity. Both men and women have issues to address on their own side of the dualistic gender-fence, but these are different, and the fundamental inequality of the notion that men are superior to women involves a reclamation for women of their lives, bodies and minds which is of a very different order, and entails a drive which we identify as feminism.

The three shared aims of feminism are defined in different ways within three main tendencies.

Radical feminism (cultural feminism)

There is a radical feminist in each and every woman. She is there even in the tiniest response of irritation, frustration, anger with which women react when they encounter oppression in any form. The throwaway 'Oh, men' springs from this gut response to the gender imbalances in our culture. Collective radical feminism encourages women to unite, to develop solidarity on the basis of their gender, no matter what their race or class. It asserts that women are strong and powerful, not weak and passive. It responds to our conventionally dualist gender assumptions (men 'are' one thing, women 'are' another) by reversing the arguments, and asserting that so-called female qualities (nurturing, emotionality) are superior to so-called male qualities (aggression, competitiveness, individualism).

Active radical feminism can be exciting; encouraging women to act, creating stimulating all-female ways of being (separatism) – social, sexual, cultural; but its more passive and dangerous form can collapse the entire world into an alternative dualism: denying the importance of race and class, it can assert that men are responsible for everything bad, and women for everything good. Ergo, everything bad has been created by men, and the only possible good future will be one controlled by women. The power struggle here is absolute, and gender the determining social difference.

Power is seen as male, and therefore bad *per se*. Language and artistic forms are seen as 'male'. Given that the only political tactic is an alternative, culturally this takes the form of asserting that there is a 'feminist' aesthetic, that there are 'female' forms, that there is a female 'language'. This is complex, since we are all born into the same language, even though there are many different forms of usage, tone, dialect, register. It is a paradoxical and contentious area, since, in practice, these ideas have informed an exciting array of separate explorations, in theatre and the other arts. In theory, however, it is ultimately a sterile and ironically bankrupt set of ideas. Ironically so, because we are never free of the culture which forms us, and even alternatives are, to some extent, symbiotically linked to the forces to which they are opposed. It is a paradox closely linked to the paradox of artistic authorship and 'creativity' – where what is known and controlled is also always in dialogue with what is unknown, unthought, unconscious. The relationship between 'separate' creations and 'separatist' dualism lies at the heart of the radical feminist drive.

It is partly for this reason that I would argue strongly against there being such an easily co-optable notion as a 'feminist aesthetic'. The idea (attractive to some) that there is something inherently 'male' about the structure of a play is clearly nonsense. The way in which drama becomes form is far too complex for such crudities. Structure is a consequence of context, and can never have any abstract meaning in its own right.

Bourgeois feminism

By definition, this is both rarely used and rarely recognised as an ideology by its promulgators. Bourgeois feminism is seductively simpler. It questions neither the fundamental social nor sexual division of labour, and therefore accepts the dominant ideology that the male is the 'norm'. Thus it sees the main challenge as equalling up with men, getting more shares of the power cake – more women at the top, more women running things. It is largely concerned with individual achievement and success, assuming the 'you can do it if you really want to' approach, seeing 'femininity' not as a social construct which keeps the little woman down, but rather as a tactic for women to get around men in order to obtain what they want.

Like radical feminism, bourgeois feminism addresses the issue of women and power, but whereas radical feminism urges women to join together for solidarity and against male power, bourgeois feminism atomises women, seeing them (her) always in relation to men, and to the dominant order. Paradoxically, like radical feminism, bourgeois feminism also has a space in it for hatred of the male – arguing that women can get around men to obtain what they want because ultimately men are weaker. This results in the 'power behind the throne' compensation for women who relate to male power.

At the same time, of course, bourgeois feminism does speak to the existential issue for each woman: how to control one's own life. Its problem is that it is caught in the double bind of insufficient analytic vision about the causes of the initial gender imbalance. In the end bourgeois feminism relates to men rather than to other women. The 1990s legacy of Girl Power exactly fits this category, although it too, of course, contains a radical feminist component in the feisty, sexually in-your-face streetwiseness of women.

In theatre, while radical feminism is there in the impulse to form all-women groups, the bourgeois feminist impulse has translated itself into the increasingly common practice of referring to women performers as 'actors', as if using the male-gendered form somehow confers on them the accolade of being the 'real thing'. In fact, it would be more radical if they re-appropriated the term 'actress', since that is both an accepted term (no longer significantly connoting actress = whore, as it did in earlier times), and one which is gender-specific. Or there is the gender-free 'performer', which, while it may not specify the genre (dance, play, etc.), at least relates to the activity. Using the term 'actor' is not empowering but actually enfeebling, because it is the same as calling a woman a man. The terms 'writer', 'composer', 'poet' do not have this problem, since they are not gender-specific. Debates about whether to alter the term 'chairman' to either the gender-specific form, as relevant, or to the neutral 'chair' are different, because historically the term 'chairman' came first, whereas to subsume 'actress' into 'actor' is to capitulate to the 'male' label as the norm, i.e. to bourgeois feminism. It is therefore a denial of the specificity of the actress as a female performer. It may appear that for a woman to refer to herself as an 'actor' is to assert pride, whereas in reality it accords with the notion that the female is subsumed into the norm of the male. Names and labels matter.

Socialist feminism

These days, this is also called in the absence of empowering socialist movements, materialist-feminism, because it derives from an approach which aims to take the whole of the material world into account, not merely individual phenomena. In theory, the socialist–feminist dynamic is the most far-reaching, because it integrates gender into an understanding of all the other complex factors which create our lives – class, race, culture, geography, work, family, sexuality, etc. Socialist feminism can potentially link the concerns and struggles of women with other kinds of oppression or inequality, such as those of class, race or culture.

Socialist feminism can incorporate the need for anti-male reaction, for women to be creative without men, and it can also deal with the importance of ensuring that more women occupy more positions of power; but this does not make it merely a catch-all for any form of feminism. Because of its far-reaching analysis, it recognises that fundamental social changes are necessary for a world in which difference and fairness can co-exist. Unlike radical feminism which dismisses men by blaming them for all ills – war, violence, etc. – and unlike bourgeois feminism which has a love-hate relationship with men, socialist-feminism asserts that alongside achieving self-determination (individual and collective), women and men have to struggle together to reach a new accommodation. This has to be undertaken both in personal relationships and at social, political, work and organisational level. Consequently, men have to take on challenges about gender identity themselves, as well as in support of women.

This is, in theory, unaffected by sexual orientation. While radical feminism creates a celebratory space for lesbianism as viable and genuine, bourgeois feminism can 'allow' lesbianism as part of the notion of 'individual choice', and socialist feminism can accept that different sexual orientations are part of the complexity of human relations.

While radical and bourgeois feminism have genuinely radical moments, in the different ways in which they challenge male power bases, and argue for female creativity and independence, only socialist feminism can develop an understanding of the functions and imperatives of gender in their social and political contexts. Radical and bourgeois feminism can both let men off the hook: radical feminism says men are irrelevant, bourgeois feminism pleads to become (lipsticked) one of the boys, whereas socialist feminism argues not only for a genuine equality but for a reassessment of both sides of the gendered coin of life. Life must be different for both men and women. The one cannot change without the other.

Consciously or not, it is socialist feminism which informs the existence of gender studies within academia, whereas it is usually a mix of radical and bourgeois feminism which informs the desire to discover and prescribe the more nebulous categories of 'feminist' or 'women's' theatre. Not that this is merely dismissive; since 1968 some of the most exciting theatre work and much interesting reclamatory scholarship has come from these two approaches.

All-female groups are vital, both as a reaction against male dominance and because of the new imaginative realities they can create. The discovery of forgotten women playwrights expands our horizons and celebrates women's achievements, but it cannot imply a totally female tradition or aesthetic. Ultimately, radical and bourgeois feminism are circumscribed by their own self-referential limitations, as will be seen in the discussion in the final chapter. At times they can actually obstruct understanding, both historical and hermeneutic.

The feminine

The development of these categories of feminism, phoenixes which rise from the bedrock of gender relations as we traditionally know them, inevitably also creates another category to account for ways of identifying more conventional, in some respects, reactionary representations of women in the stage world. The feminine dynamic remains as one which re-presents women in precisely the kinds of role which all three of the feminist dynamics challenge. In this dynamic, women retain their traditional roles: secondary to men, less valued, demoted to a sexuality which serves men, co-optable as symbols economically dependent and powerless. Here women are simultaneously desired and feared, and therefore despised.

It should be clear that my own approach is contained within the socialist–feminist set of ideas. In the second half of this book, part of the enterprise (along with continuing to identify the gender dynamic) will be to identify how these different dynamics (feminist and feminine) manifest themselves in drama after 1968. I begin with a play which is pivotal to this moment of transition, Brecht's *The Mother*, which demonstrates particularly vividly the nexus of issues that bring together notions about gender, the domestic and the social, and the relationship between gender and the nature of politics itself. I have chosen this play because it unites two influential elements: the importance of Brecht in the British theatre landscape, and the fact that it has been seen as a 'model' play which highlights vividly the way the very definition of politics itself is gender-formed.

In this part of the book, the earlier themes are also traced. What has happened to the family? The figure of the mother? The sense of individual identity in a changing world? How do the personal and political relate in the drama of the new political consciousness?

Chapter 8

A theatrical legacy

Mother on a pedestal – a doubtful chivalry

The Mother (1930–31) by Bertold Brecht

Brecht's theory of epic theatre involved repositioning the individual in his or her social setting, as opposed to working from the illusion that individual consciousness and action were somehow independent of social and material location. Brecht's own plays – some of which were didactic Socratic dialogues, many of which included captions telling the audience what was happening in history, as well as moments when characters stepped 'outside' themselves to address the audience directly, songs and music – all these 'alienation' techniques involved attempts to make the theatrical experience 'strange', to encourage the audience to become detached from the emotional experience and think about the ideas, rather than merely identify, empathise. In practice, of course, because Brecht was a superb stage craftsperson, he never avoided arousing empathy, sympathy. Even the anger which the messages in his plays might provoke was an indicator of the fact that ideas and emotions can never be completely separated from one another.

His play *The Mother* was written between 1930 and 1931, and based on the novel of the same name by Maxim Gorky. This play was a direct influence on some of the 1970s theatre work in two ways: first, as a model for a didactic theatre piece about political consciousness-raising – an individual is chosen who is supposedly as apolitical and ignorant as you can get, and we witness his or her apocalyptic journey to socialist hero/heroine. The plays itself had a number of productions in Britain at this time. Second, as a play it was credited as a point of departure for Red Ladder's play (already discussed), and for a play performed by the 7:84 theatre company, *Yobbo Nowt,* written by John McGrath.

The story is set between the years of 1905 and 1917, during the transition from Russia to the Soviet Union. The blurb of the published English translation summarises the plot as being about the way 'an ordinary working-class woman is drawn by her son into the revolutionary movement'.

The play opens with Vlasova speaking either a soliloquy or to herself, depending on how the production angles it. The speech is followed by a chorus of revolutionary workers, establishing individual thought and life in the context of a collective musical message. Vlasova's opening words 'I'm almost ashamed to offer my son this soup' – establish her poverty and her desire to nurture her son. She defines herself in relation to men very clearly: 'What can I, Pelagea Vlasova, a worker's widow and a worker's mother, do?' Her son, Pavel, rejects the poor soup, turning instead to a book, asserting the primacy of intellectual, revolutionary thought over mere food.

The first two scenes are set in Vlasova's house, but it is clear that her son's activities are the real subject of the action (cf. *Look Back in Anger*). When a group of his worker friends arrive to make leaflets, Vlasova reveals her political 'backwardness': 'I don't like seeing my son Pavel in these people's company. They'll end up taking him away from me completely.' She is shown at the beginning as a well-meaning mother, defensive about her son, not terribly bright (no Sarah Kahn here), for whom politics threatens what is left of her family life. When the police raid the house, she still does not respond politically. She agrees to distribute leaflets at the factory, not because she supports the cause (she is illiterate) but in order to protect Pavel from being arrested. Here her maternal instincts and domestic experience come in handy; she pretends to be an old woman bringing food to the workers, and she wraps food in the leaflets.

Vlasova, as a political *tabula rasa*, learns through experience. In a brilliantly structured scene she learns the basics of capitalism, with concepts of ownership and property explained. There is a difference between her table, which she uses at home, and a table owned by a factory owner, the means with which to exploit and underpay his workers. She still does not see any need for violence, until she goes on a demonstration which turns nasty when a worker is shot; her consciousness develops from a bewildered personalised response: 'I didn't want to cause a strike. I wanted to help a man. Why do people get arrested for reading leaflets?' Like Sarah Kahn, however, the impetus towards socialism (support of the group) stems for her, as a woman, from the maternal desire to nurture the individual. (One could argue, *pace* an imaginative radical feminism, that this makes all women – i.e. mothers – potentially 'natural' socialists. . . .)

Vlasova becomes politicised when she witnesses police violence; picking up the flag the shot man has dropped, she says: 'All this is going to be changed.'

All is, indeed, changed. Pavel is arrested and Vlasova is thrown out of her flat. Her 'female' and newly acquired 'male' skills and concerns are briefly joined: she gets a room in a teacher's flat in return for doing his housekeeping, and she obtains her Communist Party membership card. Now nurturing and politics can be combined for her: 'Communism's good for people like us . . . I don't know if they're giving him enough food . . . I'm very proud of him. I'm lucky. I have a son who's needed.'

She visits Pavel in prison. They are forbidden to talk about politics, and, as in the factory leaflet scene, the personal is validated as a saving device: under the cover of chit-chat Pavel manages to pass her addresses to memorise. During the 1905 peasant strikes, Vlasova, now with a reputation as a feisty old politico, demonstrates the unity between industrial and agricultural workers.

In 1912 Pavel returns from Siberia, to find his mother busy producing leaflets. In a moment which echoes and reverses the opening scene of the play, Pavel makes a speech full of ironic pride that his mother is now too busy being political to be personal:

> Does she look after him? No chance. Does she make him a cup of tea, does she run his bath for him? . . . Fleeing from Siberia to Finland amid the icy blasts of the north wind, the salvos of the gendarmes in his ears, he finds no refuge where he can lay his head down except in an illegal printing shop. And his mother, instead of stroking his hair, takes the finished pages out.

Before he leaves again, Vlasova comments: 'Next time let's hope I can slice the bread for you.' This is, of course, painfully ironic, for the next we hear is that Pavel has been arrested and shot. Three women come to console Vlasova, bringing food and a Bible. Now the tables are further turned. Vlasova is no longer the woman who feeds, but the woman who is fed. As a politico, she is no longer a woman who cooks. The ambiguous function of food is linked with a Christianity which Vlasova rejects, along with emotional expressions of grief. The women cry and Vlasova comforts them, rejecting personal grief and elevating 'rationality': 'My weeping wasn't rational, but when I stopped, my stopping was rational.'

After Pavel's death, Vlasova becomes ill. This can be symbolically seen as a mixture of gender-based social comment – once Pavel is no longer there to infuse her with male-dominated Communism, she herself 'decays', and perhaps in a post-Freudian sense as Vlasova displacing her unexpressed grief on to her body, which 'mourns'. However, she does not give up her politics, going on demonstrations, being beaten up, and in 1916 remonstrating with women who are handing in copper for the war effort. Here, castigating her fellow women with powerful references to motherhood, she articulates the play's central hidden gender-biased agenda:

> No animal would give up its young the way you have yours, without sense and understanding for a bad cause. You deserve to have the wombs torn out of you. They should dry up and you become sterile where you stand. Your sons don't need to come back to mothers like you, shooting for a bad cause. They should be shot for a bad cause. But you are the murderesses.

Disentangling the messages of this paragraph are complex. We can clearly see the Lady Macbeth Syndrome at work here. Motherhood is extolled as a potentially vital role which has been betrayed. ('Mother Russia' was a potent slogan.) The wrong choices which sons make are laid at the doors of the mothers, and this means that in the end the women are to blame for the war. The punishment is to make them sterile (cf. Lady Macbeth's 'unsex me here' speech), removing their power which lies in their capacity for motherhood (cf. Jimmy Porter and Alison). Ultimately, then, motherhood is simultaneously elevated to nobility and condemned for its evil potential, both material and symbolic.

This accords well with the somewhat ambiguous but ultimately destructive meanings given to the domestic, the emotional, the traditional concerns of the womanly sphere – Vlasova's initial habitat. The domestic is useful when it involves political ends – leaflets for wrapping food, personal mother–son chat to conceal information – but otherwise it is to be brushed aside and denied: Vlasova leaves her own home, denied the ultimate emotion of grief at her son's death in favour of political pride, and despite her great journey of political consciousness and her own self-sacrifice, defines herself at the end as she did at the beginning: 'For I, Pelagea Vlasova, a worker's widow and a worker's mother, still have a lot of things to do.'

Politics is thus defined at this period as something which involves workers outside the home, those workers being mainly men. Reason is elevated above emotion. In addition, Vlasova, as an old woman, is not a sexual presence, and can be safely surrounded by men. Her de-sexing has happened before the play starts, and her de-mothering is an essential corollary of her journey from most backward to most progressive. She has to become a symbolic 'man' (a man in drag), while at the same time carrying with her the leftover signs of the creative and nurturing powers of motherhood which are then appropriated by Communism, which, by taking on her 'caring' face, has to annihilate her and the signs of her female gender.

Because we as audience still perceive her as a woman, and because the 'character' has taken us with her on her journey, she is, of course, at one level, genuinely heroic, and this is why the play is so powerful, despite its dangerous, and at one level inadvertent, anti-female agenda. She is 'liberated' from sexuality and motherhood (biologically defining characteristics of femaleness) to become a symbol, a mascot, for men. By removing her biological features from relevance, along with their emotional corollaries, she becomes a *tabula rasa* on two counts: a neutral social being on whom is inscribed a view of Communist politics, and a subtextual message which celebrates the male and denies the female.

We can see from this the way in which some later plays modified the message to incorporate some recognition that femaleness and the 'women's sphere' must be taken on board, leading to some acknowledgement of the function of gender: Sarah Kahn links family and Communism, Red Ladder and John MacGrath incorporated the home as a site for 'political' struggle.

The double agenda of *The Mother* leaves us with a clear-cut definition of politics as gendered, only belonging to the sphere of men. Women, in order to become political, have to deny their gender, which means, of course, that they are symbolically (or actually, in this case) stripped of sexuality and motherhood. As we have already seen in the analysis of the plays by male writers from the 1950s, the notion of politics which comes through Brecht's play can be redefined as male identity needing to be predicated on an equally vigorous denial of female identity, which is still seen as coterminous with motherhood (or the capacity for motherhood), and within the stage world, on a gender-driven dynamic which conducts the story according to the demands of the male protagonist(s). In *The Mother*, interestingly, the plot is driven by the exigencies of political events, something which is bigger than both Vlasova and Pavel, but, since we already know that war and politics belong to men (except that women will be blamed if they get it wrong – the Eve syndrome), the overarching narrator is still a male-dominated political machine.

As I have described, Brecht's general influence fed into the melting-pot of post-1968 theatre with a new vigour, since so many people defined themselves as in some way socialist. Specifically, a small handful of plays redressed the gender imbalance in response to the critiques of feminism, but it is significant that these largely tended to come out of the cut and thrust of group theatre work. The legacy of Brecht, invigorating as it has been in many ways, still needed to be tested in the litmus of individually authored plays.

Part IV

Chapter 9

The 1970s

Whose territory?

Vagina Rex and the Gas Oven (1969)
by Jane Arden

The play's cast list suggests mythical archetypes – the Woman, the Man, a chorus of Furies. Like Ann Jellicoe, Arden appeals to Greek mythology to find metaphors for issues she cannot yet name clearly. However, Jane Arden's language throughout this fluid and fragmented play is very different from Ann Jellicoe's in one important respect: Arden reaches for a poetic polemic about the position of women which was not available to Jellicoe from any political movement at the time.

The play takes place simultaneously in a surreal representation of the most public and private of areas – the individual psyche of a woman situated in her feminine conditioning:

> At fifteen the alternatives presented themselves – fight – submit – or go mad. . . . We have no language, the words of women have yet to be written. . . . Woman's use of speech amounts to an assenting silence or an unheard shriek . . . centuries of oppression have made of us cowards and defeatists.

This polemic came from American feminist critiques of women's oppression, and parallels are drawn between the oppression of women and that of blacks, the sense of being colonised and needing to break out. Arden's version of the need to 'disrupt the spectacle' and shock the audience is here translated into an approach to women's relationship to society: 'We must destroy the language.' In other words, before the public spectacle is disrupted we must have a private language which women can call their own.

The Furies are ordinary men and women: 'people off the streets – those who live faceless – exposed to violence – the homeless who haunt the wastelands of the world – telling us of our lost lives.' The Furies recall the gang in Bond's *Saved*, alienated youth of the 1950s and 1960s, the symbol of people in search of territory and identity. However, in Arden's play the woman is unequivocally at the centre. The correlative to this is that men are largely represented as brutish and oppressive, although there is a moment of sympathy when Man and Woman say together: 'Are we forced to play these roles for life?'

The title of the play connects Vagina (naming the unnameable) with Rex, the powerful masculine. By saying that the vagina is king, i.e. the vagina rules, and by adding the reference to genocide (the gas oven), female sexuality is associated with power and the fear of destruction.

The play's fragmented form reflects the message about the need to break down language, sequence and narrative in order to make sense of oppressive experiences. The use of slide projections, music, light shows and strobe lights to represent the woman's madness provides a cacophony of sensations. The violence which the play says is inflicted on women is reflected in the violence of the stage imagery inflicted on the audience, similar to the 'theatre of cruelty' devices used in the American Living theatre play *The Brig* where the production re-created the atmosphere of a military prison, designed to discomfort the audience.

The negativity of feminine conditioning is demonstrated through a satirical mock-marriage ceremony and a song about Daddy's girl in which the singer advises her to break out of her expected role:

> Break your dollies
> burn their dresses
> and the house you keep them in.

A series of Brechtian captions on a screen asks the women in the audience: 'Do you believe in penis envy?' 'Are you one of the great mass of women exploited as cheap labour?'

A mother image appears, the male actor becoming a little boy, and a dummy ('the omnipotent mother goddess') making the male fear of female power explicit. As in Jellicoe's work, the woman's roles as mother and whore are brought together, but here she is not surrounded by male characters but allowed to exert her power as a female performer in the stage space, although she is left alone at the end. While many feminist critiques are woven into the generally visceral nature of the play, its ability to make political arguments is confined by its own fragmentation, so that the woman remains at the end much as she was at the beginning: alone, with only a relationship to a (weaker) man to make any sense in her world. The play lays out the connection between the material oppression of women and the inner psyche and sexual lack of identity which they experience, in a radical feminist dynamic. As an expression of defiant rebellion, the play is a series of sensory experiences which assert woman as subject matter, as a being acted upon by men and societal conditioning.

On female territory

Rites (1969) by Maureen Duffy

In her Introduction to the published play, Maureen Duffy, like Ann Jellicoe, refers to the contradictory nature of private life and conduct:

> There is a Peeping Tom in all of us. We should all like to be able to eavesdrop, to know how people behave, alone or in groups when they can really be themselves. By watching them we can enjoy the vicarious pleasure of their 'shameful behaviour' and the breaking of innumerable taboos.

She too appeals to myth:

> The Greek gods and heroes form a huge family encompassing every human emotion, every sexual combination and variation. There is no need for us to commit incest or murder, they have done it already. There is no need for us to feel guilty for homosexual or adulterous fantasies.

This notion suggests that the 'real' family, within which we either conceal emotions or experience the taboos on other emotions, is private, and 'outed' via the validating framework of Greek myth. It is interesting that both Jellicoe and Duffy appeal explicitly to myth, in a way which also enables them to focus on more conscious gender-based choices than their male counterparts. For Jellicoe, of course, there was no contemporary feminist critique of the family, and for Duffy it was barely there (this does not imply a comment on any ideas they may have held already). Myth is a respectable device within which to place the unrespectable, the taboo, the new. Myth can provide 'archetypal' characters, and free them from the real social family, in its domestic setting. The 'message' thus can be polemical and suggestive, as well as rooted in recognisable relationships and dynamics.

Whereas Jellicoe creates a surreal and absurdist no-person's-land, Duffy takes the setting by the jugular, and sets the play in the women-only world of a ladies' lavatory (see *Steaming* later for a similar decision) as a self-consciously gendered choice:

> In a world of stereotypes and attitudes (men do this, women are like that, feminine reaction, masculine response) . . . all reduction of people to objects, all imposition of labels and patterns to which they must conform, all segregation can lead only to destruction.

As with Jellicoe, the male-dominated framework of this all-women world is indicated by the device of male stage-hands, in full view of the audience, building the set at the beginning and taking it down at the end (cf. Steve in Jellicoe). Of course, these stage directions do not need to be observed, but the impact if they are is to reinforce the transitional nature, not only of the stage time, but also of the very world in which the women can find some sort of sanctuary away from the prying eyes of men. At the same time, the women are only 'allowed' this space by virtue of it having been structured by 'men', materially and symbolically. This suggests a feminine dynamic, in which men have structural power (cf. Dunn).

The women's world is full of female chat: make-up, work and so on. Meg, who with Ada looks after the toilets, takes a pride in her work. In a demonstration of single-sex chat about the opposite, Ada comments on last night's man: 'Not bad. All right for a week night. . . . No dash. I like a bit of dash of a weekend. Not much staying power either.'

In this all-female world, various taboos are broken. The set confronts us with a public lavatory building on stage (we cannot actually see the toilets), and we eavesdrop on the 'private' world of women who talk about men with the same sort of fear, attraction, dependence and contempt which is a feature of the more familiar public world of male-only camaraderie. By contrast, an all-female camaraderie is evoked; three office girls come in (a kind of giggling Greek chorus).

Two more women enter, bringing with them a life-sized boy doll. The appearance of a male figure, even though it is not real, brings a

threat into the women's world. In an uneasily distasteful game, Ada
undresses him:

> Well, he's life size.
> Made to measure.
> Just like my Willy.
> Mummy's big boy.
> Looks so harmless all quiet there.

Ada's predatory approach to men seems to confirm the fears of female
sexuality expressed by Jimmy Porter some fifteen years earlier:

> Bastard men! . . . He thinks just because I'm flat on my back he's
> got me, but I've got him; caught, clenched as if I had my teeth in
> him. 'Come in,' I say, all soft, and I squeeze him tight, loving as a
> boa constrictor. And they're wild for it. They swoon and cry in my
> arms and come back for more.

A girl cuts her wrist in one of the lavatories, and sanitary towels are
used as bandages (see the Women's Street Theatre Group and *Once a
Catholic* for similar taboo-breaking images on stage). The climax
comes when all the women join together in a ritual anti-men dance,
and, when they have reached a collective frenzy, 'suddenly a
FIGURE appears from [cubicle] number seven and tries to get to the
exit. . . . Head bent; it is suited and coated, short-haired and masculine.'
The women fall on this figure, beating it to a bloody pulp, and only
then does one of them realise that it is a woman, clearly a lesbian,
wearing male-type clothes. The play becomes like a Greek tragedy,
where conventional gender roles, women defining themselves as man-
haters and simultaneously dependent on them, result in literally deadly
prejudice. The women's solidarity, resilience, wit, control of their own
territory, are revealed as mere 'ghetto' security, in which gender bigotry
still festers.

Transgressors – either boy doll or masculine woman – must be
destroyed. By the end everyone has gone, and Ada and Meg are once
more in command. Glancingly, motherhood is revealed as problematic
when the child is a boy; otherise the maternal roles which Ada and
Meg fulfil for the other women in the toilets is a substitute for any
other kind of family, which, given their attitude to men, is clearly
impossible.

Women here are removed from the kitchen sink and put into the toilets, as it were, but at least they have (temporary) total control over the inner workings of their territory. The feminine dynamic (men building the set) allows a space for a radical feminist solidarity, which is paradoxical. In order to achieve it, they have to destroy all signs of maleness, actual (boy doll) or implied (butch lesbian) when invasion is threatened. Within the hermetic world, hatred of men and homosexuality are revealed as the new taboo. War between the sexes has been declared.

Womb envy

Occupations (1970) by Trevor Griffiths

The play is set in a Turin hotel room (a home from home), where the stage is dominated by a large bed in the background. Here Angelica lies ill with cancer of the womb. The opening images are those of Polya, the maid, injecting 'the writhing Angelica' with cocaine, while in the background the 'Internationale' is being sung. The juxtaposition of celebratory public commitment in the song with the private, physical agony of a woman sets the metaphor for a transaction between gender and politics.

Kabak, a political activist, in Turin to visit the Italian left-wing theorist Gramsci, is presented in the stage directions as a somewhat contradictory figure: 'dressed as he is in impeccable bourgeois style, there is something not quite right about him as though the form were somehow at war with the content.' Kabak has come to discuss political unrest in the city, and has brought his dying wife with him. Polya tries to tell him the truth about Angelica's illness: 'It's a woman's thing . . . it's private.' She cries, while Kabak is 'fierce but contained'. While one must, of course, always be deeply sceptical about the absoluteness of stage directions, it is an indication that Kabak is meant to be emotionally opaque: 'There is barely a clue as to his mental state. There is a tenseness, a coldness about his movement.' The tension between Kabak and Angelica is compounded by her pretence about her situation: 'I can't . . . love you . . . tonight. . . . It's the time of the month.' Kabak talks about the revolution while she sleeps; she screams wordlessly in her sleep, and he replies: 'No place for you, my love. No place at all.'

The political and personal stories run parallel. Kabak meets Gramsci, who makes public speeches, in which he describes the homeland of the

Italian factory owners, with a comparative gloss on the metaphor of motherhood: 'their motherland is not Italy, that fat-headed, sore-arsed sow: the motherland is Capital, sleek, dark-haired, bright, warm, passionate Capital. Who wouldn't defend her, the young delicious whore.' The factory audience to whom he is speaking is assumed to be all-male, and they laugh at the joke. While this castigation of motherhood and female promiscuity happens, the stage space is still dominated by the incapacitated woman lying in bed.

In the hotel, the truth becomes clearer. Polya tells Kabak that Angelica started bleeding when he left her. The use of the female metaphor for country and politics comes out into the personal open when Kabak makes the connection between the cancer in Angelica's womb and the cancer in the body politic: 'She has a cancer in her womb. A lonely fruit for a womb. We occupied the family estate in Kiev, 1918. Her husband fled. She . . . remained.' Like Alison in Osborne's *Look Back in Anger,* Angelica is a military hostage; a prisoner of war whose bed is the camp of the conqueror. However, because she carries the 'sickness' of the old regime in her body, she is infected in every way: 'It's here. . . . Under the skin. It's not a part of me. It's foreign. I can feel it moving. Underneath. In the hands. In the legs.' The old Russian regime (Mother Russia) is imaginatively destroyed through this tortured and tortuously imagined image of a woman who carries within her womb the decay of the state, which is synonymous with the decay of motherhood.

Although Angelica is dying, Kabak refuses to stay with her. Angelica injects herself, and in her final delirious stream-of-consciousness even her voice is taken over (shades of the dybbuk) as she babbles about the Tsar, bread riots, and finally, as her dying screams continue in full view of the audience, we see slides of the Tsar, Lenin, Mussolini and Hitler. Her rotting 'bourgeois' – and let me stress *female* – body is what enables the birth of socialism into a new kind of (male-centred) history.

This is an appalling and powerful, virtually pornographic image. A more 'liberated' (because uncensored) version of Orton's dead mother lies on stage, divides with extraordinary and shocking potency the concept of politics being all-male and all-important, and the domestic and the decaying as all-female. The mother as symbol is not even allowed the redeeming feature of being able to join the men on their own terms. Polya is a nurse, and a sexual servicer for Kabak's loneliness. Angelica is a representative of the decadent order, but her destruction is on the site of her woman- and motherhood, within her body, not on the basis of her class location. She has, after all, been captured as a hostage of war.

The image is a consciously politicised and logical extension of Osborne's conflation of class politics with Alison's body. However, here the issue is not that of individual male identity but rather that of the body politic, diseased (and female), contrasted with the new healthy regime (male). It is a poignant and painful irony that the female is also equated with the reactionary, and the male with the progressive; Angelica is not even allowed a partial recuperation in the way that Vlasova is. Woman here is both total symbol and a totally destroyed reality.

Whose public school?

Slag (1970) by David Hare

The title of this play reverberates with a mixture of meanings: 'slag', as in the pile of waste outside a coalmine, and a term of abuse hurled at women. Hare's play is set in a girls' public school which is on the verge of closing – it has only seven pupils left. In the common-room, the three remaining staff commune in an odd sort of all-female environment, where Joanne (23) leads the vow to:

> ... abstain from all forms and varieties of sexual intercourse. ... To keep my body intact in order to register my protest against the way our society is run by men for men whose aim is the subjugation of the female and the enslavement of the working woman ... in order to work towards the establishment of a truly socialist society.

Ann (32) has a slightly different aim: 'We will build a new sort of school where what people feel for people will be the basis of their relationship. No politics.' Elise (26), by contrast, does not spout political ideals, but is concerned with her femininity; all looks and sexual magnetism, she speaks of 'the great rush of air to my legs that sucks men to me'.

Hare's sharp-edged, satirical, quick-fire dialogue kills two birds with one stone. The first, the hermetic and incestuous nature of the minor public school (male), and the second, a widely flung series of brickbats at the new feminism, where – as in the opening quotes – he makes no attempt (or at least, his female characters do not) to distil the differences between the various strands of feminism.

Throughout the play there is a running gag about dogs (the school is going to the dogs, geddit?) crapping everywhere. The women bicker, call each other names and try to undermine each other in all sorts of ways. Joanne calls Elise by the scabrous names which men call women, and announces that for her the school represents an ideal separatist community: 'Brackenhurst is the community of women. Nothing is pointed, nothing perverts . . . I'm talking about women being really women, being different from men.' Her idea of 'real women' means celibacy: 'masturbation is the only form of sexual expression left to the authentic woman.'

Interestingly, Joanne is the least conventionally attractive of the three, and whenever she expresses any of her ideas she is theatrically undermined, as the other two play practical jokes on her. Meanwhile Ann and Elise, in a series of rituals which recall Sister George and Childie, enact sado-masochistic gender games. In this odd, 'unnatural' family set-up, Ann is the mother-figure, Joanne the bullying father and Elise the vulnerable and submissive child. The institutionalised home, which is falling apart, is revealed as bankrupt – an ironic comment on Joanne's ideals, since she 'left everything I loved' in order to find 'a different way of life'. She is also obsessed with the world of film, representing the male-dominated world which she claims to have abandoned, implying that women who turn away from male-dominated forms of creativity become merely 'ugly', bankrupt and destructive.

Joanne claims to be a virgin, and her hostility to sexuality and motherhood are expressed in a dream about Elise, who claims she is pregnant:

> You lay down on the table and the first animal came out. There was some discussion among us as to who should have the first bit, but a man interrupted and you ate your first child which was a chicken. The second was a fish and I had some. You lay on the table and the wet animals came regularly from you. And we all ate.

At the end Elise's pregnancy is revealed to be phantom, in the last complete sentence spoken in the play: 'It's gone. There was a great wet fart and it had gone.'

Motherhood, which in this environment is entirely sterile – no men, no meaningful sexual relationships – is evaluated as merely a 'wet fart'. The site of the play's narrative is that of a decaying public school. All the rituals are debased, and no one is being educated. As Elise comments: 'There was no virgin birth, there are simply declining standards in private education and that is all.'

If the play operates primarily as a satire on the public school system run by and for men, then using women and feminism as metaphor (there are, of course, public schools for girls) adds another dimension to the satire, since they are clearly so inept, self-seeking and promulgating propagandist ideologies which they cannot live out. Women cannot run anything, they are incapable of wielding power. In addition, they represent some kind of loony, stereotyped amalgam of scraps of ideas and slogans drawn from different feminisms.

In these twin capacities – as those responsible for education, and as feminists – they are shown as bickering, disturbingly antisocial women, whose sexuality is either absent, distortedly frustrated, with phantom motherhood expelled as if it were a defecatory act. The play has an articulate, compulsive power to it, driven by educated, witty and sardonic dialogue which moves fast even when very little else is happening on stage. The banter between the women is competitive and ultimately destructive; there is none of the brief solidarity of Duffy's *Rites*, since the territory is simply an imitation male environment.

Their crime is the twin one of refusing to 'be' women and have relationships with men, and of trying to imitate men by running a school and attempting to exert social power. While, at the level of satire, an effective demolition job may be done on the public school system, because the metaphor is based on an 'unnatural' gender reversal as the objective correlative for the satire, women and their 'feminism' are themselves demolished. We are left with nothing at the end – the beginning of a sentence by Joanne, which is interrupted by the final curtain.

The question really is whether feminism is being satirised and the public school is the metaphor. Whichever, the substitute family which the three women constitute is on quicksand, since at every level they have transgressed. The only outcome is that everything they represent that is female – sexuality, potential motherhood and newly acquired feminism – is shown as ludicrous and disgusting.

The sexual psyche

AC/DC (1970) by Heathcote Williams

The mixture of new hallucinatory poetic and polemic, seen in *Vagina Rex* associating women's rights with creativity, also appeared in this play. It too is set everywhere and nowhere, in the cosmos and the psyche, the new psychedelic world of the imagination. The language is inventively energetic, a kind of techno-mediaspeak, drawing on different sexual and technological argots which reflected the counter-culture of the 1960s. The play explores the way the human brain deals with the technology it has invented. The text even has different typefaces for characters, with Sadie, the woman at the centre, in italics throughout.

The title is one of the phrases used for bisexuality, an introduction to the idea of sexual flexibility. Sadie is, in many senses, the equal of the men. They are all media freaks – stoned, spaced-out people testing the boundaries between sanity and madness, coherence and the wildness of an improvisatory imagination. The freeing of language is symbolic of the desire for freedom from fixed social roles. Maurice at one point comments on Perowne: 'He's a lesbian.' We never know what to take literally, as the characters are all capable of extraordinary shifts of consciousness. Occasionally the disquisition about gender roles comes into the open: 'Do you know why women can never deliver good epigrams? It's because of the nature of the orgasm. A man's orgasm is intensive, right. And a woman's orgasm is extensive.'

Gary and Melody represent conventional male and female roles. Melody fears Sadie and taunts her into having sex with them. Sadie rejects them:

> My vaginal walls were built in Berlin. There's no sensation there. There's no such thing as a vaginal orgasm, dig? That's a three billion year old male supremacist con. . . . Well, dig this, my clitoris is a transistorised prick. Everything's tending towards greater and greater miniaturisation, right? And my clitoris is a security leak from the future . . . MY WHOLE BODY IS A COCK.

Sadie is American, a new outsider who brings the power of the new media with her. This play also allows conflict between the women, Sadie acting as a burgeoning feminist voice, furious about the power of media images: 'The thing to do is to colonise them (pointing to the wall) before they colonise you.' Sadie is the focus of the final section of the play. She attacks Maurice and takes on the role of liberating Perowne into a new experience through the painful process of drilling a hole (trepanning) in his head to liberate the 'third eye'. Sadie's aim is to 'get you responding to undiscovered electro-magnetic fields', and Maurice feels no pain. Perhaps Sadie's name refers to 'sadism'. In a curious way, at the end the trepanning is a birth fantasy with Sadie as psychic midwife-guru, enabling Perowne to give birth to himself.

Sadie figures as a new and positively powerful concept of mind-motherhood, which in the vocabulary of the play gives her a significance above that of the men while still isolating her from any communication with other women.

Whose sexual freedoms?

Lay-By (1971) by Howard Brenton, Brian Clark, Trevor Griffiths, David Hare, Stephen Poliakoff, Hugh Stoddart and Snoo Wilson

This play is an exception among the plays discussed, as it was co-authored by a group of male writers who were commissioned by Portable Theatre, a writers' group started by David Hare and Nick Bicat when they came down from Cambridge University. The published introduction says that the play was: 'inspired by a case of rape and indecent assault for which a man was convicted, perhaps unjustly, and sentenced to eight years jail.' Two sides of the story are told, beginning with two women, Joy and Lesley, who pose provocatively as they discuss going for a swim. Lesley describes what happened to her: 'I sucked him off . . . and then the dirty bugger goes and rapes me.'

Lesley is on drugs, and sleeps around, but she claims she was forcibly assaulted. We hear the other side of the story when Jack says that Lesley was willing. An investigative figure called Barber mediates, acting as devil's advocate, trying to goad Lesley into admitting that she agreed to everything.

At the end of the play, Lesley is brought in on a stretcher, unconscious, just as she was found in the lay-by after the rape. She is stripped naked and examined by a (male) doctor, in a mixture of pornographic and necrophiliac imagery. She dies, and is then washed with a bucket of blood by two 'orderlies' in white coats, who then hoist her body up into a Christlike pose. One of the orderlies relates a parable about too many mice being crammed together in too small a space: 'And then it all starts to fall apart. Anarchy, chaos, total irreversible breakdown. Nothing. Void, the whole thing.'

Jack and his partner Marge (who simply sat powdering her nose during the rape) are also brought on, dead and naked, and they too are washed in blood. At the end we are left with the two orderlies, bewildered, not really knowing what they are doing.

The imagery, the action and the questions raised by the play are complex and intriguingly of their time. There is a nihilist attitude to the nature of social order (Beckett), in which authority, in the form of white coats and the interrogator, is mixed with religious imagery (washing in blood) to present a picture of an almost mystical, proto-religious order which demands sacrifice and victims. In one sense, ultimately, all three involved in the incident – Lesley, Jack and Marge – end up as sacrifical victims to some kind of nameless order (Godot never appears here either!), implemented by a kind of 'management' which simply follows orders. There is no morality or legal code here. Guilt seems to be attributed simply by association.

There is a social, agitprop dimension to the piece; at one level it is a demonstration play, asking an audience to speculate on the nature of rape: What is it? How is it defined? Is the man merely guilty? Did the woman collude? Was she raped? Who is responsible? With the new stage freedoms comes another challenge for performers and audience. Nakedness, nudity, disaffected, drug and sex-free lifestyles, the shocking image of blood being used to wash naked 'dead' bodies – all these disrupt the spectacle of theatre in a way which offers challenging and taboo images.

However, in its gender dynamic and implications, the play also reveals a further textual and subtextual problematic. Apart from some very brief moments, the active protagonists are all men, and Lesley, as chief victim, is acted on both verbally and physically. She is isolated from the other women – Joy, her friend, is hardly a supportive presence, and Marge, Jack's sidekick, is, on his side, colluding in the event which precedes the play. The figure of Lesley comes to represent the generic meanings of a society which is sexy, available, and therefore, presumably, dangerous.

Paradoxically, despite its apparently 'liberated' imagery, the final message is somewhat puritanical – Lesley, after having been ogled and handled by the men in the play (and ogled vicariously by us, the audience), is passive, dead and an example to us all – a warning, along with Jack and Marge. But Lesley carries the central message: the body politic symbolised again by the female body (as in Griffiths, and in a more minor way by Hare), which has to be destroyed to exorcise the danger and the 'evil', both to expose a set of moral questions, which themselves do not refer to femaleness as such; Lesley is simply taken for granted as sexually vulnerable and dangerous, never as the agent of her own actions.

Biology and property values

Owners (1972) by Caryl Churchill

Caryl Churchill's play has at its centre Marion, a successful estate agent. Clegg, her husband, who runs a butcher's shop (more meat and blood), finds this both attractive and threatening to his own notions of what a real man, head of a real family, should be:

> She's physically a strong woman. And mentally in some respects. . . . She can stand on her own two feet which is something I abominate in a woman. Added to which she has what you might call a magnetic personality.
>
> We were taught to look up to my father. My mother literally worshipped him. . . .
>
> I was thrusting. I envisaged a chain, Clegg and Son. I was still the son at the time. I would have liked a son myself once I was the Clegg, but now I've no business I don't need a son. Having no son, I don't need a business. . . . And another satisfaction of my shame is the proof that it's she who is infertile.

The knot of property (implied in the play's title), ownership, money and control are set up in both the contexts of work and marriage. The link between family and the continuation of property (and ego in the family name) is made by virtue of its impossibility – Marion may be successful, but she is infertile and cannot become a mother. There is a running gag through the play in the form of Clegg's ineffective plans to murder Marion. His final reassurance, as he plunges a knife into a piece of meat, is that 'She is legally mine and one day she'll die knowing it'.

Marion is also a landlady, and the pregnant Lisa and her husband Alec, their children and his mother all rent a house from her. A series of gruelling emotional scenes culminate in Lisa offering to give Marion her baby in exchange for somewhere to live. We also learn that Marion has been in a mental hospital, where she met Worsley, a man who is continually bandaged or physically damaged in some other way.

The complex plotting moves fast: Marion and Clegg take the baby, and in a role reversal, Clegg stays at home to look after it. Worsley, meanwhile, becomes even more damaged – his neck is bandaged, his hand gets blown off. Clegg, still concerned about his manhood, remembers National Service, and having killed a man twenty years before:

'Manhood . . . some of us may think we have it when really it is someone else.'

Money and ownership, business and personal life, are knotted around the displaced baby. Lisa wants the baby back, with Marion trying to force her to sign adoption papers: 'I don't see that signing a bit of paper makes him hers. He is mine. His blood and everything. His look . . . he's yours and mine.' Lisa also has to negotiate with Clegg, who allows her to see the baby if she will have sex with him: 'On your back and underneath is where I like to see a lady, and a man on top. Right on top of the world . . . I didn't say you mustn't move at all, but just in response.'

The baby is the object of the central struggle, with Marion still determined:

> The more you want it, the more it's worth keeping . . . every one of you thinks I'll give in. Because I'm a woman, is it? I'm meant to be kind. I'm meant to understand a woman's feelings wanting her baby back. I don't. I won't. I can be as terrible as anyone.

In the final scene, which mirrors the opening, Clegg has a new butcher's shop, Worsley has burned down Alec's house and Alec is dead – the sacrificial victim to the propery values which dominate all their lives. Lisa gets her baby back, and Worsley, Clegg and Marion return to their odd 'family' set-up.

One can see in the imagery links with some of the legacies of the 1950s and 1960s: the 'outsider' figure in Worsley, who is also the damaged male (although he is not the husband), and a Cliff-like surrogate son in a family which cannot have its own biological children. The family and interpersonal relationships are at the core of the play, with the Brechtian placing of the characters not only in their social contexts, but also in their ideological framework, where capitalist ownership controls everything.

The end re-establishes a kind of truce-like order: the real mother gets her real baby back, but her nice marriage has gone. Marion and Co resume their *modus vivendi* as an unwillingly unconventional family, but a family nevertheless.

The style of the dialogue – a self-knowing Brechtian-type consciousness – (which makes it easy to find quotes!) enhances the satirical barbs. Worsley, for example, spells out the legal starting point of the play's title: 'the law is not for morals so much as property. The legal system

was made by owners. A man can do what he likes with his own.'
Yet ownership is revealed as permeating every aspect of human relationships, not just inanimate property. Marion is a contradictory case;
she accedes to the dominant values of property, bullying and bargaining
to get what she wants because she has the money and power to do so.
She is, however, a woman – and so she is, in a sense, imaginatively
punished, by not being able to 'own' biological motherhood. Churchill
hoists her with her own petard, as it were, and this imaginative 'punishment' lends the play its moral tone. At the same time (Churchill is
adept at posing opposites to test absolutes), she transgresses. She is a
woman, and the corollary to her being powerful is that her husband is
not. There is no room for shared power. Marion also transgresses emotionally – in a bourgeois feminist bid for the right to feel 'as terrible as
anyone', i.e. any man. Like some of the figures in earlier decades, the
powerful woman is barren. At the same time, because she has power,
Clegg has a crisis of manhood, and Worsley carries the damaged male
image as an implied symbol of male weakness in the presence of
female power.

Marion is juxtaposed with Lisa, who is far from barren. Lisa retrieves
tenderness through her maternal love, and she gets the baby back as
well. However, we have seen in the course of the story that this is at
a price; she loses Alec, she has no material power base, and she is therefore passive and open to further exploitation in the future. The 'happy'
ending is only a temporary resolution.

Gender conflict and a bewildered sense of gender identity are self-
consciously threaded through the play. The undermining of 'manliness'
is as much an issue (in terms of the way people feel about themselves) as
the transgression beyond 'womanliness'. The play shifts from the
domestic (home) to the public (shop) to the institutional (office),
and it demonstrates in agitprop effect, though not in literary style,
that notions of property permeate both our public and private lives.
Marion dominates the play, and while in some ways she gets her
come-uppance, she is not destroyed, and she loses out with the baby.
Her relationship with Lisa is absolutely on its own solid territory. The
symbolic victims are both male – Alec, the innocent, and Worsley,
the perpetually damaged. The values debated in the play are always
firmly rooted in the gender of each character, and the one never
becomes a symbol or cipher for the other. The fact that a woman is
at the centre of the play, and that a woman wrote this play, is not
accidental.

Gender and creativity: the Ophelia syndrome

Teeth 'n' Smiles (1975) by David Hare

The play is set during a single night in the summer of 1968, at a Cambridge May Ball. The opening stage directions present us with a romantic image:

> ARTHUR is lying on a bench, staring. He is wearing a silver top hat and a silk suit, but the effect is oddly discreet. He is tall, thin and twenty-six.

He lies there, relaxed, while Inch arranges the sound equipment for the May Ball band, for which Arthur is the song writer. One man does the manual work, while the other is there, charismatic and immaculate. Gradually the rest of the cast congregate: Laura, who cooks and sews for the pop group, describes Maggie, the group's singer, whom they're all awaiting:

> She starts drinking at breakfast, she passes out after lunch, then she's up for supper ready for the show. Then after the show she starts drinking. At two-thirty she's out again. Morning she gets up. And drinks. She's a great professional. Never misses a show.

Laura's function is a mixture of office and welfare manager, wardrobe mistress, supplier of food – general mum and bottle-washer to the all-male (apart from Maggie) group. As we wait for Maggie, Arthur also gives us information and a buildup: he met Maggie when she was 16 and an uneducated folk-singer. In Svengali fashion he made her into the extraordinary singer she is. They had a relationship which has turned sour.

When Maggie appears, her main power is evoked through the songs she sings – songs which are (pace Ronnie in Wesker) a version of Arthur's voice and art. There is a kind of artistic partnership between them, in which the division of labour between inchoate emotion and artistic formulation is clear: 'He invents me. . . . The words and music are Arthur's but the pain is mine. The pain is real. The quality of the singing depends on the quality of the pain.'

The division of attributes along gender lines is clear: Arthur is art, intellect, Maggie is interpreter, emotion. Where Arthur is immensely

articulate in his physical and mental control, Maggie is equally articulate in her lack of control:

> I only sleep with very stupid men . . . they never understand a word
> I say. That makes me trust them. . . . So each one gets told a dif-
> ferent secret, some terrible piece of my life that only they will
> know. . . . Then the day I die, every man I've known will make
> for Wembley stadium. And each in turn will recount his special
> bit. And when they are joined, they will lighten up the sky.

The image is powerful; the self, fragmented (and female) in life, can
only be reunited in some kind of death. Saraffian, the group's manager,
has a more cynical view of her anguish, believing that she drinks 'so as to
stop any nasty little outbreaks of happiness among her acquaintances'.
  The play is full of self-referential commentary from these articulate
characters about themselves and each other. Maggie, seeing herself as
'one of the boys', is unpleasant towards Laura, but the latter nevertheless has an interesting comment to make about her, linking the fact of
her hedonism with victim/sacrifice:

> It's just possible anywhere, at any time, to decide to be a tragic
> figure. It's just an absolute determination to go down. The reasons
> are arbitrary, it may almost be pride, just not wanting to be like
> everyone else. I think you can die to avoid cliché. And you can
> let people die to avoid cliché.

Despite the fact that Arthur and Maggie meet after a long separation,
we hardly see them alone together. Saraffian arrives, fed up with
Maggie's unreliability, and fires her; to add insult to injury, the band
hide their drugs in her bag, and she is arrested. She ends up (*pace*
Annie in Arden) with no job, no relationship, no identity.
  Her one chance for some kind of resolution with Arthur is muddied
by Laura, with whom she is in sexual competition. Laura challenges
Maggie: 'If you really wanted rid of him you wouldn't sing his songs.
And you wouldn't be afraid to tell him to his face.' This competition
effectively anatomises Maggie, who is isolated as a woman among
men, with no real friend or colleague. She is, of course, ascribed
power, as a dominating personality, and as an expressive artist, who
can move an audience, but her iconoclasm is too threatening – literally,
to the band's survival, and figuratively, precisely because of her
inchoate, emotional strengths. She therefore has to be removed from

the action (by being arrested) rather than finding any resolution through it, or even being allowed to remain within the bounds of social life, like the others. Her self-sacrifice has an apocalyptic hollowness, like someone who makes an altruistic speech from the stake:

> So I go to jail. Nobody is to think about me. . . . Nobody is to remember. Nobody is to feel guilty. Nobody is to feel they might have done better. Remember, I'm nobody's excuse. If you love me, keep on the move.

Arthur confirms this in his own words: 'The music remains the same.'

What remains the same is that men control the world of creativity, with a little help from a servicing female, and the occasional wild pure emotion (female) which must be annihilated after it has served its purpose. After all, the music is still there, even though the singer is not.

Arthur's explanation for Maggie's 'self-destructiveness' is similar to Saraffian's:

> Her problem is: she's frightened of being happy. And if ever it looked as if she might make it, if the clouds cleared and I, or some other man fell perfectly into place, if everyone loved her and the music came good, that's when she'd kill herself.

As a tragic figure, Maggie is assigned desires for the impossible, but we never gain any insight into what they are; she has no relationship with another peer or equal, she never confronts the central tussle with Arthur. The crisis with the band is relatively arbitrary – this is only one of a whole number of similar events. Unlike Beatie who begins (apocalyptically) to find her own voice, Maggie never finds hers – she merely continues to use Arthur's. Like Angelica (for whom the opening image of the reclining Arthur provides a potent gender contrast), her sexuality and her talent are threats, and she must therefore be removed lest her chaos be too contagious. This is, of course, fairly ironic, given how off the wall the rest of the band are.

Arthur, with his stylish cynicism, is free to continue creating immaculately, white suit and all. Maggie is constantly changing out of one dress into another, while he remains cool and immaculate. She is physically a mess – the men constantly have to carry her around, as if she is visibly disintegrating. With no real voice of her own (she sings Arthur's songs), and unable to cope with the physical world, Maggie is banished into the mad world of the Ophelia Syndrome – the mad woman who sings. In the face of this, Arthur, the Svengali-Frankenstein figure, must destroy his creation in order to continue creating himself. His cry (even if somewhat ironic) is: 'Where is the money and where are the girls?'

The artist as male is vindicated. It is a curious hark back to nineteenth-century notions about men and rationality and creativity in the face of the dangers of creative women, who inevitably were supposed to get their messy emotions and hormones muddled with their creative forces. Here the play literally enacts a solution; the creative (even when she is interpretive) woman has to be symbolically destroyed, and the only woman who can be tolerated is the servicing 'wife' figure.

The absent centre of this play is the relationship between Maggie and Arthur. This is partly enabled and reinforced by the public setting, as well as the exigencies of the plot – the show must go on. Yet there is a central emotional evasion, which leaves Maggie (like so many other women in plays by men) as overdeterminedly symbolic, the only space she can occupy when she has not been given a sound hold on the stage reality.

Gender and the Left

Destiny (1976) by David Edgar

The play opens in 1947, with a speech from Nehru:

> A moment comes, which comes but rarely in history, when we step out from the old to the new, when an age ends, and when the soul of a nation, long oppressed, finds utterance.

Three men – Turner, a soldier, a Colonel, and an Indian, Khera – come to Britain from India, returning 'home' after the war. The Colonel, in self-conscious Brechtian style, identifies himself as 'always a little liberal, a great conservative'. He also speaks in rhyming couplets, a literary and story-book (and pantomime) device which allies him with a nostalgic past.

The scene then switches to a drawing-room, where a young Tory, Peter Crosby, is discussing a by-election. His aunt, Mrs Chandler, defines the changes taking place in Britain: 'Once we stood for patriotism, Empire. Now it's all sharp young men, with coloured shirts and cockney accents reading *The Economist*.'

To complete the political line-up, we go to the Labour Club, where Bob and his wife, Sandy, are playing darts (good working-class-signed leisure activity). They have a double act, where she asks questions about politics and he provides her with answers. The gendered division of labour, which makes the man the one with the knowledge and the woman the ignorant one, is already a familiar device from Brecht.

An old-style Conservative, Major Rolfe, pronounces on the new society:

> . . . it's not true we've lost an Empire, haven't found a role. We have a role. As Europe's whipping boy. . . . And for those – the people that I come from – that is a betrayal.

We move on quickly to 1970, where Turner now runs an antique shop. He has a Tory poster on his wall, and rejoices at the 'end of six years of Socialist misrule'. Meanwhile, the racial tables have been somewhat turned; Turner's landlord is Razak, a Pakistani with a cockney accent, who in his turn speaks to the audience: 'So told him. Idea was to conceal a whole row being bought by one developer. . . . But nothing he could do, and liked his face, so told him.' Here the absence of personal pronouns indicates an assimilation to an upper-class order, which denies emotion and therefore human presence. The play moves back to the far Right, dissecting its relationship to Conservatism:

> Beware the man – the Right Conservative, the disillusioned military man – who'd take the Socialism out of National Socialism. But also, even more, beware the man – the passionate young man who would take the National out of National Socialism.

In these scenes of the Right, the women serve tea, take messages, and represent ordinary, simple politics: 'I want to know why to have children.'

The play is constructed around an array of different political 'types', with one woman as the old-fashioned Conservative, Mrs Chandler. The other women are either ordinary, anonymous servicers or, in Sandy's case (because she supports her husband's Labour position) a slightly more elevated, but nevertheless secondary and largely ignorant figure, useful as a device to convey expositional and ideological information to the audience. In the final big scene with Peter, she suddenly speaks up: 'I do have a name, Bob. And being your wife isn't the sum total of my existence.'

Later in the scene, she voices apparent anger: 'if you don't think there are real problems in integrating large numbers of people from a totally different cultural background, then you need your head examining.' However, at the end of the play, despite these tiny, schematic indications of independence, one personal, the other political, Sandy is once again solidly behind Bob.

In keeping with the plays of the 1970s, the locations shift as necessary. The majority of the play, which moves around according to the dictates of historical 'story' (cf. Brecht) rather than the fortunes of individuals, is located in public spaces. The content of the play is a series of declarations of political positions, and the tactics and strategies that have to be adopted in the democratic process, where victory is not necessarily fair or desirable. Here, group allegiances and alliances are what matter – the Brechtian individual in the social context. Again, it is very much the context and narrative drive of the men's stories.

The political candidates (and therefore the candidates for politics) are all men; the women either a token right-wing woman (who could just as easily have been a man), anonymous women who service men and meetings, and Sandy, whose dominant device is the question, handy not only as mediator between audience and information, but – in terms of 'character' – also a device which prevents her from saying what she thinks, let alone arguing for it; at most she represents a mild conscience (cf. John Arden). These categories of women are all marginal to the play. They could be removed from the script and, with minor adjustments, it would still be the same play.

This is confirmed – and perhaps also a consequence of – the fact that, despite a nod at the domestic setting, essentially there are no personal/sexual relationships which form part of the play's questions or dilemmas. Sandy does not need to be de-sexed, because to all intents and purposes she has no relevant sexuality. The nuclear family is not the arbiter of relationships here; politics is; and here 'families' are matters of expediency and alliance. This, of course, is part of what is fascinating and effective about the play, but it can only be 'read' as applying to the 'real' world of men. The personal is implied by the presence of the women, but they never engage with the action or the politics. The personal neither matches nor contrasts with the political, since it does not effectively exist on any territory of its own – which does not need to be domestic. Similarly, the men have no personal/ sexual being, although they do at least control and operate in the public, political arena. The women have and do neither.

Rites of passage

Once a Catholic (1977) by Mary O'Malley

The play is set in a north London convent. It reverses the usual gender cast bias, and has ten women and four men. Each nun has a man's name (e.g. Mother Peter), while all the girls are called Mary. Message? Girls are potentially holy virgins, and then they grow up to be asexual, male-defined beings.

The time is the mid-1950s. While Jimmy Porter was railing out of his top floor window, the girls of Willesden were being taught to become good wives and mothers. They are taught that:

> . . . every ordinary baby comes into the world with a stain upon its soul, the big black stain of original sin . . . and remember no sin ever goes unrecorded. Every little lapse will be brought to judgement.

Three of the girls hate school, and plan ways to get expelled. One suggests: 'you could make a big long willy out of plasticine and stick it on the crucifix in the chapel.'

One of the girls, Mary Mooney, is rather simple, the only one who is truly religious, with a beautiful voice. She wants to become a nun: 'I want to be as perfect as I possibly can and be sure of getting a high place in heaven.' Out of innocence she asks in a biology lesson how sperm gets into the vagina, and is thrown out of the classroom, since the nuns assume she is just trying to embarrass them. They assume that 'such ignorance is inexcusable in a girl of fifteen', but are not prepared to tell her the truth about sex. Eventually the other girls tell her.

Mary McGinty's boyfriend, Derek, assumes sex is OK before marriage for boys but not for girls. Mary Gallagher's boyfriend drinks and smokes, and knows all about lesbians: 'They all have very short hair and big gruff voices.' Mary Mooney resorts to reading the Bible in the lavatory, to find out about menstruation and nakedness, and Mother Basil finds a box of Tampax in there: 'No self-respecting girl would abuse her body with such a contraption, and that's a fact.'

In the denouement, when the plasticine penis is stuck on the crucifix, all the nuns assume Mary Mooney is responsible. She becomes the scapegoat, while the others go free.

There are elements in this rites-of-passage play that recall Duffy, which also has a scapegoat in it, except that this time the irony is that it is the girl who represents most of what the nuns want who is targeted. The movers of the action are all women – though there is one interesting male who is drafted in as a supporter of Mary Mooney: Mr Emanuelli, the organist, who teaches her to sing:

> You must learn to stand up for yourself or you'll find yourself trampled right into the ruddy ground. It will be better for you when you go away from this dump, this sanctimonious institution.

However, he has no power in the institution, and to boot (as it were) he has a gammy leg – a damaged male in an all-female community, and therefore symbolically impotent. The play is powerful because of its sharp wit, and the poignancy of the central irony. The world of the convent is, of course, controlled by women because it is an all-female institution, and it is realistically approached (cf. *Slag*). To all intents and purposes, the nuns are entirely responsible for the teaching of the faith, and in a sense are the lovable 'baddies' in the play. Any tensions they might experience are not part of the drama: the play belongs to the girls, to the women of the future, most of whom are shown to be rebellious, resilient, and – so far – not prepared to be dictated to either by men or the church.

The fluidity of setting shifts between the convent (controlled by the nuns and the Fathers), the street or the boys' houses. There are no scenes in any of the girls' houses; they meet in school (beleaguered), in the street (in transit) or *chez* the boys (on 'male' territory). They have as yet no territory of their own, and their striving for identity consists of small subversions on institutional and/or male territory. These are their tactics for survival during their teenage years – momentary freedoms within the radical feminist dynamic of a solidarity among women, both real and defensive. This is reinforced by the breaking of theatrical and public taboos, in the appearance of the box of Tampax and the plasticine penis, both signs of power within female-defined identity.

In terms of implied promise for the future, the prospects fall imaginatively into a feminine dynamic; no homes of their own, and the only role models those of female repression (nuns) or of a sexuality within male-dominating patterns (the boys we are shown). The one possible escapee into art, Mary Mooney, while she shares a space with a damaged male, has few visible prospects: her passions (God and music) are virtually denied her.

The paradoxes of the play's meanings hover between the witty, accurate and alternately entertaining and poignant rebellions, and the world which awaits the girls, hedged around with censorship and repression. The feminine dynamic operates effectively with the import of a moral warning: an exposure of the way Catholicism (and social expectation) both limits the girls' horizons, and also creates a tragic figure in Mary Mooney, the most committed to all these conventional ideas. Thus the feminine dynamic, if effectively illustrated, need not necessarily carry a 'reactionary' message, but rather reveal the ethical dilemmas for women in a conventional world.

In addition, there is an interesting issue raised here about the relatively hermetic community of women. Duffy's public lavatory is, in a way, a place of retreat for the women. The convent, however, is virtually a place for incarceration. From the point of view of the girls (the point of view of the play), the action operates a socialist–feminist dynamic, revealing the contradictions and conflicts in religion, social potential and in explorations of sexuality. At the same time, a radical feminist dynamic exposes the potentially exploitative nature of (most) men's expectations for women in the persons of the boyfriends. Only the damaged male (cf. Churchill, Wesker) who is powerless represents an alternative (male) poignant point of view.

Utopias

Cloud Nine *(1979) by Caryl Churchill*

The first half of this play is set in colonial Victorian Africa, where paterfamilias Clive heads a family of three generations. The values of authoritarian British imperialism are presented in rhyming couplets (cf. Edgar) as Clive introduces himself and the family:

> Clive: This is my family. Though far from home
> We serve the Queen wherever we may roam
> I am a father to the natives here,
> And father to my family so dear.

Integrated into the fabric of the play are stage directions that Clive's wife Betty is played by a man, to indicate that she is made in her husband's image; also, a black servant, Joshua, is played by a white man. The casting in these cases (and in the second half where 5-year-old Cathy is played by a man) externalises, and literally embodies, the values espoused by the relevant characters, so that their biology, age and race change to suit what is in their heads, and thus by reversing the norms, draw attention to those stereotyped concepts. Son Edward is played by a woman, highlighting Clive's futile attempts to bring him up as a 'man', and daughter Victoria is a dummy, since that is what girls are expected to be.

The cast sing a patriotic song, and a series of fast-moving set pieces (characters are constantly rushing on and off stage in Act 1) reveal some of the knots of repression and hypocrisy in Victorian ideology. Betty has a passion for explorer Harry Bagley, Clive cannot keep his hands off the widow Mrs Saunders, crawling under her skirts to satisfy himself. Harry, meanwhile, is the object of Edward's pubertal affections, and Ellen, the governess, expresses her love for Betty.

Clive finds out about Betty and Harry, but chooses to ignore it, with a warning to Betty: 'We must resist this dark female lust, Betty, or it will swallow us up.' He makes an offer to Harry: 'I know the friendship between us, Harry, is not something that could be spoiled by the weaker sex. Friendship between men is a fine thing. It is the noblest form of relationship.' However, as Harry assumes that Clive means sex as well, the two struggle with the demands of manliness – Harry abject because of his homosexuality, Clive punitive and imperialist: 'Rivers will be named after you, it's unthinkable. You must save yourself from depravity. You must get married.'

The second half of the play catapults us into the present day, where the characters are twenty-five biological years older. Victoria is now a single mother, and makes friends with Lin, a lesbian mother. Edward arrives, and Lin immediately recognises that he is gay. Edward has a relationship with Gerry, a gardener, and Victoria lives with Martin. Betty, meanwhile, has left Clive, although she still holds quite conventional views about boys and girls, preferring men's company to women's. Victoria and Lin fall in love, and Edward tells Victoria that he would rather have been a woman and fondles her – she enjoys it.

Late at night in the park Lin, Victoria and Edward, all drunk, engage in a goddess-worshipping session. They are interrupted by Martin, and by the ghost of a dead British soldier, Lin's brother. Victoria moves in with Lin, and as we near the end of the play, Betty makes a speech about discovering her body and masturbation. The closing moments of the play remind us of the paradoxical presence of Clive:

> You're not that sort of woman, Betty. . . . And Africa is to be communist I suppose. I used to be proud to be British. There was a high ideal. I came out on to the verandah and looked at the stars.

The Betty (male) from the first half embraces Betty (female) from the second half, in a utopian image of reconciliation between opposites. This image, a resolution between the two wives and mothers, combines the nurturing roles with the bid for personal and sexual independence, both contained within an image of a mother, albeit one who holds very traditional views about gender roles.

The stagecraft of the piece plays very clear games with our perceptions of the signs of gender – the male or female body, the deep-voiced man playing a little girl, the woman playing a gay man, black versus white – and each appearance, as it lulls us into a suspension of disbelief as we engage in the relationships and actions, asks us implicitly to question what these 'roles' are. We see in the first half how personal and sexual possibilities are repressed by an imperialist ideology which has to depend on very clearly demarcated gender roles in the interests of the family, which is itself a microcosm of the British Empire. The patriotic songs which punctuate the action are a hot line from the mother country.

Churchill tackles the family head-on, by encasing it in its macro-political ideology, and giving it a self-contained outsiderness (with total power) on conquered territory. It is notable in this respect that all the action takes place outside the house, in both halves of the play. The interconnections between class, race and gender, enmeshed in tightly woven scenes which ring the permutations on all the various sexualities bursting to get out, work almost as a kind of thriller. Each desire, if unleashed, will undermine the family, and so in the end, the 'happy ever after' empire wins back to a 'normality' which equals repression. The gender mixing, the balancing of stage priorities and plot between all genders and sexual proclivities, proclaims the first half as embodying a socialist–feminist dynamic, which shows us how desire and choice are at odds with the prevailing ideology.

In the second half of the play, however, the family has gone, in the interests of more liberated lifestyles which are no longer subject to empirical control. The structure of the second half matches this 'liberation'; it is looser, shifts between park and the domestic, even has a rogue ghost who fits nowhere, except that he represents a token reference to Ireland, almost the last piece of Britain's colonial empire. Apart from this ineffective military moment, there is no link at all between macro-politics and the personal. Thus while we see a number of people finding ways to follow their desires in the libertarian 1970s, which look like heaven compared with the repression of the nineteenth century, we have no overarching political system into which to fit them, no ideology either to work against or contain these new ways of being, no way of understanding how the change has come about – no politics, in fact, which weakens the impact of the play as a whole.

Analytically, there are a number of questions about the 'feminist dynamic' of this piece, and also about its form, structure and the way it creates its world(s) – and, in effect, makes its 'argument'. Formally, the tightly meshed linkage between class, race, gender and sexuality in the first half is reinforced by the placing of the family – there to represent class and racial domination – and within the family to establish and enforce traditional gender roles. The excitement, tension and drama lie in the way these parameters are constantly either actually breached, or on the brink of being breached.

It is as if we are back in the censored theatre world of the 1960s, when repression led to odd and fantastic expressions of the taboo. The socialist–feminist dynamic is such because the gender functions of both men and women are placed within their social and political context, and the contradictions teased out both in the story-lines and the physical subversion of gender–body representation on stage. This taut ideological framing is reinforced by the relay-race feel to the structure, and the tight, line-for-line dialogue. Cause and effect are constantly clear.

In the second half of the play, there is no overarching political structure, no dominant social values within which the characters live. Libertarianism – the ability to choose their own life and sexual styles – seems to be prevalent and accepted. There is a kind of utopianism about this, free and wistful at the same time (common to much of Churchill's other work), but the libertarianism translates into an individualistic bourgeois feminist dynamic, dotted with a radical feminist dynamic, in the occasional moment when women are free of men (the lesbian relationship, Betty's discovery of masturbation).

Given the conceptual framework of the first half, it is impossible not to carry the question of context forward; but there is none, only (literally) the 'ghost' of one. There is continuity between the two halves in the characters and their relationships, so there must be some kind of cause and effect, unless the implied statement is that the 1970s are merely anarchic, a society with no system, which is clearly nonsense (as we can tell from the presence of the Irish soldier anyway). The second half also, interestingly, isolates characters from their contexts; where the first half has cohesive songs which everyone sings, here individuals emerge for soliloquies, more than hinting at a vulnerable isolation in their 'new' choices. The relationship between personal and political is offered in the first half and denied in the second, thus conflating the bourgeois feminist with the feminine.

The issue of how the personal derives from, or is reflected in the political is raised by implication in the time gap/character continuity between the two halves of the play, with no answer for the present day. This means that the gender parity, the cross-dressing and subversion of gender expectation in the first half is contradicted by what becomes utopian (and, as we have already seen from the first half), by definition impossible. At least the impossibility is based on parity of gender, with the mother used as a symbolic union of hope which carries the poignancy of impossibility within it. Yet there is a sense in which one can argue that generally (as opposed to small, specific exceptions), the first half is 'progressive' in its illuminations and representations, and the second half 'reactionary' in its reinforcement of a separation between personal and political, which leaves the framework of the characters' lives invisible and untouched. This is important because we have seen from the first half of the play that a framework can be touched and evoked.

Whatever the motivation of this tactic for the second half – perhaps to encourage the audience to 'think' about its own times and mores – in terms of the text (whatever its complex impacts on an audience) this division remains, and the final message is that gender, class and race are explicable in terms of the past, but not in terms of the present. Both feminist and feminine dynamics are so powerful that they come into conflict, rather than augmenting or transforming one another.

Daring loves

Bent (1979) by Martin Sherman

This play is set in the 1930s, beginning briefly in a domestic location – Max and Rudi's home. They are a gay couple, living together, going to gay clubs, already in 1934 under threat from Nazi persecution. They hide out briefly in a club run by Greta, a transvestite: 'Me? Everyone knows I'm not queer, I got a wife and kids.' S/he comments: 'Now you're like Jews, unloved, baby, unloved.'

Max and Rudi obtain papers and tickets, but are caught and put on a prisoner transport train, where Rudi is tortured and killed. Max, to save his own skin, does not interfere, and even colludes in the torture merely to be able to survive.

In the prison camp Max claims to be Jewish, knowing he would otherwise have to wear a pink triangle, the symbol of homosexuality. He has no illusions about his opportunism: 'I'm a rotten person. . . . I'm going to work a lot of deals. . . . I'm only under protective custody, that's what they told me, I'm going to stay alive.'

He becomes involved with the pink-triangled Horst, and the two work together, breaking rocks, talking secretly so as to not be over-heard by the guards. During an extraordinary and unusual scene, the two, standing to attention during their brief rest time, make love through words.

Max: We can't look at each other, we can't touch.
Horst: We can feel . . . each other without looking, without touching.

The taboo and the possible are made explicit and joined in this simple moment, but there is danger involved, and Max warns Horst not to love him. When Horst is ill, Max gets medicine for him, even though he has to perform fellatio on the SS captain for it. The irony here is that the captain thinks Max is Jewish, and therefore the homosexual act is intended as a different kind of 'degradation'. Max comments: 'Do you think that SS bastard would let a queer go down on him?'

At the end, Horst is killed, and Max touches him for the first time. He puts on Horst's jacket with the pink triangle and walks into the electric fence, prepared to embrace both his own 'real' identity and the terrible consequences of his historic circumstances.

The journey from home to prison camp is, in one sense, a journey from the meaningful personal to the most depersonalising institutional. It is, of course, a history play about the persecution of homosexuals and Jews by the Nazis, and with its chilling, uncompromising ending it is also about living personal, moral truth. In a world of such annihilating censorship personal relationships are excised, and the scene of erotic communication between the two men also celebrates by implication the fact that, even though such emotions cannot be suppressed, they will always find a way to be expressed. Here friendship is everything, and is both sexual and interpersonal.

The settings move from the most personal (home) to the most horrifically impersonal, and yet, through the latter, the most intimate of personal relationships still survives, but at a price. Heroism consists in simply asserting the right of the individual to love, knowing that death is one of the material consequences. Its socialist dynamic is both Brechtian in its historic sense, and acutely imbued with a gay sexual-political dynamic.

Chronicling gender

The Romans in Britain (1980) by Howard Brenton

This is a chronicle play with a vengeance – ranging from 54 BC to 1980 – about the relationship between England and Ireland. It opens in the dark, in limbo. Two Irish criminals have abandoned 'the meal, the fire, the family'. They find a young woman slave and question her about her family, talking about her and referring to her as 'it'. They have been thrown off the land, and their misogyny is partly a consequence of having been separated from their own family: 'Our souls taken away by the priests.'

A local indigenous British matriarch, simply called the Mother, comes on. She too refers to the family, and the link between family, property and rights: 'You kill people on my family's field? You take that right away from members of my family?' The Romans are coming, to conscript men, and the envoys who bring the Mother this news try to define this new political force: 'They are – a nation. . . . A great family? No. A people? No. They are one, huge thing.'

Three naked Druid soldiers play in the sun. This pastoral image of supposedly innocent boyish happiness is dispelled when three Roman soldiers arrive, assaulting them, voicing obscenities about their mothers, and finally trying (and failing) to bugger one of them. This attempt at rape is not done out of sexual desire but as an act of scato-logical humiliation, a metaphor for the political rape of Britain by the Romans. It is interesting that the homosexual rape attempt happens on stage, whereas later, when one of the criminals rapes a woman, the rape happens off stage. In terms of metaphorical priorities, therefore, the rape of man by man operates with more resonance than the rape of a woman by a man. The symbolism of sexual violence is here dis-placed on to homosexuality, and the way it evokes traditional notions of homosexuality as 'unnatural'.

The second half of the play is divided between AD 515 and Ireland in 1980. Chichester, a British officer in the present, waits fearfully near the Irish border, reaching for comforting thoughts:

> Could see my mother – coming out of the trees now. Telling me to get my hair cut – that I'm drinking too much. . . . Hard men can weep for home . . . Mummy! Mummy! Mummy! Can I have a British Soldier to play with at Christmas. . . . If I get bumped off, ask my mother to throw my ashes on the Old Acre field . . . my mother is a stern old cow. Insist.

The British public school male, deprived of many of his personal pronouns (cf. Edgar) by his stiff-upper-lip training, still needs his Mummy, and is trapped between her and the macho manhood he is expected to display (cf. Osborne). However, in the end this does not lead to anything enlightening: the play parallels the conquest of Ancient Britain by the Romans, with the current occupation of Northern Ireland by British troops. The imperialist presence is seen as brutal, but then there is also little distinction between the conquered and the conquering, both brutal, with the differences being those of scale and degrees of power.

There is a spirit of resistance, represented by some of the women. The slave woman who is raped later kills her assaulter with a stone. In the second part of the play, two daughters attack a father who has been abusing them, and one finally kills him:

> *Corda*: I hated him. Ever since he lifted my skirt when I was only just a woman.

Corda's heroinism is balanced by Adona, a disfigured Roman matron, who (like Angelica in Griffiths) represents the decay of the old order. These women fight back against individual men. They have no access to political power, and figures like the Mother and Adona, who do, are quickly despatched; their power is minimal and temporary. Like Brecht's Mother, their status as procreators is morally ambiguous; their motherhood is implicitly responsible for evil: 'A mother of killers. . . . Of children to kill the English. Children brought up right. Like stoats, like weasels, like otters.'

The family here has an ambiguous and interesting symbolism; the anthropological notion of family as tribe or clan is the one appealed to here, and it is also inexorably linked to property and geographical/

national rights. When characters do not 'belong' and have no personal location, notions of individuality also paradoxically disappear: gender distinctions, the uses of personal pronouns. Within this new, nationally defined family, however, all sexual relations are problematic; both heterosexuality and homosexuality exist as forms of rape, and sexual relations themselves become the central, and extraordinarily potent, political metaphor for the political parallel messages. Sexuality – the personal – has itself become symbolic (cf. *Lay-By*) rather than narratively 'real'.

Somewhere, deeply buried, is the need for a loving but dangerous mother who can transmute suddenly into a 'stern old cow', the kind of stern old cow who, presumably, can become 'A mother of killers'. It is a no-win situation. The central story configures the world of politics as male, with all forms of sexuality (signs of individual, emotional relationships) consigned to the realm of political metaphor within which women are confined.

Interestingly, this raises a further analytical question, related to a determinist Marxist approach to social structure. Here the material base (power relations between nations/men) is the most important force. Sexuality (superstructure) and women are imaginatively available to be purloined for use as metaphor, rather than as anything which determines in its own right. The male bias, even while providing potent and shocking theatrical images and accounts of imperialism, still leaves women with, at best, a token presence, at ambiguous worst (ambiguous because the use of rape as a metaphor is indeed effective, precisely because it is so repellent) filleted of their real-life referents, to become available as metaphor.

Chapter 10

The 1970s

Conclusions

The first plays discussed in this section show very vividly some of the radical shift in both content and form in post-censorship theatre. Sexuality, the representation of the body (male and female), 'strong' language is there in all of them. Nudity in Arden, blood, tampons and a nearly naked male in Duffy, masturbation in Williams, rape in Lay-By, physical decay in Griffiths, sexual imagery in Hare.

The expansion of content is also marked by a new approach to the stage space: nothing traditionally domestic in sight. With the influences of Brecht now more explicitly tangible, the public or abstractly fluid space takes over. This is most obvious in the epic sweeps of the modern chronicle plays (Edgar and Brenton), but it is also there as a public or institutional backdrop even to plays where the intimate, the personal, the sexual is part of the matter: Griffiths uses a hotel room, Hare and O'Malley a school/convent, Churchill's plays are mostly out in the open, Williams and Arden create a 'cosmic' space, Duffy a public lavatory, Sherman a concentration camp.

Where the subject matter is itself historical/political, this rationale makes sense: Griffiths, Edgar, Sherman and Brenton all situate their pieces at specific historic moments, and cover degrees of expansiveness in time. Where the subject matter is more mixed, the shift becomes more complex. On the one hand, the influences of feminism provide a rationale (radical feminist in its dynamic) for examining women's relationships to their world. At one level, this corresponds to the feminist clamour to see women not just as confined as dependants in the home; by taking them out of the home and on to the stage, they are – quite literally – being let out into the public arena. Freed from the involuntary biological ties of Delaney, the manless emancipation of Lessing, they acquire theatrical control in Arden, move on to their own (temporary) territory in Duffy and O'Malley, and into a world where their roles and identities are examined along with those of men (cf. Churchill). Domestic scenes, where they occur, are used to make a narrative point, rather than to explore the intertwining of place and personal relationships (cf. Bond).

The role of the mother is therefore also affected, since her territory (*pace* Delaney, Jellicoe, Bond, Osborne, etc.) is largely defined on domestic territory (whether realistically or otherwise represented). In Arden and Williams she leads a psychic rebirth; in Duffy and O'Malley she is the custodian of dominant and alternative values (Vi and the nuns). Apart from Williams, these last are all women writers. When it comes to the men, we are still stuck in a metaphorical allegiance to the Lady Macbeth Syndrome. Hare and Griffiths both coruscatingly destroy the female body and its mothering potential. Motherhood is not an issue in Edgar (no reason why it should be); and for Sherman writing about male–male relations, there is no need to bus in a female metaphor, since his narrative draws resonance from its internal constituents. Churchill is an exception here; using the same kind of stage fluidity as the other playwrights, motherhood, mothering, control within adult–baby relationships are included in her overarching exploration of the painful way in which economic ideas about owner-ship and control are applied to interpersonal relationships, but she too does this at the level of polemics and schematic action rather than exploring any relationships in depth.

Of course, in many ways this is an expansive and liberating develop-ment; with epic and historical potential, by taking personal relation-ships explicitly out into the social structures which help to form them, the interests and gains of the public or neutral settings are immense, both for men and women playwrights. These high-art radical plays are no longer about love, jealousy, interpersonal interaction, but about social roles and the ways these roles shape individual lives. Perhaps this is also a reason why the outsider figure is no longer neces-sary. Everyone has become an 'outsider' – an individual separated from personal/familial ties, surviving in the world outside.

In terms of the issues of individual identity, there are also marked differences from the previous decade. Unlike the male-centred plays of the 1950s and 1960s, Kabak (Griffiths) is absolutely sure of his political allegiances, as are the men in Edgar's world. They may appear to be unsure, but they know what they are unsure about. Kabak's dilemma is that he cannot reconcile his political beliefs with his love for his wife – she is in any case a class 'enemy'. Not only is her body rotting from within (cancer), but she is imaginatively destroyed as her dying cries are drowned by the slogans of Communism. The clear message is that woman = reactionary = enemy, and must be destroyed so that man can = progressive = hero.

Although the content of plays has broadened to include any place, any time, any image, any language, the gender divide is still clearly there. Only in all-female plays are women the central subjects (even when framed within male control – Duffy, O'Malley), as women playwrights begin to find their voices. Paradoxically, in the overtly 'political' plays by men, however, women are even more marginalised and metaphoricised than before. Above all, the dominant message is that the political is at most the social, but certainly not the personal; as if Brecht's message in *The Mother* is thoroughly vindicated. Men still inhabit the world of ideas, and try to work out how to control the world; but at least now more women are concerned about their own survival.

A version of the 'personal' for women is now possible, in the context of all-female 'ghetto' space. This is paradoxical, because by virtue of the fact that it is staged in a public space, it is no longer private-secret, but now rather private-public. This is an imaginatively reclamatory act, a radical feminist assertion that women must and do have their own spaces and relationships. These hermetic spaces, however, because they are contextualised in 'the world', provide a necessary imaginative function for the outsider, who is now specifically male and generally represents a threat to female freedom; he also represents the male power structures outside the (temporary) women's worlds.

The dividing line between the 1970s and the 1980s is not merely a matter of arbitrary dates. It coincides, rather neatly, with the return of a Conservative government, headed by Margaret Thatcher, in 1979. This parliamentary success produced, in terms of the arts, and theatre in particular, a difficult situation. The end of censorship, increases in subsidy and the lively politics/culture debates had generated a whole new field of work. After a mere decade, this work came heavily under the pressure of consumerist ideology, where everything was meant to pay its way and aim at making financial profit. Subsidy ceased to be an expanding force for the development of theatrical work, and many of the touring theatre companies were forced to shut up shop. At the same time, at least some of the playwrights who cut their theatrical teeth during the 1970s, managing to earn something of a living from the theatre, became more confident as writers, developing their own interests and ideas alongside their responses to the world of the 1980s.

Neatly, the political relations between England and Ireland, which formed the content of the final play discussed in this section, also form the substance of the first play to be discussed from the 1980s proper.

Part V

Chapter II

The 1980s

Ireland, imperialism and language

Translations (1980) by Brian Friel

This play is set in County Donegal in 1833, and opens in a barn full of farming implements which is 'comfortless and dusty and functional – there is no trace of a woman's hand.'

Hugh runs a hedge school in the barn, conducted in the Irish language. As the play opens, Manus, his son, is teaching a speech-impaired girl, Sarah, to say her name. In the background, Jimmy, the local drunk, lecher and Latin and Greek scholar, is reading Homer. Sarah manages to pronounce her name, and this sets up the central theme of the play: two officers from the British army, Captain Lancey and Lieutenant Yolland, have arrived to map the whole country and to rename the places in English. Various acts of anonymous sabotage try to prevent this cultural takeover. At the same time, a national school is due to open up locally, where all education will be conducted in English. The culture and its language are under attack – ironically, since the apparently 'primitive' Irish are shown to be fluent in Latin and Greek, a far cry from the ignorant peasants the British assume they are.

Matters hot up when Owen, Hugh's other son, arrives. He has been away for six years in the city, and is now employed by the army as a translator: 'My job is to translate the quaint, archaic tongue you people persist in speaking into the King's good English.'

The personal is represented by the tension between Maire, mother of ten, and Manus; the latter does not want to apply for a job in the new school, and Maire does not want a man with no job or prospects.

The second half of the play opens with Owen and Yolland working out new names in English, and at the same time Yolland learns to pronounce Irish, saying he would even like to live there:

> Even if I did speak Irish I'd always be an outsider here, wouldn't I? I may learn the password but the language of the tribe will always elude me, won't it? The private core will always be . . . hermetic, won't it?

Yolland begins to have a conscience about what he is doing – 'It's an eviction of sorts' – but even he has been getting Owen's name wrong, calling him 'Roland'. When Maire arrives, Owen has to interpret for both of them as they talk about a forthcoming village dance. At the dance, the two of them go outside and try to communicate, each speaking their own language, Maire now and again breaking into Latin. She finally recovers the only (archaic) English sentence she knows: 'In Norfolk we besport ourselves around the maypole.'

They end up communicating by reciting a litany of Irish place names as the only shared language they have, which, in the absence of anything else, becomes a poignant language of love. Manus sees them, and decides to leave. However, the British army has shipped in more troops to try and catch the saboteurs, and Manus is under suspicion. Yolland, after the scene with Maire, has also left the army. As the village is in disarray, news comes that the soldiers' tents have been set on fire.

At the end, Maire asks Hugh to teach her English, against the time when Yolland returns, and he agrees. Jimmy, the scholarly drunk, expounds on marriage:

> Do you know the Greek word endogamein? It means to marry within the tribe. And the word exogamein means to marry outside the tribe. And you don't cross those borders casually – both sides get very angry.

The play ends with Hugh reciting remembered Latin texts.

The core of the story revolves around the three men – Hugh and his sons, who each represent a different take on history, culture and belonging. Hugh is of the old school, but in the end accedes to progress, acknowledging that Maire needs to learn English. Manus, by trying to sustain the past, is stymied both personally and socially: he loses Maire and is chased by the army. Owen, the 'traitor' to his own kind, becomes an outsider, and is a survivor, a literal translator between two worlds, who has himself been translated into the other, opposing world.

Meanwhile Yolland, the real outsider, is desperate to find a way to belong, but as a member of the occupying army he can never be accepted, except, perhaps, through the salvation of love. The theme of colonisation and cultural theft and destruction is filtered down into familial relations between men, the succession of generations itself also about historical succession. The women here, tenderly portrayed, still remain marginal; in both Irish and English worlds, it is the men who are in charge of knowledge and naming, except in the most basic sense which is represented by Sarah. She is an alternative, personalised Vlasova, moving from inarticulacy (literally) to speech, a Beatie for whom language represents belonging.

Maire's affections are quickly transferred from Manus to Yolland (love at first sight is always possible!), and she, like Owen, capitulates to the dominant culture and language for the sake of love and opportunism (she has already expressed a desire to go to America). The lovemaking scene between Yolland and Maire (cf. Sherman) seamlessly dovetails personal, cultural and imperialist relations.

Here the interplay between individual and social is more subtle than the English epic dramatists; language itself is both the agent and subject of the symbolic and real ways in which imperialism and cultural colonisation work. Sexuality thus becomes something of a subject in its own right, although the core of the gender dynamic is still centred around the three men alongside its sensitive socialist dynamic.

Taking gender out of the ring

Trafford Tanzi (1980) by Claire Luckham

In this play, Luckham takes a different tack from fellow women playwrights Duffy and Dunn. Rather than open out female territory to the public gaze, she appropriates the almost exclusively male territory of the wrestling ring. This confined, public space, with its own rules and conventions, becomes the site of, and metaphor for, relations between the sexes. The symbol reversal here takes something from the world of men, and seeks to harness it as a metaphor for the lives of women. A referee (male), who also doubles as other male authority figures, such as a psychiatrist, uses a microphone throughout, and controls the relationship between performers and audience (cf. Jellicoe). He announces, for the first time ever, 'a man and woman fighting to the finish.'

Accompanied by appropriate circus-type music, and punctuated with pastiche numbers such as 'Stand by Your Man', the play proceeds, in ten rounds, to tell us the story of Tanzi's life. Born to a working-class family, she disappointed her mother who wanted a boy:

> a girl is just plain boring,
> Unless she's very pretty,
> Which she isn't more's the pity,
> And you can't forgive her cos you know
> She'll never grow
> Into a man.

We meet Sue, Tanzi's childhood friend who is into clothes and boys, her father who loves his pretty daughter, and her boyfriend Dean Rebel, a professional wrestler. Throughout, Tanzi rebels, throwing food at her mother, refusing to wear girlie clothes, behaving like a 'tomboy', and finally falling for Dean and supporting him in his wrestling – until, that is, she discovers that Dean has slept with Sue. She goes back to Mum, who 'consoles' her: 'Dean may be a swine, and a brutish monster but so are all men. And we love them for it.'

However, Tanzi decides to go back to Dean on new terms; she is going to become a wrestler, and make good use of her experience. She wins all sorts of championships, while Dean complains more and more that she is not at home being a good little wife. Tanzi finally challenges him to a wrestling match, the loser to do the housework. In the final round, Tanzi and Dean wrestle, and she wins, using her special hold, the Venus Flytrap. Dean's last words are a demand for a rematch, so although Tanzi has won a victory, the loser will not lie down.

As the piece nears its final round, the audience is whipped up into support of the contestants, the cast asking the audience to take sides in the gender contest. Obviously this need not mean that the audience will polarise completely along gender lines, but because of the invitation to participate in this play-within-a-play, each member of the audience is being asked to think about and act upon their gender identification. If they do not wish to cheer and boo, then they are likely to be surrounded by others who do, so they cannot opt out of the experience completely.

In terms of theories about the gendered gaze, this device disrupts on two counts: first, invading the metaphor of the wrestling ring, and making it 'real' for the audience, by asking them (us) to behave as though we are a real, wrestling audience. Second, it inevitably urges each member of the audience to take a stand on the issue of gender roles – do you support the member of your own sex in the ring, or do you deliberately support the other? The theatrical experience, because the play itself is so tightly and effectively wrought, begins to incorporate something of a political experience, seductive and risky. Although anecdotal evidence is never more than just that (it does not 'prove' much), the three performances which I saw all provoked a mixture of laughter, pleasure, and a handful of arguments from people sitting near me, when couples divided, the woman cheering Tanzi, the man, Dean. This was a rare occasion when theatre became consciousness-raising, before returning to being pure theatre.

The objective correlative – the metaphor – here, the wrestling ring, adds another radical element to the experience. Every phase and stage of conflict in each 'round' is accompanied by physicalisation; wrestling holds and throws are as much part of the fabric of the script as the dialogue. The story follows Tanzi's life – the main female protagonist leading the narrative – but she is contained within this microcosm of the man's world (the ring), structured and controlled by a man (the referee), and we see her conquering it on its own terms. However, the ambiguity of the end raises the question of whether Dean will honour the bet, or, even if he does, whether he will continually insist on a rematch to offload domestic responsibilities, thus reflecting the dominant order – the 'way it is'.

The consequence in terms of the gender/feminist dynamic is interesting. Tanzi reaches the top, beating men at their own game in a bourgeois feminist triumph. She (and the other women in the cast including sexy Sue) challenges all the received stereotypes that women are just decorative, passive and weak, by wrestling as well as acting. We see strong, physically fit women giving as good as they get, a radical feminist dynamic demonstrating physical strength and agility, where there is no one sex superior to the other. The paradox is highlighted, because they are, at the same time (e.g. Sue and Mum) conforming (performing) feminine stereotypical roles. Form and content are in conflict, in an exhilarating theatrical coup.

However, the terms of the metaphor remain controlled by the men (Dad briefly becomes Tanzi's manager). This is, of course, part of the theme of the play. The terms of the bet are based on housework being undesirable (and in effect, women's) work. Dean has to be beaten (a metaphor for battles which take place between men and women), but housework still remains despised. This frames the action in a traditional sexist (feminine) dynamic, where the world of men's work (wrestling) is valued, and the world of women's is not.

These very tensions of different feminist dynamics, within a sexist (and feminine) framework, serve to enhance the tautness of the metaphor; Tanzi fights to achieve the apparently impossible, and in a utopian moment won with great courage and strength, she achieves it. The world, of course, remains the same. The final round, which may either be provocative or cathartic for the audience (or perhaps both!), places the issues fairly back in the world, with the theatrical metaphor of the wrestling ring safe in its own text.

Foreign customs

Tibetan Inroads (1981) by Stephen Lowe

This play is set in feudal Tibet, centring around a self-sufficient community which is taken over by the Chinese Liberation Army (military and ideological outsiders). In the beginning, we see an event at the margins of accepted family life. Genyen, a young woman married to an older landowner, Jamyang, is having a relationship with Dorja, a butcher and blacksmith. In an opening love scene they use gentle, poetic language, the two dress each other and Genyen builds a stone shrine to love. Intercut with this is a scene where we see monks renouncing everything material.

Back at home, Dorja's mother goes on at him about getting married, giving him a gendered identity as either a son or a husband: 'I'm talking business, It's my business as well. We need a woman.' Dorja's brother, Tashi, is a monk, and, placing Buddhism before his family, is sent to arrest Dorja. The very test of loyalty – between family and religion – is part of Tashi's training: 'I have been sent to understand my duty. It's a test for me, and if I fail, I fail you and all my teachers.' Dorja's transgression is his affair with Genyen. The abbot, also in charge of religious 'order', castigates sexual desire. The punishment is fundamental and final:

> You need to be free of those desires that torment you. The judgement: all that he earns to be confiscated to Jamyang and the prisoner himself to be emasculated. . . . You are to be castrated.

Material property, the family and sexuality are objects of social control. As part of the punishment, Dorja's mother is given to Jamyang as a servant. As Dorja recovers from the punishment, he equates sexual potency with the life force: 'Why am I not dead? You took life from me.' Tashi, on the other hand, sees it as liberation from desire: 'We have lifted the rock. You are free of it. The traces of desire that still haunt you will soon fade away.'

Dorja travels, trying to reconstruct himself after the castration, and he dreams that Genyen appears to him, her back scarred where her husband beat her till she confessed to the affair. Because Dorja is now sexually impotent, he is forced to try and define the combination of emotional and social forces which make him a 'man':

> They said I'd never feel like this again. I can't do anything. I'm not a man. I can't feel like a man. That's the only way I can bear the weight . . . I want to enter you. To join you. Devil. You've worked your magic, go back to Jamyang. Let him laugh round the fire. You've brought me hell.

He 'rolls into a tight foetal ball', regressing into babyhood. Then, while he performs a ritual dance with a magic dagger, members of the Chinese Liberation Army appear.

The second half of the play takes place after the Chinese Revolution. Education and technology have improved material life in the village. Now the tables are turned and the monastery has been taken over, its monks left to beg. Dorja still wants revenge for what was done to him. Genyen, on the other hand, in spite of Jamyang's actions, still wants to bury him in the old way:

> He understood nothing in this life. But in the end he prayed for someone to guide him back with a new understanding. . . . There was still a desire there. . . . Not to be born the same. Not to make mistakes the same. To grow.

Dorja helps, cutting up Jamyang's body with his butcher's knife, in keeping with the old traditions. At the end, he works on the road, still struggling to understand the relationship between desire and reality:

> I work on the road, but I work like a donkey not like a man. My mind is full of dreams. I do not ask myself all the time who is this road for? Is it for the people . . . I should ask these questions more often, and out loud, so that my comrades can help me in answering them.

The shocking central image of Dorja's life after castration invades the male-gender stereotype equating intellectual with sexual potency. Dorja continues to 'desire' as intensely as before. He feels passion – sexual and intellectual; he continues to question the benefits of a new regime which is differently repressive – he loses none of his intellectual, emotional or moral power just because he is sexually impotent. The transition to more enlightened (in some way) political systems produces other scars – yet 'history' in this play is not defined by specific dates, but rather moments in which manhood itself comes under investigation. Although the story follows Dorja, Genyen is given her space within her scenes and never becomes a symbol, since Dorja becomes his own symbol, as it were – his theatrical potency compensating for the potency he has lost. He contains and conveys the use of sexuality and desire as both real, transgressive events, and as events symbolic of political and visionary desire. By extension, we are led to question whether political forces are potent or impotent.

The enmeshing of tribe, family and social system is more focused than in Brenton or Churchill, even though we span two discrete historical periods. The ideas recall some of Churchill's preoccupations. The 'otherness' of the Tibetan setting and the Chinese politics enable the 'outsider' nature of the subject matter to become itself representative and resonant with some of the same questions on home territory. It is interesting that the male-gender dynamic is observed (we follow Dorja's story), but this very fact is itself under interrogation, in the way that Lowe confronts issues of manhood while placing them clearly within their social context. From the male-gendered perspective, this is one of the rare plays in which the personal and political are not driven violently apart, and where, because the interface between male sexual and social identities are at the heart of the play, women do not need to be appropriated as metaphor.

Cleaning up the act

Steaming (1981) by Nell Dunn

A 1909 Turkish baths is the all-female setting for this play. The cast of six are buttressed by Bill, 'a man who is heard but not seen'. Unlike the rather more functional setting in Duffy, here the baths are homely: 'to one side is a small table with some knitting and a radio on it and an armchair.'

Violet, who manages the baths, has the kettle boiling and the radio on, and is a substitute mother-figure for the women who come here. A group of women gather: Josie, a sparky woman with little more than sex on her mind, Mrs Meadows and her daughter Dawn, who live in poverty; Nancy and Jane, two middle-class friends. Dawn and her mother are completely dependent on one another – Dawn claims to have been raped by a policeman when she was 16, and appears to be retarded. Mrs Meadows will not allow her to take her clothes off, even in the baths: 'no, my Dawn's never even kissed me, we're not a kissing family.'

Tension comes from the fact that there is no hot water; Bill is in charge, and although Violet is the centre of the baths, looking after its moment-to-moment workings, she is dependent on a man's authority to enable the place to function. Eventually, Violet, fed up with Bill's refusals, tries to mend the pipes herself.

In keeping with the leisure atmosphere of the baths, the women chat freely, establishing friendships and interest in each other built up over their weekly visits. Jane and Nancy discuss past and present lovers, Mrs Meadows misses her long-gone husband. Josie's pride and exhibitionism are contrasted with Dawn's shyness. When Violet threatens to complain to the town hall about poor maintenance, Bill appears behind a glass door to tell the women that the baths are to be closed in six weeks' time.

In the second half of the play, the women's friendship coheres into solidarity to stop the baths being closed. Jane and Nancy plan to go to a meeting to protest. On a more personal note, the women look after Mrs Meadows who is ill in bed in one of the cubicles. While all this is going on, Dawn achieves a moment of personal liberation when Josie gets her to take all her clothes off. Dawn cavorts around in great pleasure at being free from her mother's repressiveness.

Towards the end of the play, Bill's shadow appears again behind the glass. Josie, Vi and Dawn return from the town hall, to announce that the women have lost their struggle. As Bill comes downstairs, Violet bolts the door and the women decide to occupy the building. Jane's comment to Nancy sums it up: 'Go for what you want, Nancy! We must put up a fight, even if we lose, we'll go down fighting.'

The final stage direction gives us an image of simultaneous strength and vulnerability: 'The stage goes misty as the women begin to undress.'

As in O'Malley and Duffy, the play creates a hermetic (and, it turns out, transitory) space for women to engage with one another. Here too, there is an alternative 'family' set-up: Violet makes the baths homely, and creates the environment within which the women function. Here – in a radical feminist dynamic – the oppositions of class and social position are forgotten, as the women are all equal in nudity, and where solidarity in the face of the baths' closure unites them all. Within this there are various personal odysseys, such as Dawn's awakening, and a mixture of friendships and conflicts free of the distraction of the male presence.

However, the very shadowiness of Bill's presence – the faceless, formless man behind the glass door – represents not just control over the hardware of the baths (hot water), but also the bureaucratic world outside which has no concern for women's needs, friendships and pleasures. In the face of such 'hard'-ship, the women's nakedness is both freedom and vulnerability. The only possible end (judging from evidence within the play) to the story is that they will eventually be thrown out of the baths, and have lost not only the value of a Turkish bath but the *raison d'être* of their relationships. The mother has been usurped, and the fledglings thrown out of the nest.

The radical feminist dynamic is absolutely contained here within the feminine (and ultimately powerless), and operates as an essential set of tactics for survival. The overarching dynamic is the traditional, feminine dynamic, exposed only by implication, and made more poignant because we have seen what strengths are about to be destroyed. Bill recalls Steve in Jellicoe, and the spectre of the male-dominated church in Dunn. The framework of the feminine is both security and vulnerability. The drama itself leaves us with an elegiac reminder of the women's freedom.

There is an additional issue here: because the play is set in the Turkish baths, the women are either actually or (more often) potentially naked. The predominance (but *not* exclusivity) of the male gaze/perspective in our culture leaves us with a rather different set of dilemmas from those which we encounter in *Tanzi*. Given the way the female body appeals differently to men and women – to men as objects of desire, to women as the image they desire to be for the male gaze – the play potentially reinforces its 'feminine' dynamic by potentially dividing the audience.

Women and men in the audience are likely to 'see' and 'read' the nudity differently, and, since the issue of what the women look like naked must be thought about in casting and performance, the ambiguities about the representation of the female body come into operation. The performers (naked and vulnerable) enable men to 'eavesdrop' on women's territory as erotic voyeurs, and this again possibly undermines and contradicts the strength of the radical feminist detail simultaneously created within the play's friendships and subversions.

Women, on the other hand, are looking at themselves being looked at, without the participatory liberation of the wrestling ring audience. On the other side of the footlights, actresses and director also have to deal with these same issues. Is a body a body, or is the appearance (especially of the naked female body) itself hedged round with expectations, notions of the ideal, notions of the acceptable? In the end, the play is suspended between the mixture of the radical feminist dynamic, a brief moment of socialist–feminist dynamic, and the framing feminine dynamic.

The right legacy

Maydays (1983) by David Edgar

This play spans the period between 1945 to the early 1980s. At the opening we hear the Internationale sung on May Day 'beautifully – by working class voices'.

Jeremy Crowther, aged 17, a member of the British Communist Party, celebrates the Labour government and the victory of socialism in a speech delivered directly to the audience. We leap to 1956 and the Hungarian uprising against Soviet control. The army, in the person of Lermontov and a female stenographer, is engaged in helping quell the rebellion. Lermontov allows a young man to escape.

We return to Britain in 1962, where Crowther, now a teacher at a minor public school, has to deal with a rebel of his own: Martin, sporting a CND badge. The two strike up a rapport, with Martin affirming the rational, manly nature of the political sensibility, rejecting both the 'emotional' and psychoanalytic (psychological) approaches: 'I imagine you'd resent as much as I do the idea you want to ban the bomb because you want to kill your mother.'

Jeremy tells Martin how he left the party over Hungary, and he talks about those who struggled in the 1930s in a way which recalls a rather more intellectual Jimmy Porter:

> And what we'd missed, of course, was all the glory. And indeed the confidence that once you'd cracked the shackles of the system, every man indeed would be an Aristotle or a Michelangelo. Because in a way, it had already happened. And it hadn't turned

out how we thought it would at all. Oh, it was decent, sure, and reasonably caring in its bureaucratic way. . . . But you realise there's something missing. The working class is freer than it's ever been. . . . But somewhere. . . . You hear a kind of scream. The scream of the possessed. And you realise there's all the difference in the world between liberty and liberation.

However, while Jeremy looks back to the past, Martin is looking to the future. In 1967 he is in Californnia with the hippies and the Vietnam War draft resisters. In 1968 he is in the thick of British student protest in a Midlands' commune, whose living room contains not just a washing line with nappies, but also a stencilling machine. Domesticity and politics appear to be cohabiting; but this is a visual illusion.

Amanda (Martin's other half) comes in carrying a tray of mugs, bantering about a conference she could not attend because she was looking after the children. A political friend, James, tries to persuade Martin to join the Socialist Vanguard, whose slogan includes 'the festival of the oppressed'. Amanda's throwaway comment – 'Well, I suppose – it's only rock and roll' – is a part ironic, part affectionate comment on the stage of history within which they all live. Part of the ammunition James uses to try and persuade Martin is used to deny his individual conscience, echoing a phrase used earlier by Jeremy:

I frankly couldn't give a toss about your guilty conscience, I don't even care if you're repressing latent homosexuality, or if you really want to kill your mother . . . until you sacrifice your individual conscience, then you will be frankly useless to the building of a party.

Amanda agrees with this, and when she and James are alone, she acts confidently again: 'Let's go and fuck, okay?'

Although this sounds very like a woman in control of her desire, it sits oddly at a moment when the individual has been thrown out with the political bathwater. We have also seen far less of Amanda (we follow Martin's historical story), so we know far less about her than we do about Martin. Logically it simply appears that for Amanda, sexuality is a matter of rational, non-individual desire, whatever that is. However, in 1970, during the invasion of Cambodia, Martin does join the Socialist Vanguard: 'I want to be a traitor to my class.' Amanda gets his membership card for him, which suggests that either she is already a member or has better access to the party.

When Jeremy visits Martin in 1972, asking: 'Oh, is there a Mrs Glass?' Martin has no doubt about his reply: 'The Party.'

Politics now replaces – indeed, becomes – the personal, even to the point of being the wife. To some extent this tension between the individual and the group, the personal and the political, enters the fabric of the play. James comments at one point on the contradiction between subjective and objective positioning of the self: 'He may think he's a revolutionary. Objectively he is nothing of the kind.' Martin himself is expelled from the party for not thinking and doing the right things, and for feelings that are at odds with policy, although it is never clear what these are.

In 1974 Amanda again appears, this time carrying glasses and a bottle of whisky. She has left the party (we do not know why), and is again on child-minding duty. At one point during their conversation, Amanda starts to tell Martin about the way she used to cry – but her emotional confession is blocked by the arrival of a group of friends. Later she tells James why she used to cry:

> All those opportunities, those bold bright schools and gleaming universities. That our folks had never had themselves, but had been through a slump and then a war to win for us. And if we didn't finish it, if we didn't get it right this time, if we didn't actually complete the building of the New Jerusalem, for them, for us, then what the fuck were we about?
>
> And I left your party when I realised the one absolute condition of my membership was checking in those feelings at the door.

In 1975, at the end of the Vietnam War, Amanda and Martin go to a party. Martin is going through yet another crisis of conscience, with Amanda as the strong reassuring one, calling him 'lovey'. She then explodes, out of the blue:

> Martin, I'm not sure that I'm presently that interested in what you think. . . . Or what you feel . . . the problem does come down to what you are . . . try to imagine what life would be like if you didn't have a cock. I think that would be really helpful. Actually.

There is no context, no lead-up to this remark; there has been no gender conflict, no presence of feminism as any kind of force in the socialist world they inhabit, no debate between them. It is only Martin who seems to see himself as part of history, and, in keeping with the way that familial roles have been hijacked for politics (the party is the wife), disasters take on the imagery of mothering:

> And as once again the proofs pile up that we are catastrophically wrong, we change the question . . . that all the stillbirths, all the monstrous misbegottens with no legs or stomachs but with all those twitching ears and beady little eyes, that they're the deviation and that therefore somewhere in the future there must be a norm.

Meanwhile, Amanda simply seems to move with the political times. During the late 1970s she is at an anti-Nazi League rock and roll festival. When Martin meets her later, he asks: 'So what's your present bag, then? Apart, that is, from battered lesbians against the bomb.'

Martin himself travels if not quite full circle, then pretty close, back to something like his parents' politics, and ends up working for a Tory think-tank. The play closes with him and Amanda at a Greenham Common-type demonstration outside an American air-force base, where the hardware – the guns, loudspeakers, sirens, searchlights and wire – are contrasted with the vulnerability of unarmed female bodies in protest. Amanda summarises:

> But I think in fact that in the end they are doing, what we all are trying to do, in our many different ways, can only be accounted for by something in the nature of our species which resents, rejects and ultimately will resist a world that is demonstrably and in this case dramatically wrong and mad and unjust and unfair.

The secondary plot, about Lermontov, reveals that he was imprisoned as a dissident, betrayed by the stenographer. She did it because he had sneered at her for being an ignorant peasant girl. His response when he discovers this is: 'But what was visited on me broke all the rules. . . . That wasn't faceless. It was sharp and real and personal.' It is interesting that this fleeting moment articulates a character's consciousness about the links between the personal and the political, something which echoes Amanda's earlier speech about continuing to fight for a better world in the way her parents did. Otherwise, politics is split along the conventional lines of group/intellectual, individual/ emotional, with the woman guess where on this divide.

Martin moves through different sets of left-wing ideas, engaging in argument and carrying some kind of conscience, although we never really know what the conscience is about at any point. Amanda, on the other hand, is ruled by some sort of gut response which is linked back to her working-class origins, but equally, we have no idea why she goes from one party to another. She never engages intellectually with anything or anyone, and in the apocalyptic speech at the end appeals to a biologistic/cultural line that the desire for justice is 'in the nature of our species'. She seems to be always one move ahead of Martin, and so appears to 'lead' his politics, but because she does so 'instinctively', without any visible intellectual back-up, she subsides, as do so many women in drama, into the mixed haven and blessing of metaphorical importance. In the context of a piece whose drive and language celebrate the passion and power of the intellectual, Amanda is excluded from these kinds of rationale behind her actions. She is too much needed as metaphor to be given adequate stage reality.

It may look as though this is a chivalric nod in the direction of women's ability to lead political passion and protest, but it has no power base, either social or aesthetic. Amanda is not part of any kind of feminist grouping as far as we know, she does not struggle within any relationship, sex appears to be something she gets when she wants it. There is no built-in rational journey for her to travel. Dramatically, she is merely reactive, responding to wherever Martin is at. Rebellion, for her, is therefore correlated with un- (and therefore anti-) intellectual ballast, infantile and linked with women and children. At the end of the play Amanda's daughter carries on the torch: 'it's only rock and roll.'

When rebels grow up they must leave it all behind; as indeed Martin does and Jeremy did before him. Women, of course, do not grow up, because they simply move on to the next bit of gut response protest, and hence remain 'eternal' rebels and, in terms of rationality, eternal children; a mixed blessing, since this means they can never develop any real understanding of any social reality. Rebellion itself is thus merely an 'infantile disorder', to be moved on from by men who 'grow up'.

In the context of the play, where the dates (cf. Brecht) of each scene in the life are determined by the male protagonist, his intellectual/ political ideas and conscience are given greater value, because clearly dominant. The world of politics belongs to the men, who argue and debate and have congruence with one another. Amanda is isolated from other women; indeed, according to this traditionally imagined 'politics', she must be, in order to function as a symbol for the men, and to remain only in touch with a motherhood which is handing on the torch to the next generation of female symbols. Motherhood in this context cannot be problematic (or even that interesting), because it is only a biologistic means of maintaining emotional rebellion.

Because the play so potently denies familial ties, interpersonal relationships and sexualities, it does, of course, have a polemical force and magnetism; but one of the consequences is that a critical core of maleness is also denied. These men, like the women, are asexual, apparently unable to have personal relationships (as far as one can tell from the agenda of the play). They have transferred the force of personal feeling on to their politics – reversing the Jimmy Porter syndrome, but also, like him, they have had to find a way to annihilate the women along with the feelings. The Lady Macbeth Syndrome still hovers.

The solution, which appears to be more symbolically chivalrous, is to give women the voice of occasional conscience, and thus rethink (along seemingly more 'positive' lines) the traditional notion of woman = emotion. Imaginatively, however, it comes to the same thing, even if the imagery is not quite so violent – woman as relating to the 'real' is denied, and therefore 'real' women cannot be imaginatively represented.

Pornographics

Masterpieces (1983) by Sarah Daniels

The opening, polemical scene of this play gives us a group of middle-class people out for dinner. Juxtaposed with their socialising, we hear a monologue in three parts, spoken by the same male actor. The first is from someone who makes big money out of pornography, the second from a man who works in a sex shop, the third from a male customer.

Jennifer and Clive are the middle-aged couple, she a snob; Rowena is her daughter, a social worker, there with Trevor, her husband. Rowena's friend is a teacher, there with her husband Ron. The scene is expositional chat; a series of jokes about rape prompt various ideological responses: Rowena says where's the harm in it, Yvonne confesses to being disturbed because the boys at school bring in pornographic magazines. Clive also has various magazines, and in response to all of this

Yvonne comes up with an analytical feminist response: 'Crimes committed against women have never been credible.' Jennifer, very much acting the 'batty' mother, counters Clive's misogyny with descriptions of flower arranging, using her contraceptive diaphragm as part of the display.

The scene switches forward to a court, in which Rowena is being arraigned for pushing a man under a tube train. We shift to a school, where the mother of a rapist son has come to talk to Yvonne, bringing with her a bag full of pornographic magazines which belong to the son, saying also that her husband 'has a drawerful of his own'. Rowena meanwhile visits Hilary, a single mother on a housing estate, who talks about her 'men friends', and says that all she wants is a job, and someone to look after her son, Heathcliff. On her way home, Rowena is followed by a man. Later Trevor defends Hilary for being on the game: '. . . they've been wanting to tax it for years – just haven't found a way – short of inventing accountants to accumulate sperm returns.'

Rowena suddenly asks Trevor to bring her some pornographic magazines to look at, and he lets slip the fact that Ron has told him that his and Yvonne's sex life is in trouble. We shift to an unpleasant row between Ron and Yvonne; apparently she will not respond to him physically. He swears at her, then cajoles, then finally says he loves her and she, when he has gone, says: 'I hate you.'

There follows a very long monologue from Hilary about her awful childhood, how she slept around, and then got pregnant. Yvonne comes around to visit Rowena, and confesses that she hates Ron: 'Men, it's all to do with the way men are taught to view women.' She has some confiscated magazines in her bag, and Rowena looks at them. While she is doing so – 'in such a way that the audience is not exposed to their contents' – there are three voice-over monologues from women who have posed for the magazines. When Trevor comes back, Rowena explodes with anger and shock, and he says she's being 'hysterical', appealing to his own non-discriminatory behaviour: 'I've never raped anyone. I've never so much as attacked a single woman.'

He says there is nothing that can be done about pornography. The action flashes forward again, to an interview between Rowena and a court psychiatrist, in which it is revealed that she has left her husband and wears jeans. She answers back, with angry speeches about the mutilation and exploitation of women's bodies for entertainment. Back in the 'present' she visits Jennifer, who informs her that Clive has had affairs for years, that she played various sexual games to try and keep him interested, but has given that up. Meanwhile Hilary has taken a job with Ron (set up by Rowena) but has left because he tried to pull her. The foursome meet for dinner, which ends up in a huge row about attitudes to sex, and the two men storm out. Yvonne decides to leave Ron.

An idyllic scene by the sea follows: Jennifer, Rowena and Yvonne are having a picnic. After some nostalgic chat about childhood, Jennifer invites them both to go on holiday to Greece with her. In a wordless scene, Rowena waits on the tube platform, a man comes towards her, and she pushes him violently on to the track. An angry confrontation between Hilary and Rowena reveals class antagonism, and Hilary tells Rowena to go back to her nice dinner parties. Finally, we are back in court. Psychiatric reports say Rowena is frigid and cold. In her defence, she says she had been to see a snuff movie and was angry, and that she did not want to be harassed by the man. She cannot remember what he said to her. The judge suggests that she killed in cold blood, and invites the jury to give its verdict.

The last scene is in a side room where Rowena is being guarded by a policewoman, who asks her what the film was like. Rowena describes it in graphic and gruesome detail, and the policewoman confirms the 'reality' of it by describing photographs she has seen. Rowena intimates that she is going to have a long time to think about it, implying that she will be found guilty. Her final speech is:

> I don't want anything to do with men who have knives or whips or men who look at photos of women tied and bound, or men who say relax and enjoy it. Or men who tell misogynist jokes.

Structurally, the play interweaves three strands; there are the realistic scenes: domestic, work, restaurant, court. Then there are the monologues, which at the beginning give us the apologias of three men for pornography, ditto for three women who take part in pornography, and then the life story of Hilary, and her sexual encounters. Third is the flash-forward technique, showing us Rowena on trial before we either know what she has done or what leads up to it. At the end, past and present catch up with each other, and we are left with Rowena, with no idea about anyone else's response to her actions.

The game with time compounds the complexity of distentangling the play's themes, its 'message', and the gender dynamic which informs, and finally determines, it. First of all, on the gender trajectory, it is clear that there is a continuum between the liberal Trevor and his unthinking misogyny, and Ron the rude-joke rapist. Along the way, Clive, the male psychiatrist, the prosecutor and the three opening monologues, all point to the snuff movie as the logical end of their hatred of women.

The three women, whose stories drive the action, represent different stages in their consciousness of pornography and misogyny. Rowena begins in ignorance and, as soon as she glimpses her first magazine, becomes a convert to militant anti-pornography, although it is not at all clear where she gets her ideas from, so we must assume they are somehow gut responses which result in anti-pornography comments, which second-guess pamphlet slogans. Yvonne is already bowed down by pornography, hates her husband, and then suddenly decides to leave him. Jennifer has played along with a misogynistic male, and then makes a bid for freedom and a holiday without him. Rowena travels the longest journey (cf. Brecht): from ignorance to the ultimate action – murder without apparent provable cause, just a reflex lashing out, as far as we know.

It is here that issues about form are interestingly raised. The polemical devices and the realistic scenes are – formally – at odds with each other. The understanding of institutionalised pornography's effects on people's lives relies on the dramatised, realistic 'scenes'. The polemical monologues may thus appear to disrupt, but they are, despite their important content, secondary to the motivating dramatic texture; they have to be, since this is theatre and not journalism. Relationships are at the core of theatre, no matter what the form or the 'disruptive' devices. That is why, ultimately, the dynamic here is a dangerous mix of the radical feminist and the feminine, the latter ultimately co-opting the former, and looking, hearing (though not necessarily 'seeing') with the male-spectored gaze. Disruption here is merely interruption.

The conversions in each case are sudden, just like Rowena's actions and change of consciousness. The realism set up by the main conventions of the play are constantly interrupted by non-realistic (not based on developed emotional logic) decisions, and similarly the naturalistic dialogue is constantly interrupted by polemical segments (cf. Edgar) which sound (and read) as if they come out of anti-pornography writings. Thus the 'unsettled' world of the writing is disrupted. The problem here is not the mixing of discourses, but because one discourse (the realistic) is dominant, and builds the argument. The monologues function merely as illustrations; they cannot really drive forward the interaction between characters, or even act as direct commentary on the action.

The interruptions therefore appear as inconsistency rather than challenge. We are led along in the play's argument one way – realistic representations of members of a particular nexus where emotional cause and effect attempt to make sense, but are too schematic to do so – and then we are effectively bullied by shock tactics which deny that cause and effect are relevant, by simply asserting individual experience.

The resolution of the play is divided into two parts: the first, the idyllic (seaside) picnic with the three women alone. Here they appeal to a past mother–daughter–friend triad, with no men around to shatter the atmosphere. For the present, there is a promise of a holiday without the men to match the earlier idyll, but this is followed by the arrest and trial, so we do not know if the holiday ever happens. The second part of the resolution is the very end: here Rowena announces she will have nothing to do with any men – the continuum between 'men with knives' and 'men who tell misogynist jokes' is confirmed – but this can have no force, since Rowena appears to be about to be sent to prison for a very long time, and there will be no men there anyway.

The gender dynamics thus become very interesting. We are presented with all men as misogynists, some violent. We are presented with all women as objects or victims of this misogyny. We then, apocalyptically and polemically, see each woman rebelling against this misogyny, with moments of rapport between them (Rowena/Yvonne, Rowena/Jennifer, Jennifer/Rowena/Yvonne, Rowena/Policewoman). This radical feminist dynamic enables the women to find small oases of safety in a misogynistic and sexist world. Jennifer and Yvonne also make small bourgeois feminist gestures in their lives to give them individual space and freedom.

However, as far as we know, the vision of the holiday does not carry forward. It is more a fantasy idyll than a space for radical feminist solidarity, and more seriously, Rowena's murderous outburst is at best some kind of generalised revenge against a total stranger who may or may not have been harassing her. The three women, in their different ways, remain powerless (Rowena herself the ultimate victim) while the men all continue to live their lives. Power is thus absolutely divided, with the men more or less having it all, Jennifer and Yvonne taking small initial steps, and Rowena driven to homicide and therefore now totally powerless. The effect – shocking, because it is the opposite of what it appears to be – is that the case against pornography is never made within the means of the play, a realistic story, told through a basically realistic mode. The accounts of pornography are all at one remove. The soliloquies are confessional, journalistic and non-interactive.

The feminine dynamic (particularly with the impossible paradox of the final speech) is thus completely reinforced, and the momentary disruptions of form (monologue, polemical quotations) and small radical feminist oases fail to impact on the apparent theme, which is supposed to be the nature and impact of pornography. Pornography (and therefore misogyny) in effect continues to rule, and the momentary solidarities between women (including the mother/daughter–Jennifer/Rowena) are powerless to impact upon it.

Indeed, one could argue that the very dramatic inadequacy of the unintegrated theatrical form vindicates pornography in general. In this context, Rowena's apparently irrational action leaves her isolated, at the mercy of the court, and in any case, on the verge of being sent to a female ghetto (prison) not of her own choosing. The apparent momentary rapport between Rowena and the policewoman (radical feminist dynamic) is subsumed in their institutional relations of prisoner and warder. One of the morals appears to be that if you take action against pornography, you end up in prison. Another implies that if you take up feminism, you could end up as irrational, and the murderer of random male victims.

Myth revisited

The Love of the Nightingale *(1988) by* Timberlake Wertenbaker

Like Maureen Duffy decades before, Wertenbaker takes a Greek myth as her point of departure. The play opens with two juxtaposed scenes/worlds: the public/outdoor world of soldiers and the male world, and then a tender, passionate scene between two sisters, Procne and Philomele. Procne, the elder, knows she is to marry; the two talk about men, and Philomele comments indirectly on the safety of the women's world: 'I'm frightened. I don't want to leave this room, ever.'

Procne, the Athenian, goes north with her husband Tereus; here she is alone, surrounded by women from another culture. She has a son. Tereus goes back to ask her parents to allow Philomele to visit her. During the course of this scene, the play itself 'plays' with self-referential elements from Greek myth: two Greek choruses, male and female, comment and join in the discussion. In plays within plays, characters from Greek tragedy – Phaedra and Hippolytus – impart their own implicit comment on the play. As the Queen (not terribly subtly) puts it: 'Listen to the chorus. The playwright always speaks through the chorus.'

The choruses' polemical functions accompany the plot as it moves along. Philomele and Tereus sail north, and the male chorus pontificates on the power of myth that leaves women silent. When Philomele is attracted to the ship's Captain, Tereus kills him. The male chorus see 'nothing', passive bystanders as the human agents proceed with the story. Tereus tells Philomele that Procne is dead, and effectively rapes her: 'I will have you in fear.'

Her maid, Niobe, like the male chorus, has stood by. Tereus arrives home, covered in blood, implying that Philomele is dead. Procne welcomes him. Tereus gets between the two sisters, and when Philomele rages and upbraids him, he cuts out her tongue. Niobe has again stood by as Philomele is silenced, this time literally.

During the feast of Bacchus, at a puppet show, Procne sees Philomele, and realises what has happened. During the revels, Procne's son Itys, together with the soldiers, watches the women have a good time, but when he attacks Philomele, the women close in and kill him. Finally, when Itys' body is revealed, Procne admits that she did nothing: 'As usual. Let the violence sweep around me.' Tereus, on the other hand, elides love of his country with love for Philomele and for Itys. Procne counters that he merely found a way to take what he wanted, and Tereus claims he could not tell right from wrong, because no one explained.

The play ends by retreating again to the commentating cover of the chorus. As the male chorus begins the play, the female chorus ends it. We see the conclusion of the original myth: Philomele becomes the nightingale, Procne the swallow, and Itys asks Philomele lots of questions. This time it is Procne who is silent, since the swallow does not sing. Like Tereus, Itys cannot understand the difference between right and wrong, and the play ends with his bewildered question: 'Didn't you want me to ask questions?'

The story becomes a rationale within which to display certain ideas about the relationship between culture, morality, power and gender. The conventional male/female dualism is there: men wage war, violence, lack conscience. Women love one another and feel desire for men, express themselves poetically, and yet are also politically passive, powerless. Within this dualism, the play gives greater theatrical power to the women. The plot follows their needs and desires. War is referred to, but we spend no time on the battlefield, we hear no discussion between the men about war.

In addition, the male chorus is undifferentiated, whereas the members of the female chorus have names; they represent both general and individual voices. The play, if it does anything, demonstrates the dualism, but focuses on exploring some of the dilemmas this dualism creates for the women. The final 'word', as it were, is Philomele's, to whom a voice has been restored. Curiously, both Tereus and Itys are also represented as helpless, unaware of either moral or political ideas.

A radical feminist dynamic focuses strongly on the women's stories, while at the same time a socialist–feminist dynamic informs the play's clear demonstration that the worlds of men and women are existentially, morally and emotionally separate. The powerless, male or female, are helpless (the Captain killed by Tereus), the soldiers mere servants, the women slaves also helpless bystanders to brutality.

There is further a bourgeois feminist dynamic in Procne's awareness that she herself has been passive in her fate and, by implication, in that of her sister. There is an overall terseness in the style of the play, which evokes Brechtian echoes in the way characters step outside their immediate situations to question – but the questioning is largely undertaken by the women. The use of the chorus, too, while it has polemical and narrative purpose, also functions to 'tell' us when chunks of time pass, or when events happen off stage. This enhances the sense of the piece as a modern morality play, in which issues of gender join the issues of social and moral power that underlie the original Greek myth, but in which the fundamental political imperatives remain unquestioned. Thus both men and women remain victims in the light of a greater destiny – the gods? The way the play halts at the edge of the material, political questions perhaps implies that it hides behind a theology which is itself inadequate for the issues raisesd in the play.

Chapter 12

The 1980s

Conclusions

By the end of the 1980s, the Brechtian convention of situating the individual in his or her context was well and truly established with its theatrical corollary of the stage as representing public spaces. This does not necessarily mean that playwrights are all self-consciously trying to interpret Brecht; it is simply an easy theatrical convention, no longer challenging to the audience, but absorbed into the imaginative possibilities of form. It is there in the historical/epic sweep of Edgar, in the mythic world of Wertenbaker, in the historically foreign worlds of Friel and Lowe. The use of neutral public space as setting is there in the wrestling ring (Luckham), the baths (Dunn) and the constantly shifting locations (Daniels).

With the foreign no longer simply 'exotic', as it were, immediate issues can be more subtly addressed. Friel sculpts his dilemmas and relationships through his uses of language/communication, both public and personal, on Britain's imperialist doorstep. His play gently, if somewhat schematically, also shows how family relationships (fathers and sons) can be destroyed by political conflict, and how love has to struggle to find some means of communication in a world full of hostilities. Here men are clearly the centre of the action, but are dealt with without recourse to the use of women as metaphor. As a consequence, the men have to deal themselves – and between themselves – with direct expressions of emotion.

Lowe goes further afield to explore a revolutionary moment which becomes a template for a study of the constraints of masculinity – recalling some of Sherman's courage, and with a new freedom in the way its male characters understand maleness – a very different aesthetic world from the plays of the 1950s and 1960s.

The subtleties of sexual politics are now more fully articulated and conceptualised in the way Dorja's personal heroic crisis is given its narrative. Unlike Jimmy Porter, Dorja is himself invested with an intellect which struggles to come to terms with ideas, while his body and emotions are also engaged in their existential struggles. This is not a value judgement in favour of Lowe over Osborne, since both have a totality and coherence which makes them powerful and important plays. However, there is a very clear change of stress, from the bewildered individual in his domestic eyrie, aware only of his immediate extended environment, to the plains of the Far East, where politics, religion and sexuality converge in the lives of ordinary people in a more fully self-conscious way.

The trails laid by the female rites-of-passage play continue in both Luckham and Dunn's plays, while the male-defined epic political play continues in Edgar's work. During the 1980s issues surrounding sexual politics (sexuality, relations between the sexes) enter the fabric of the work, and yet the narratives themselves remain 'public' narratives, with the personal and domestic inserted into public spaces, and with a predominantly similar gender divide in the narrative drives of the plays.

It is demonstrable that domestic privacy has continued to be abolished/eschewed in these plays. The family no longer has its own setting. We are not discussing 'dysfunctional' views of the family; we do not have a context within which 'family', of whatever kind, is seen. Where interpersonal relations briefly appear, they punctuate the public world. It is almost as if the stoning of the baby in Bond's *Saved* has become a symbol of the destruction of the vulnerable self revealed in interpersonal relationships which previously formed the bedrock of the old-fashioned, domestic, 'drawing-room' narrative. There are exceptions to this, but by and large, these exceptions do not appear in the high-art repertory. More on this in the final chapter.

Love, motherhood, the figure of the outsider, all still hover hazily behind the plays of the 1980s, but are no longer centre stage, significant as themes or as metaphors for other issues. Instead issues of male identity are occasionally more clearly gender-specific: in both Edgar and Lowe, men are concerned with their own place in the world. These playwrights articulate the place of women differently, Edgar continuing to sideline, to exclude the personal, using female characters as devices, while Lowe allows his women secondary but more individualised voices.

At the same time, the influences of feminist critiques and experiences are present in the way the three general feminist dynamics inform plays by some women. The mix is complex, and the dominant message is not always as clear-cut as it might at first appear. The mix in Churchill's

Cloud Nine, for example, can arguably cloud (!) and weaken the overall strength of the piece. In Daniels' *Masterpieces*, the mix turns what looks like a radical feminist take on important issues into a demonstration which rebounds and attacks the very ideas it appears to promulgate, resulting in the assertion of a feminine tendency which structurally undermines the play's apparent thesis. This may make for a poor and unsatisfactory play; a drama using schematic agitprop techniques which weaken the dramatic case. Pornography is an extraordinarily difficult issue to represent and deal with, because of the political questions surrounding its representation.

It is particularly important to stress this, since there is no imaginative law which says that plays by women will all be the same as each other, or contain the same degree of gender bias or content. The danger is only there if this is taken to be the one, definitive play about pornography. Tokenism, both in terms of the 'allowed' successful woman playwright and subject matter, spells implied censorship of other voices, as well as being detrimental to the richness of theatre itself.

Part VI

Chapter 13

The 1990s

Down on the estate

Beautiful Thing *(1993) by Jonathan Harvey*

This play is set almost entirely outside three flats in south-east London, on the walkway joining and dividing them. Here Sandra lives with her 15-year-old son Jamie. She is visited by her middle-class (and therefore slightly better spoken) boyfriend Tony. Ste, aged 16, lives on one side, and Leah, obsessed with Mama Cass, on the other. Sandra is hostile to Leah; Ste is constantly being beaten up by his violent father and takes refuge with Sandra and Jamie, sharing the latter's bed. Leah hates her mother, Sandra and Jamie bicker, and at one point they have a serious physical fight; emotions are raw and direct: 'Okay, so you got me for a mother, but who said life was easy?'

The young ones mostly bunk off school, though Ste is keen on sport. Tony and Jamie are able to establish a rapport, Jamie talking about Sandra's other boy-friends who beat her up. As the action progresses, Ste and Jamie fall in love and go off to a gay club. Sandra is at first angry and shocked. In a series of scenes after the revelation, Tony consoles Sandra and, when Leah turns up, seemingly on a bad acid trip, they help her, feeding her orange juice. At the end of the play, Sandra, while getting ready to go out, basically gives Tony the brush-off, and the remaining four dance, Jamie and Ste together, Sandra and Leah together: 'The music turns up of its own accord, blasting out. A glitter-ball spins above the stage, casting millions of dance hall lights.'

In this nexus of relationships, one in particular stands out as unusual: mother–son. Here we have a Delaney-like mother, on her own, still wanting a good time, in knots, which express themselves abrasively, about her maternal role. We also have the male rites-of-passage which challenge taboos – Jamie and Ste discovering their homosexuality.

On the edges are two figures: Tony, the articulate, middle-class outsider, who is useful as a device because he acts as confidant to Jamie and Sandra; and Leah, the girl who is isolated from school and parents in the fantasy world of music and drugs. Tony, having fulfilled a helpful outsider role, is imaginatively dismissed (he is also the 'wrong' class), and Leah, after the peer bickering of the two young men and the hostility from Sandra, is integrated into a new extended 'family', deciding not to go after men, finally beginning to find a way out:

> I gets up in the morning, bake me face in half a ton o'slap. Tong me hair wi' yesterday's lacquer . . . and that's it. Same every bleedin' day. Fuck all to look forward to except Mama Bloody Cass. Nothing ever happens. Nothing ever changes.
> I intend to find meself a nice dyke tonight. . . . I'm through with men.

The solution, or redemption, for all four is in coming out, in same-sex relationships, sanctioned and participated in by Sandra the mother, literal and surrogate. The closing image combines the utopian and escapist world of music and the dance-hall (Leah's and Sandra's worlds) with the council estate. The middle-class, heterosexual male has gone. Mother–son relations are allowed, and indeed resolved; when push comes to shove, Sandra supports Jamie and Ste, and indeed, joins them in the new world of gay relationships. Although the focus of the action is mainly on Jamie and Ste, Sandra's presence is always looming (on or off stage), and Leah's role becomes directly influential in the way her music (woman associated with emotion still) becomes the means whereby all four find an idyllic moment. The gender balance, despite certain stereotypical associations, shifts in a cumulative way from male to female, and this is boosted by the class dynamic. The main sexual focus is still on the men, and the sexual drive from hetero- to homosexuality.

Unusually, in the context of male playwrights, this piece delicately charts personal, working-class lives with emotional frankness and abrasiveness. It is, of course, no coincidence that the emotional heart of the play focuses on homosexuality in a heterosexual context. However, what is also interesting is that the mother-figure not only does not have to be imaginatively annihilated, but can be integrated into the lives not only of the next generation, but into a world of young men and their defiant sexualities. In the process, the conventional hetero-family is redundant – the heterosexual mother now free to find a sexuality outside the dictates of procreation.

New urban disaffection

Shopping and Fucking (1996) by Mark Ravenhill

The personal anarchy and social disaffection which marks this piece, with its jagged fluency, is (unlike Harvey) nevertheless centred around a kind of parodied family. The living room which places the opening scene is 'once stylish, now almost entirely stripped bare'. This descent from a secure, 'stylish' home to a bare space heralds the emotional barrenness which shapes these people's lives. In this space live Lulu and Robbie who, at the beginning, are, parent-like, trying to persuade Mark to eat some takeaway food. Mark is a junkie, and has decided to go into detox. When he goes, we see Lulu being interviewed by Brian for some sort of job, which turns out to be selling Ecstasy tablets.

In an almost unnoticeable time shift Mark comes back, off junk, still wanting sex and relationships, but on a different basis, as he tells Gary, a 14-year-old who has run away from an abusive stepfather. Mark uses the language of psychological insight, very different from the fragmented, street argot of the rest of the play:

> I have a tendency to define myself purely in terms of my relationship to others. I have no definition of myself you see. So I attach myself to others as a means of avoidance, of avoiding knowing the self . . . if I don't stop myself I repeat the patterns. Get attached to people to these emotions then I'm back to where I started.

The play does not follow an explicit narrative, but, in keeping with the meandering nature of these people's lives, we see episodes: Gary steals credit cards and he and Mark go shopping (to Harrods, among other places). Lulu and Robbie end up in debt to Brian, who brings a violent video to threaten them with, and they then earn money by working on sex chat lines. Brian's values, all money, are countered by his capacity to cry at the beauty of a boy playing the cello on video, and the beauty of the music elides with the kind of moneyed background which enables a child to have access to expensive education and training.

Gary tells Mark the story of his background: he is looking for a father, a strong dad, and against his better judgement, Mark begins to fall in love with him. Meanwhile Robbie too has glimpses of an alternative – against wars and suffering in the world, he has a vision of living only for peace and beauty. He is interrupted by a man wanting to buy Es, who then beats him up.

When he tells this story to Lulu, she fondles him in a way which is as much violent as consolatory. Indeed, the chief and most intense mode of interchange between the characters is sexual, and that mainly male homosexual. Both Mark and Robbie at different times have violent, consensual sex with the passive Gary on stage, and the climax (*sic*) of the play (and its denouement) is at the end when (the 'family', now with another 'son' among them) Robbie and Mark, egged on by Lulu, in turn bugger Gary, who finally begs them to use a knife, as his step-father did. They (fortunately for us) draw the line at that, and at the end Mark tells a futuristic story about a mutant who wants to remain a slave because it is afraid it will die if it is set free. The closing image is of Lulu, Robbie and Mark back in their opening family unit, feeding each other takeaway food. The outsider, Gary, has served his purpose, which in part is to bind the odd, lost, nuclear family even closer together.

In one sense the takeaway image is central to the overview: our culture is dispensable, consumerism absorbs both shopping and fucking. No-one is really able to look after themselves. The former involves theft and ownership, the latter continuous physical, homosexual violation. At the centre are semi-homeless, parentless, unloved young people. The only older figure is the exploitative, cruel, emotionally hypocritical Brian, who represents the male-dominated society outside (cf. Dunn).

However, there is, even in the representation of disaffection, a gender imbalance. Most of the time, Lulu is the one feeding the others. She is the only woman in this all-male world. She has her own cruelties, and sexually she may fumble Robbie, but none of the men have a sexual relationship with her. In one sense, she is superfluous (except perhaps in the early scene with Brian, when he gets her to strip for the job). The real relationships are homosexual, and between men; the young looking for a father-figure, both afraid of emotional entanglement and dependent upon it.

It could be argued that the relative absence of women and total absence of meaningful heterosexuality (even of a cruel nature) might imply that women have less of a problem than men. Lulu is certainly less powerful than any of the men, and has no conflict within her relationships. Robbie is jealous of Gary, Mark and Gary tussle to find terms, but Lulu is just there, joining in as necessary, and feeding the men. The men's overwhelming need is both for meaningful affection as young adults and for a father who will look after them. This suspension between child- and adulthood lends the dilemmas of the men a poignancy, but in the process inevitably excludes the woman. As I have suggested (cf. Edgar), Lulu could be excised from the play and it would not be substantially different (cf. also Frayn below).

The fragmented and basically irrelevant time scheme is built largely around Gary's arrival and departure. He, the outsider, catapults the others into an episode after which their relationships are reinforced. The men feed alongside Lulu, and perhaps Mark has found his father-figure. Lulu appears to need nothing except to be there, and she has not moved. The three are something of a defensive cohort against the invasions of Brian (the 'man', older, social power) but as far as we can tell, this is only temporary.

The overall vision is profoundly nihilistic – as far as men are concerned. Neither shopping nor fucking appear to bring anything desirable with them, and the focus appears to impute blame to inadequate earlier families, so that subsequent parenting becomes impossible. In the face of this, even homosexuality offers only a series of further exploitative and violent possibilities for men. Women do not exist here – except as implicitly absent mothers.

Intellectual life

Copenhagen (1998) by Michael Frayn

The language, location and concerns of Frayn's play are very far removed from the bleak immediacy of Ravenhill and Daniels. Frayn's play operates as a series of intertwined conceits. At the level of subject matter, it is about a possible/imagined meeting between the German physicist Werner Heisenberg and his Danish counterpart Niels Bohr. After working as colleagues in the 1920s, the two men are on opposite sides during the Second World War.

The play has no specific location, in keeping with the fluid, abstract movement between past and present, between memory and historical fact. The Danes, Bohr and his wife Margrethe, under German occupation, are visited by Heisenberg. The role of Margrethe is particularly interesting. The dialogue, poised and highly literate, is full of expositional elements, giving the audience background information and facts. In the opening moments of the play this is largely Margrethe's role, enacted through a series of questions which she asks, about the past, about what is likely to happen (cf. Edgar).

The central dramatic event is the meeting between the two men. When this happens, Margrethe becomes a narrating participant-observer, alternately commenting on events from the side of the action, and joining in the conversation now and then.

At first, Margrethe is angry at the prospect of Heisenberg's visit, because of the possibility that he might be harnessing the discovery of nuclear fission for the benefit of the German government. She is the voice of conscience, while Bohr still feels nostalgia for his past friendship and thus has divided loyalties. Bohr is 'half Jewish', which compounds matters.

During dinner, the old friends reminisce (more exposition), and Margrethe casually remarks that she typed Bohr's work, which explains why she understands quite a lot about it, and can also, when dramatically required, operate as the 'innocent' spectator to whom things need to be explained, a useful mediation device for the audience. Heisenberg compliments the couple on their closeness, to which Bohr replies, using science as metaphor: 'I was formed by nature to be a mathematically curious entity: not one but half of two.'

Frayn's games with time, with 'real' conversation and inner thoughts, works to moving advantage in the sections which refer to the death of one of the Bohrs' children; when the two men go out for a walk, Margrethe again becomes narrator, continuing the pattern set up at the beginning of the play.

The second theatrical conceit operates at a more profound philosophical level. This is related to the 'uncertainty principle', which derives from Heisenberg's notion about quantum physics, that, in Frayn's words:

> The more precisely you measure one variable . . . the less precise your measurement of the related variable can be; and this ratio, the uncertainty relationship, is itself precisely formulable.

'Uncertainty' here operates in a number of playful senses. It is first of all a scientific concept. Then it is about the uncertainty of memory at every level: did the men meet in September or October? How, exactly, does each of them remember the details of how they made their scientific discoveries? How much of it really happened anyway? How much does it matter in Frayn's imaginative enterprise, which is to re-examine and re-imagine some important ethical issues about the relationship between science and politics?

Although it is the matter between the two men which is the stuff of the play, predictably, it is Margrethe who bursts out in anger, with virtually no warning (cf. Edgar), at the possibility that Heisenberg wants to persuade Bohr to persuade the Americans to stop developing the nuclear bomb. In the event, this turns out to be Margrethe operating functionally as an emotional safety-valve in the discussion. The men do not directly face this conflict to any real extent. The end of Act 1 rewinds in time to show the men greeting one another as they did at the beginning.

The format of Act 2 is very similar; Margrethe again punctuates the discussion, occasionally engaging with the ideas (which she has grasped because she is an intelligent typist). She takes over the stage at one point when she becomes carried away with psychological and emotional interpretations of Heisenberg's motivation. The following interchange between Margrethe and Bohr succinctly defines her role:

Bohr: Not to criticise, Margrethe, but you have a tendency to make everything personal.

Margrethe: Because everything *is* personal! . . . I'm sorry, but you want to make everything seem abstract and logical. . . . It's confusion and rage and jealousy and tears and no-one knowing what things mean or which way they're going to go.

However, this is mere polemic; the play manifests no confusion, rage, jealousy or tears between the two men.

The argument continues, with Margrethe defending Bohr, and attacking the emotional syndrome which has made Heisenberg into a clever, aberrant, ersatz son-figure in their lives. Having completed her emotional intervention, the debate cools and returns to the two men, about how much Heisenberg had understood about the bomb.

The play concludes with an elegant replay of the opening moments, with Margrethe's contribution an image about silence and 'lost children on the road'. It is left to Bohr to give us the philosophical message at the end about 'that final core of uncertainty at the heart of things'.

The play is an intricately woven Socratic verbal dance. It is, in this form, curiously untheatrical, despite the games with time, with interior monologue and dialogue, narrative commentary and free-standing dialogue. It is, quite deliberately, a highly verbal play, since it is in part precisely about conversation as an act which operates to recall historic events. However, in part this diminution of theatricality is determined precisely because of Margrethe's function in the play.

To come at this in another way; if Margrethe had not been in the play, everything would have to be (literally) enacted between the two men. Margrethe is actually not at all necessary. She functions as a receptacle for conscience, as a dramatic device, representing the audience, for exposition and explanation, and she accrues unto herself the function of expressing powerful emotion, of seeing the 'personal' (i.e. the emotional), and of allowing the softer side of memory in her sadness at her son's death. She gets in the way of emotion between the two men because she becomes the repository, the symbol of emotional response.

Clearly, the play is what it seems. Merely reattributing Margrethe's lines would not solve the problem, but the gendered separation between attributes/emotions weakens both the stage drama and the relationship between the two men. In addition, as has been shown in the analysis of some of the plays written by men in the 1970s, simply 'using' a woman character as a repository for 'other' traits maintains a separation between notions of maleness and femaleness, and – in a very palpable sense – denies the woman character her selfhood. It reinforces the stereotype that ideas and politics belong to men, and emotions and conscience belong to women. In this equation, women can never have executive power, however elegantly they sit on the intellectual sidelines.

New brutalism

Cleansed (1998) by Sarah Kane

The scene settings here veer between the relatively realistic – 'inside the perimeter fence of a university', which later is more defined as 'a patch of mud inside' – and a series of stylised, coloured spaces: the White room, which is the university sanatorium, the Black room, the sports' showers converted into peep-shows, the Round room, the university library, an unspecified Red room, where people are beaten up. At moments we hear the reassuring sounds of England in the background, for example, cricket being played (cf. the backdrop to *Slag*).

The people in this play are young, with one distinguished as (possibly older?) the one with power, an amalgam of doctor, dealer, torturer, undertaker. At the opening, Tinker is preparing smack (cocaine) for

Graham, who is trying to get off the drug, but also wants more. We then meet Rod and Carl, a gay couple, with Carl keen for the relationship to be binding.

Then we meet Grace, here to collect clothes from Graham, her dead brother. Another young man, Robin, is wearing the clothes, and after he strips naked, Grace puts on Graham's clothes. Robin has been suicidal; Tinker puts Grace to bed and injects her with sedatives. A series of horrific tortures are imposed on Carl as the play progresses, all controlled by Tinker. He has a pole pushed up his anus, his tongue is cut out, his hands and feet chopped off, and he and Rod, still trying to find a space for loving, are attacked by rats. Meanwhile, Grace and Graham appear together, Graham possibly a figment of Grace's imagination, while Robin begins to fancy Grace. For relaxation from his onerous labours, Tinker regularly visits a peep-show and masturbates while watching a woman dancing. Eventually they fuck. At the end, the other various mutilated, cross-dressed characters sit with the rats chewing at them, with Grace/Graham closing the picture:

> Felt it.
> Here. Inside. Here.
>
> And when I don't feel it, it's pointless.
> Think about getting up it's pointless.
> Think about eating it's pointless.
> Think about dressing it's pointless.
> Think about speaking it's pointless.

The stage directions are simple and to the point, however cruel and sadistic. It would miss the point to categorise the play (as the blurb on the published text does) as set in 'an institution designed to rid society of its undesirables'.

The given setting is that of a university, and therefore, however inexplicit this may be in the action, the clear implications are that the kind of institution preparing young people for the world is sadistic, sexually punitive (Carl, the one with true homosexual love, is progressively 'castrated'), and excludes any sense of female-gendered identity (Grace can only find meaning when dressed in Graham's clothes, thinking of herself as a man). The physical horrors and violence are the objective correlative to the conditioning, or mind games, played by society (i.e. Tinker, who is himself incapable of either equal affection or real sexual expression) on everyone else, namely young people whose every desire is blocked, and who resort to disguise, drug-induced oblivion and 'taboo' feelings. Tinker and the Woman (the stripper/ dancer) are a sado-masochistic parent couple, whose mission (for whatever reasons of frustration) is to torture their children.

Here again, in the visceral fragmentation (a far more dangerous world than that of Ravenhill), the parent figures give most of their attention to their male 'offspring'. Grace and Robin never really get it together. Perhaps Carl's transgression (and therefore punishment) is the greatest, because he has dared to love another man whole-heartedly. Within this 'family', the man (Tinker) always has ultimate power, the Woman is a permanent tease, and the children have to be tamed and trained at any cost. There is no sensitivity in this world; the only emotional exchange is that of violence, and if Tinker does not get you, the rats will.

The 'university' of life and the family thus become one and the same in the maelstrom of horror. The mother is contained within her sex booth, and Grace subsumes her femaleness into the memory of Graham. At least with the men, we know what they are striving for or towards; the women remain contained or diverted. Ravenhill's nihilism is taken one stage further, into an inchoate world where the young eat and are eaten, almost literally. The world is still defined by men, with women compromised in the process.

Chapter 14

The 1990s

Conclusions

The dividing line between the 1980s and 1990s is even more arbitrary than that between the 1970s and 1980s – socially and politically speaking, that is. From 1979, the return of the Conservative government under Margaret Thatcher heralded the weakening of the power of trade unionism, and the organised and anarchic left-wing groups. The entrenchment of Conservatism and the effective disintegration of a powerful socialist movement have meant a blurring of distinctions between parliamentary positions. Vigorous ideological debates still continue, but without the supportive backing of optimistic movements for fundamental change. Culturally, theatre subsidy continues to be beleaguered, although theatrical activity and enthusiasm does not abate.

It is, of course, too early to be really sure which plays from the 1990s will remain with us as exemplary, enduring works. The plays I have chosen to discuss have made critical impact, and have come mainly from a new generation of writers, supported by our main theatre houses, and so, again, we are seeing writing which has been allowed to occupy public prominence because of the decisions of artistic directors.

In terms of the configuration of these plays, the theatre world seems to be closing in. Social and urban fragmentation move into the theatrical space; families are scorned, abrasive interpersonal relations suggest desperation in personal life for meaning, security, affection.

The new brutalism which marks the work of Ravenhill and Kane is violent, anarchic, physically and sexually brutal, on stage, in your face. Harvey is a gentler (sic) spirit, but nevertheless confronts sexual crisis in an inter-generational fashion. These newer voices can be read in a number of different ways: as youthful outburst, as predictable cynicism about the older generation, as rebellion against authority. It can be a nihilism in the face of a world which offers no principles, no ideals or vision (no good causes left again!), and the inability to give and receive love.

It can be seen as veiled political protest; neither right nor left, nor any liberal ethos in the middle affords prospects for a future, in which technology and hardcore materialism appear to offer havens of consumerism. We are in a more dangerous world than that of the 1950s, with no sense of a history which has let characters down, and certainly none of the political/utopian optimism of the 1970s. The action homes in on individuals who cling together in groupings which scarcely even imitate a dysfunctional family, let alone a traditional family model.

Here the individual of the 1950s in a (his) shifting social world, meets the disaffected (male) intellectual of the late 1960s, but without either the freshness of articulacy (new education) of the former, or the political bite and idealism of the latter. In terms of form, however, this work still operates within the epic model (the heritage of the 1970s and 1980s), bringing the personal and private into the public arena, or blurring the two so that we appear to be in a latter-day Beckettian world.

Even Harvey's play, which ends with a utopian rather than a nihilistic image, takes place largely outside everyone's front door, rather like the convention of the sixteenth-century Italian Renaissance play, privileging the public space over the private, suggesting that almost everything that happens between people is now publicly available, laid bare to general scrutiny. There are echoes here of Anthony Burgess' *Clockwork Orange*, or Orwell's futuristic fantasies.

In these plays there is either the sado-masochistic family/power structure of Kane and Ravenhill, both with a man at their head, or the fragmented family-type structure of Harvey. In the latter's case, the Mother is herself outside the conventional structure, and ultimately this enables her to be incorporated into a future where the generational differences are less important than the sharing of sexual freedom, and the discovery of a different loving. In Harvey's world the Mother no longer needs to be destroyed, since she is herself part of the fragmentation, and no longer (apparently) a threat as representative of some inchoate emotional authority – but this is predicated on her rejection of heterosexuality (i.e. the presence of any father-figure). She joins her 'children' as an equal.

In the world of politics and ideas (slimly represented by Frayn), the presence of a woman remains token. The sexual division of spheres (politics for men, emotions for women and young men) is still the name of the game. With the legacy of the epic form (however small writ), the family is bound to be fragmented because it has no territory of its own. Of course, there is nothing to say that all interpersonal, inter-sexual relations have to be set on domestic territory, but it is a rare play which manages to do so on public territory (cf. Sherman and Lowe as rare exceptions).

Because the domestic has been rejected as a structure for inter-personal relations, the subject matter becomes the atomised relation-ship between the individual and a bleak world. When the world itself is not identified politically or geographically, the consequence is that certain power relations are simply taken for granted; male dominance is not questioned, female oppression becomes invisible. Explicit feminist dynamics are absent from these plays, although this is not to say that the underlying male–female relations have changed in any significant fashion – in both Ravenhill and Kane the authority figures are male, the women always lesser.

I reiterate that this does not mean that we must suddenly all start writing domestic plays, but there is a real imaginative conundrum here about the way different kinds of interrelationships belong on different material and imaginative territories. How do we imagine worlds, relationships and ideas in dramatic settings which do not sell some aspects of life/experience short? This is an open question, and one which belongs here and at the end of this book.

At the end of the twentieth century we have an extraordinarily rich half-century of British playwriting to look back upon. The concluding section of this book will look at the patterns of gender representation which emerge from these selected exemplary plays, to see how the profound (and profoundly important) critiques of the social and sexual division of labour have affected our serious drama, and to look at what have been the predominant preoccupations of recent decades.

Part VII

Chapter 15

Turning the tables

> We each begin probably with a little bias towards our own sex, and
> upon that bias build every circumstance in favour of it.
>
> (Anne Elliot, in *Persuasion*, by Jane Austen)

This book began with two conceits: Virginia Woolf's Orlando, who begins life as a man, to be transformed half-way through into a woman; and my own speculations on what would happen to the meanings in *Hamlet*, were we to work on the assumption that the main character had changed sex and become female. Woolf implies (utopianly) that a change in gender does not have to herald a change in mental/psychical make-up. However, we see in the case of Hamlette that the aesthetic and social meanings of Shakespeare's play change dramatically (*sic*) when the central figure is not male.

To recognise that gender is an inevitable variable in the playwright's imagination, in the performative possibilities of the text and its meanings, must add richness to an understanding of the ways in which dramatic texts function, and the varied ways in which men and women 'imagine' – indeed, can imagine, in the symbols they reach for which have cultural resonance, in the new permutations they create in order to challenge some of those resonances, and set up others.

For the purposes of understanding the sweep of post-war British drama, beginning in 1956, the following check list which relates the gender focus of content and form delineates what I argue are the dominant trends in the second half of the twentieth century. While the era of group-created 1970s agitprop was profoundly radical, and culturally important, it is – for better and worse – not these plays which mark the arc of theatrical texts, images, dominant forms of representation which come to be known as the history of our theatre. By its playwrights shall it be known, even though our theatre is run by artistic directors, not the writers themselves, and even though many of the far-reaching changes were wrought by other theatre workers.

Insofar as it is possible to determine a list of canonical contemporary drama, I would argue that a very high proportion of the plays discussed in this book consist of a recognisable modern canon. It goes without saying that there are many more plays I could have chosen, many more writers who could have been represented. Readers are likely to have other individual plays which are important to them, but I am arguing here for a case for a dominant set of patternings, based on the gender dynamic and the imperative of gender, through which we can tell the extraordinary story of transformation of theatre from 1956. It is important to remember that there is another story behind this one: the explanation of the process whereby these plays rise to the peak of visibility. To do this thoroughly would have to involve an examination of the processes by which artistic directors and publishers make their decisions, and what kinds of criteria theatre critics apply when they laud new work and help set it on its successful life path.

The following checklist of elements, thematic and formal, codifies the themes discussed in this book: the way the imperative of gender informs the playwright's imagination, and the way the gender dynamic determines the narrative drive; the way the family, the mother, hetero-sexuality, homosexuality, male and female identities interact with domestic and public settings, with the representation of men and women, and the way in which the relationship between the personal and political is refracted in the imaginative landscape. The conclusions – particularly in relation to the way the gender bias works in plays by male and female playwrights – is perhaps not too surprising; however, some of the more politically articulated issues do lead to some quite startling conclusions.

PHASE 1   PHASE 2
1950s/1960s   1970s/1980s/1990s

Gender dynamic

In mixed-cast plays by male playwrights, the action (story, plot, narrative) moves with the destinies of the male characters. In mixed-cast plays by women, the action moves with the

destinies of the female characters. All-male cast plays or
male-dominated plays tend to be written by men, all-female cast
plays by women.

In plays by women, female characters function in relation to men.	In plays by women, female characters function in relation to each other.
In plays by men, male characters engage with relationships with women.	In plays by men, male characters engage in relationships – non-sexual and sexual – with men.

The Family

Pervasive in plays by men and women. Real and symbolic.	Largely absent as explicit institution, or nexus of interpersonal relationships.
As role model for other kinds of relationship, in plays by men and women.	People in groupings, defined by political or social common interests, rather than biological or sexual relationships, in plays by men and women.

The Mother

A continuing presence, largely as a symbolic role in plays by men; largely as a real social role in plays by women. Not usually in control of the action in plays by men, more so in plays by women. Motherhood – real and symbolic – as obstacle or issue in relation to definition of male identity.	Virtually absent in any realistic form of role in plays by men. Sometimes as one social role among others, in plays by women.

Heterosexuality

Frequent, fraught and significant for the definition of male identity in plays by men.

Virtually absent as explicitly addressed subject matter in plays by men.

Occasional and fraught in plays by women.

Present as fraught, rites-of-passage issue, with a mixture of dependence and contempt by characters in plays by women.

Homosexuality

Explicit in plays by men about men or women; sometimes subtextual and homo-erotic, sometimes taboo and expressed through semi-pornographic imagery.

Either totally explicit in plays by men about men, or not addressed. Lack of homo-erotic subtext.

Virtually absent in plays by and about women.

Present and celebratory in plays by and about women.

Male identity

Pervasive in plays by men, personal and political.

Absent in individual sense but more stress on being part of social group.

Occasionally touched on in plays by women.

Absent in plays by women.

Female identity

Exploration, real and symbolic, of the place of women in her familial, social world in plays by women.

Wider exploration of women in non-familial roles, and as independent, existential beings in plays by women.

Absent in plays by men.

Absent in plays by men.

Domestic settings

Pervasive, many effectively single, domestic-set plays by men and women. Little stage fluidity.	Pretty well absent as single-set convention, cursorily included as an occasional scene in plays by both men and women. Stage fluidity a hallmark.
Men in control of the domestic space in plays by men. Women in control in plays by women.	Men in control of the epic space in plays by men, women in plays by women.

Public settings

Confined to occasional plays by men and women.	Common, as both realistic and polemical spaces in plays by men and women.

Representation of women

Powerfully symbolic of sexual and maternal power in plays by men; not the subjects of the plays, and not in control of the action. Partial outsiders.	Recognition of women's sexual power, dealt with by excluding women from the main action, or by symbolic annihilation, or as symbolic of romantic/political hope in plays by men. Either symbolic, or outsiders.
As emerging subjects of drama in plays by women.	Clear subjects of drama in plays by women, in relation to other women, within structures defined by men off stage.

Representation of men

In control of the action in both domestic and public plays by men.	In control of the action across history and politics in plays by men.

As fascinating, but often secondary characters in plays by women.	Either absent from the action, or as secondary characters, sometimes still defining the world of the female characters in plays by women.

Politics and the personal

Men bewildered, unsure, in transition, looking for causes and morality in plays by men.	Men in command, whatever the dilemmas. Few personal dilemmas in plays by men.
Women actively engaged, sure of themselves in plays by men, symbolic as well as real figures.	Women absent, except in token fashion, either symbolic of hope and principle in plays by men.
Women engaged sometimes just with the domestic, sometimes also with the political in plays by women.	Women seeking choice over their histories and life choices, not engaged in national/ world politics or political ideas in plays by women.
Little sense of link between politics and anything beyond immediate post-war period in plays by men and women. Low overt intellectual content. High emotional content.	Strong sense of politics as part of the historical process, extending over a longer period of time, in plays by men and women. High in ideas-content, low in emotional content.
The political incorporated into the personal in plays by men and women. Politics itself is defined as male concern, where defined at all.	The political separated from the personal in plays by men, and rarely an engaged issue in plays by women. Elements of the personal enacted in the public space.

These patterns are significant. In both phases a clear divide based on the playwright's gender is evident. This is a predictable outcome and should in some ways be reassuring, since gender is one of the fundamental determinants of imaginative focus. It is not, *per se*, a 'problem', or a failure of the imagination. It is the way we are socially and culturally constructed. Indeed, since 'characters', personae, people in fiction must necessarily be male or female (unless subversion or conscious cross-dressing is the order of the rare day), decisions about gender (conscious or not) are bound to constitute one of the prime (not necessarily earliest) decision-making moments in writing.

Thus the dramatic action is impelled in Phase 1 according to whether it is the story of the male or female characters at the centre, in Phase 2, according to the eyes through which the span of history is seen. There are, of course, exceptions, as I have shown; an apparently central female character (good role for an actress though she be) may not mean that the play is 'about' her – or about women or women's experiences as such.

This can be read in different ways; one could argue that we have always had something of a ghettoised theatre, in which men write from the male perspective, and women from the female perspective (varied, of course). But the notion of a ghetto implies a total separation, and I hope I have shown that even where there is a fundamental gender divide, it results in an imaginative symbiosis in the plays themselves, where the interaction between the way men and women are imagined produces powerful (even when misogynist) imagery, metaphors for politics, or paradigms for the dominant power structures of our society (shadowy males controlling the structure of women's lives).

This description does not mean that I am simply advocating and accepting 'difference' as it currently works. Such difference is problematic, because it is institutionalised in the accruing to men of power in the theatre industry, and to the perspectives and contents of the imagination which come to be seen as represented by the imaginations and writings of men, and therefore not women. In other words, the important plays on important themes tend to be identified in the work of male playwrights, with the occasional token woman to mollify the dominant bias.

These gendered differences may be endemic, but being able to identify, understand and analyse them is hopefully to open up the possibilities of different kinds of imaginings. That is why I have not taken the easy path of castigating some plays by men as merely 'sexist' or 'misogynist', even though aspects of both these terms may well apply. Nor does this necessarily have to result in a moralistic dictum that men 'must' write better about women, or vice versa. The workings of the imagination, however carefully planned, can never be so coolly controlled.

I am talking here about what, and how, playwrights imagine; what imagery they draw on, create, disrupt. In the theatre journalism of the 1970s (and sometimes still today), plays by women were criticised for not 'developing' male characters fully enough. The criticism is mis-placed. The vast majority of plays present primary and secondary characters, and the primary ones determine the narrative, and often the point of view, of the action and perspective. Secondary characters are, by definition, not as fully 'developed' as their primary colleagues, and this affects how the story is refracted through the relationships between characters.

To understand and accept that men and women write from within their sector of the gender divide is to begin to understand the strengths of their perspectives, to discuss where the real subjects and themes of the plays lie, and to raise questions about representations, mostly of women, but also, to some extent, of men. How easy is it to imagine one-self and one's work from a very different set of life experiences, passions, thoughts? This question applies, of course, to other cultural fields – ethnicity, race, other cultures. It is more than just the common-sense phrase 'writing from your own experience', although it also includes that. It clarifies some of the deliberately obfuscating consequences of the notion of the simply 'universal', and enables us to begin to see what communicates to whom, and where that communication is denied or belittled. I should add that talking to the playwright, fascinat-ing though his or her account of the imagining/writing process may be, will not produce answers. In the end, they can only be found in the text itself, via a fruitful analytical approach.

In my discussion of Phase 1, as well as identifying broad themes – the family, the mother, the relationship between politics and the domestic – I concentrated mainly on identifying the structural gender dynamic. In discussing Phase 2, because of the fuller entry of women playwrights and the legacy of feminism, I have explored the way in which different feminist dynamics influence both imagery and arguments, plot and themes, and added to this the cautionary of the feminine, where appar-ently radical approaches to representing women can collapse back into a reactionary, conventional dynamic.

However, in the above checklist, there are certain preoccupations which both men and women share. Before the repeal of censorship, the domestic, the family, the significant figure of the mother, and anguish about individual, personal male identity flourish. In post-1968 drama (reaching even into the 1990s, with the virtual abandon-ment of the 1970s/1980s epic play), the family as subject and theme is virtually absent. Stage spaces are either totally public or a mixture of public and domestic, with the public not only literally predominating, but also symbolically dominating in the way that the 'public' stage space is emphasised by its very ability to represent any and every location at great speed. By the 1990s, we are back to an outspoken wasteland of interpersonal relations, in unpoliticised, impersonal settings.

This excision/exclusion of the family results in a fascinating cultural/ political conundrum. How did the slogan that 'the personal is political' – something feminists argued with a vengeance, but which initially derived from male-dominated radical ideas – appear/affect the drama of the 1970s to 1990s, whether written by men or women receptive to both socialist analyses of the family, and discussions of the position of women? In practice, it seems – except for very few exceptions – to have slipped through the imaginative worlds both of men and women.

I think the reasons for this are themselves subject to an interesting gender bias: in the case of male playwrights, engaged on their dramatic quest within the contemporary history/epic play, there was no place, to put it simply, for love-stories. In the case of the women playwrights, most of the imaginative energy on stage went towards demonstrating and writing women in situations outside the home, away from their ideologically placed 'ghetto' of the kitchen sink. Women largely explored what it was to be female outside the family context, although still more in relation to it than in plays by men.

The consequence appears to be that apparently political activism and personal life cannot go together, or at least that they have not, or cannot, be easily *imagined* together, or represented in relation to each other. This leaves a separation between the intellect and the emotions, with men still associated with the world of politics and the intellect, and women as custodians of the emotions, separated from the world of intellect and politics, or there as secondary figures. In the group-created plays of some of the touring companies it was precisely this divide which was addressed, which became part of the 'story', but this book is concerned with the work of individual playwrights, and with the greater intimacy of the imaginative process which results. It appears that insofar as the 'personal' appears in Phase 2, it consists of meaning the 'existential' in work by women playwrights – the life choices we make as individuals (the predominance of the bourgeois feminist) – and as largely irrelevant in the work of male playwrights, since the individual is important only insofar as he (*sic*) is representative of a point of view or a historical moment.

Put simply, in Phase 1, politics is taken into the home (though not always directly addressed), and in Phase 2, the personal is subsumed into the public, political relationship between the individual and his or her world. This is, of course, an extraordinary achievement, but it has resulted in sometimes curiously passionless dramatic exercises. It is not that I call for old-fashioned empathy or identification *per se*, but it is as if the passion exemplified by Sarah Kahn for a deeply felt understanding that political and personal life are inseparable has fragmented into a dualistic world where public and private are separated, and the public dominates; passion here has little or no place in the fabric of the drama, and, of course, Wesker's trilogy is precisely in part about that process of disintegration. That process writ large ends in the disaffected British urban worlds of Kane and Ravenhill, apparently peopled by orphans at the mercy of predatory and exploitative male adult figures.

When *Look Back in Gender* was published (1987), I was somewhat shocked at this conclusion, having assumed that along with insights about politics, social and sexual, the slogan that the personal is political would impact equally on the drama. It is still fascinating that it has not really been a part of the remit of those playwrights who make it to the canonical apex of the high-art ladder. The theatrical split between the personal and the political, at precisely the point where they appeared to come together in political analysis, is fascinating. In aesthetic terms, this has its corollary in the fact that the representation of the public space, or limbo spaces, has taken over from the representation of the domestic, the home, the 'private' house.

To spell out the implications of this observation: my conclusions do *not* mean that I am advocating some kind of moral return to the domestic play, or to mimetic social realism. As I have stressed earlier, prescription, of either form or content, is (1) impossible (2) not what interests me, and (3) meaningless, since the kind of theatre writing under scrutiny is not bespoke, is not written to order in any mechanistic way.

We can look back to the 1970s and 1980s and find plays which give us history in moving pageants, which encompass social satire, provide insight about political parties and ideologies, explore the workings of male-dominated institutions, demonstrate the way women have their own rites-of-passage process into adulthood and choice, but we have to look back to the plays of the 1950s and 1960s, with censorship still in force, to see families and individuals under stress and emotional stricture struggling to define their personal identity in relation to social and political configurations, and for a representation of women which, while it is loaded with many of the prejudices of male bias, still exerts a powerful theatrical symbolism, which acknowledges the power of female sexuality and the figure of the mother. When we leap-frog back into the 1990s, we have stage worlds which are not engaged with ideas or political history; but rather with individual identity in a world where there is no personal space, just a series of abstractly represented social institutions and relationships.

Of course, in one sense the subtext in the plays of the 1950s and 1960s was about 'censorship' – the censorship of individual restriction, of the power of convention – but it is also true that, despite immense social change in personal/sexual life in Britain, for most people the pattern of the life-cycle centres round the family for crucially long periods, and it is into some form of family that we are born, formed, socially constructed. It may be that the homogenising of political ideologies which has taken place in the 1990s, where you can hardly tell the difference between Left and Right sometimes, and therefore have no centres of organised rebellion, practical or theoretical, from which to critique, means that the disaffected urban play is as close as we can come to the personal. In this world the family, if referred to at all, is a shadowy, bitterly confusing backdrop to a bleak present.

In keeping with my refusal to allow description to become prescription, I want to end with a series of questions, all of which hinge on what the playwrights of 2000 and after might imagine. Before the questions, however, I must make a campaigning rallying call. The surveys referrred to earlier in the book confirm with hard facts what we all know to be the case: male playwrights far outnumber female playwrights. We cannot even begin to claim to know what is possible until this imbalance is redressed. It cannot be done suddenly, and it cannot, in the end, be done in isolation from attempts to redress the gender imbalance in other areas of theatre.

However, at the very least, it ought to be possible to request, and perhaps even make funding for new plays contingent on, a graduated quota system, which over, say, a ten- to fifteen-year period, ensures a gradual increase in the number of plays commissioned from women writers, until parity is reached. This will doubtless need active outreach encouragement from those commissioning new work, and if they have a serious commitment to new writing, that is precisely what has to happen. This could mean not only looking for the young and the new, but garnering those of us who still have a passion for theatre, even if (like me, for example) they also earn their living from other forms of writing. Theatre is a greedy medium – few playwrights can earn their living exclusively from it, but it is also ruthless, and nurtures the tiny minority at the expense of a much larger number of good writers.

The questions which remain circle around the gender divide. How much can the individual, gendered imagination leap over its bit of the divide? How will the configurations of the personal and the social (rather than the political) take issue in the next decade? What will happen to the relationship between our perceptions of our society and our experiences of our personal lives? How, if at all in high art, might the family (in its many forms) be represented in the drama of the new century? Will the earlier obsession with the figure of the mother now be balanced with a similar preoccupation with the father? How will political issues be represented in the drama of the new century? And central to all these questions, how long will it take before our theatre ceases to be dominated so overwhelmingly by plays by men, and provides a parity of representation of women both in terms of authorship and on the stage?

There are two postscripts to this book: the first, a brief coda visit to an area of theatre which provocatively gives the lie to some of my general-ising claims: about the way the personal and familial are represented. However, these plays have not fitted into the body of my study, because they are not generally considered to be in the forefront of radical, high-art drama. I suspect this ambiguity of status is due to the fact that they are all, in different ways, preoccupied with the family and interpersonal in what may at first appear to be an old-fashioned sense. These writers include Peter Nichols and Alan Ayckbourn, the latter probably the most widely performed contemporary playwright in this country.

Chapter 16

Coda

Serendipities and *alter egos*

During August 2000, when this book was completed, two theatrical events serendipitously provided me with a chance to indicate where dramatic explorations of the interpersonal have continued to be located.

Passion Play *(1981) by Peter Nichols*

Peter Nichols' *Passion Play* was first produced by the Royal Shakespeare Company in 1981, and revived for a new production in April 2000. The multiply punning title refers not only to the contemporary sexual/ emotional interplay between the characters, but also to the spiritual/ religious concepts of passion in the music played (from Mozart's *Requiem* and Bach's *Passions*) and in the kinds of paintings which James, one of the main characters, restores.

James and Eleanor have been married for decades, and have two grown-up daughters. The much younger Kate comes into their lives, and initiates an affair with James. The rest is the stuff of classic eternal triangle plotting – but with some technical twists which reveal rather more than either mere adultery or farcical treatment of different sexual priorities.

Nichols creates two *alter egos*: James has Jim, who arrives quite early on the scene; Eleanor has Nell, who arrives rather later. These perform a variety of favours: they voice unspoken desires (not acceptable in polite company) which lie beneath social convention, they express despair, passion, doubt, uncertainty. They are the 'unconsciouses' made flesh, sometimes literally hovering behind their mortal counter-part, urging him or her on, or holding them back, and occasionally they even take over, playing a scene in their own right.

The settings are divided between James and Eleanor's living room, a restaurant and art galleries, but the home dominates, since it is here that the relationships focus most strongly. The characters' work, ideas, political affiliations, are not paramount. In terms of the plot, it is James' actions and desires which lead; after an early scene in which Eleanor pleads age and a bad back, James' responses to Kate's come-on, and consequent sexual attraction to her, imply that his sexual needs are greater than Eleanor's. Any sexual peccadilloes of her own are talked about as in the past – which means, of course, that they may not be 'true'.

Eleanor is told about James' infidelity by Agnes, a mutual friend, from whom Kate also 'stole' a husband, Albert. It is at this point that Eleanor's *alter ego*, Nell, arrives. When Eleanor confronts James, she hints that she was unfaithful to him – with Albert; but since Albert is dead, we have no way of knowing whether this is true, or whether Eleanor is simply responding to Nell's urging her to hurt James. Nell also suggests that there was a man in the choir in which Eleanor sings, implying that there might have been something between them – but again, this is ambiguous.

Kate briefly disappears from their lives, but returns to say how badly she had felt, not wanting to lose either James or Eleanor as friends. Kate reveals that she is bisexual – indeed, for her what seems to matter is simply sexual expressiveness, however it happens. Eleanor forgives her.

Kate's presence in their lives provokes a rethink, in which James clumsily implies that Eleanor's age is the problem: 'Families are little countries. If they can't change they die.' Although she thinks they should both talk to a therapist, he persuades her that she needs it and he does not. By this time Eleanor no longer trusts him. Despite the fact that both James and Kate say they have stopped seeing each other, Kate lets slip some information which confirms that they still are. Eleanor takes an overdose, recovers, Christmas is celebrated, and the play ends with a party at which James is still sexually fanta-sising about Kate. Nell helps Eleanor on with her coat, and then leaves. Does Eleanor stay or go? Does James continue or stop? End of play.

The play's structural wit lies in the interplay of levels of reality between the 'real' characters and the *alter egos*, demonstrating the pain and absurdity of social conventions of behaviour. Interestingly, in all this Kate has to remain (relatively) one-dimensional, since she is only there as the plot needs her for sexual activity and social deception. There is ambivalence here about the relative ways in which Eleanor and Kate, as the two main female characters, are represented. Eleanor firstly is reactive – powerfully so, but nevertheless fully reactive. She is the one placed as 'mad' by James; she struggles and tries to make sense of her life in a way he never does. His sexual needs thus appear to be taken for granted.

Kate, however, simply floats on a wave of youthful opportunism; we never see her emotionally vulnerable, and since she only goes for older men, presumably she is pretty safe, because she is never challenged on her own territory.

Home and away

House and Garden (1999/2000) by Alan Ayckbourn

With his customary wit, Ayckbourn combines the titles of these two plays to evoke references to a middle to upper-class magazine, concerned with the appearance, status and elegance of the house and the garden. In the published version of the plays, *House* is the first in the book, perhaps in keeping with its appearance as the more substantial, coherent play. In fact, this is part of its message.

The action of *House* takes place entirely in the 'summer sitting-room' of an English country house, 'tastefully shabby, cluttered, casual'. *Garden* is set, as its title implies, in part of the garden; it is the 'lower part of a much larger garden which has been allowed to grow wild'.

The plays, first performed in Ayckbourn's own theatre, the Stephen Joseph Theatre in Scarborough, came to the National Theatre in London, where much was made of the fact that the two plays have the same casts of characters, and are performed simultaneously, with performers rushing from one theatre to the other to make entrances on time.

This is not merely a gimmick of logistics and endurance, but itself an indicator of the way in which Ayckbourn has consistently played with time frames, place and perspectives/points of view. Here the dramatic irony hinges partly on the fact that when characters in one play go 'off', we know where they are going. When they refer to events happening 'off stage' we know these events are happening somewhere accessible to us at another time in another place – if we see the performance of the other play in the other theatre.

The plays take place on the same day, between 8 a.m. and 6 p.m., the day of the village fête. The relationships and marriages between a number of characters are in turmoil. Trish Platt, the lady of the house, has not spoken to husband Teddy for weeks, because she is fed up with him. Teddy is meanwhile having an affair (involving much rustling in the bushes) with Joanna, teacher wife of doctor Giles. Pearl, the young cleaner, has been sleeping with Warn, the taciturn gardener; when he moves in with Pearl's mother Izzie, the latter decides that Warn must shift from the role of lover to that of father.

Meanwhile, two events, one social, one political, frame these personal shenanigans. Barry and Lindy race around the garden setting up the paraphernalia for the fête; Gavin Ring-Mayne, a novelist friend of Teddy's, comes down from London to persuade the latter to stand for Parliament. We never know exactly what party he represents, but we may glean from the ambience and lifestyle, and the fact that Teddy and Trish's daughter Sally is into protest and ecology, that Teddy is likely to be a Conservative, or possibly even a Liberal.

The macro conceit of these two plays is that there is always more than we can know going on. Within the parallel locations of house and garden lurk the things people keep secret from one another, find out about one another, and do not know about one another. This is reinforced by the fact that even the material setting is not what it seems. As Teddy explains to Gavin:

> This is the old library. . . . But although it's called the old library, it actually replaced the previous library which was much, much older and eventually fell down. But although this was called the old library, curiously enough it was never used as a library.

The old library is neither old nor a library. There is always a 'But' to follow any piece of knowledge or naming in Ayckbourn's world. And because interpersonal relationships are sustained within the given conventions of marriage and the family, the devices of dramatic irony, of secrets which are revealed as threats to existing relationships, are all harnessed by Ayckbourn to explore the parts of people's emotional lives which the family cannot reach.

At its most poignant and funny are the scenes (in *House*) where Trish, pretending she can neither hear nor see Teddy, repeats things he has just said. After telling Gavin about her mother's marital unhappiness, she comments:

. . . it's very difficult to break the tradition, you see. . . . My way of coping is to blot things out completely. I've started editing my life. Like a stencil, you know. You hold it over the paper and you just allow the bit you want to bleed through.

Later, talking to young Jake, who is in love with Sally, she elaborates further. Using the fête maypole as a metaphor, she says:

Clinging onto our ribbon, terrified of deviating in case we get hurt or lost or rejected . . . never for a minute do most of us ever dream of doing the obvious and just letting go.

Trish's role as commentator leads her to approach the plays' central philosophical concern more directly towards the end of *House*: 'Love is essentially a very simple business. But in the hands of human beings it often becomes monstrously complicated.'

At the end of the play, she comes on stage with a suitcase, addresses an empty room (as she and Teddy have done before), and then leaves. These moments of commentary from Trish are fully contextualised as she busies herself running the house, preparing lunch, coping with visitors and Teddy. She takes action at the end, a modern Nora in full control of her life; but this is low key, not an apocalyptic step.

In *Garden* other skirmishes are also foregrounded. Pearl, Warn and Izzie perform their rude mechanicals dances; Barry and Lindy punctiliously follow a rigid, boy-scout routine conducted by Barry. The two outsiders, Gavin, and Lucille, a French actress brought down to open the fête, also reveal their subtexts: Gavin turns out to be a nasty, manipulative piece of work, and Lucille is a scarcely recovering alcoholic.

At the end of this cathartic day, certain historic changes take place: Trish and Lindy (the latter cadging a lift to London from Gavin) both leave their impossible husbands. Only the explicitly dysfunctional family of Pearl, Izzie and Warn seem set to live happily ever after: Pearl has the father she has always wanted, and Izzie and Warn have each other. Somewhere in that is an ironically suggested message about class and marriage: the bastions of convention are falling to pieces, while the social outsiders (the below-stairs crowd) find a way to live contentedly together.

Within all this, the gender balance is excellently maintained. While it is true that it is still the man having an active sex life (cf. Nichols), in terms both of stage territory and dramatic action, all the women have strong presences. It is true that Teddy holds the lion's share of stage space across both plays (Trish has very little part in *Garden*), but interactively the play's action follows its various plot strands in a way which does not announce male-gender bias too exclusively.

There is here a fascinating set of questions. I have already commented that my analysis does not lead to a prescription for the return of the domestic play *per se*, nor for the abolition of the public, epic/historical play. It is, rather, a question of how playwrights represent what interests them about relationships in context. Here we have Nichols literally embodying the concept of the *alter ego*, of staging aspects of the subtext of dialogue and relationships, an avant-garde technique harnessed in the interests of a play about love and marriage. Ayckbourn has always played with time, perspective and motivation, and here he does so on a more expansive scale, by literally writing two plays. Of course each is complete without the other, and of course each is also incomplete without the other. Whether the two together give us the 'complete' story is yet another question: there are still questions which the plays leave unanswered. Ayckbourn deals with a fundamental philosophical issue in these popular plays: the nature of reality, how we imagine, represent and name it; he also deals with a fundamental political issue which feminism has approached from other perspectives: the nature of marriage and the family. The concerns of women here find almost as much space as the concerns of men, yet still with imaginative differences.

We have not exactly come full circle. The social institutions within which we live have not fundamentally changed in the last half-century. Many conventions and assumptions, practices and expectations have been modified. Our playwrights have found ways of breaking out of the confines of the domestic set into public and abstract spaces. Yet most have, most of the time, ignored/been unable to explore/deal with/imagine the intricacies of interpersonal relationships.

This is left to soaps (on television and radio), and drama which hovers at the edges of the high-art sphere, or is categorised in an oppositional sense as 'popular'. There is no simple conclusion to this observation. The variety in the British theatre testifies to the fact that playwrights explore their own concerns, enhanced by the aesthetic and political freedoms gained since 1968.

However, certain issues do need to be thought about and acted upon: the male-gender bias of most drama, not wrong *per se*, but too often at the expense of either female-centred or gender-balanced work. The frustratingly small number of commissions awarded to women playwrights, and the desperate need for policies which will at some point soon lead to gender parity for playwrights.

Epilogue

In 1989, a survey commissioned by the Arts Council showed that in an average period of four weeks during 1998 to 1999, 6 per cent of the adult population went to the theatre. In 1990, Sabine Durrant reported (*Independent*, 2 February) that there were an estimated 6500 amateur theatre companies in Britain. In the subsidised theatre (which includes both large national houses and small theatres/companies) funding is constantly in crisis, the last major round of which also occurred in 1990 when theatre funding was substantially devolved to regional arts boards.

In February 1955, the year before *Look Back in Anger* started something, there were thirty-eight West End theatres offering entertainment. In the issue of *Time Out* (the London listings guide) for 13–20 September 2000, there are forty-five theatres listed in the West End section, sixteen in the off-West End section, and thirty-four in the Fringe section. The tension between theatrical energy, funding, opportunity and commercial success, and the small percentage of actual theatre-goers, remains crucial to what continues to be a thriving cultural enterprise. Theatre influences television and film, directly and indirectly; it provides a space for the reassuring, the uncomfortable, the rebellious, the challenging and disturbing. It celebrates the power to make the imagination real in the immediacy and reality of the theatrical experience in a finite temporal and architectural moment.

And be assured that in every crevice of this field, the gendered imagination is at work, the gender imperative operates, and the gender dynamic infuses everything. It will not go away. It may as well be celebrated as one of the major spurs for further changes and explorations. As long as there is parity between men and women playwrights in our theatrical future.

Select bibliography

The post-war theatre scene

Anger and After – A Guide to the New British Drama by John Russell Taylor (Eyre Methuen, 1962)
A sound, discursive round-up of the playwrights of the 1950s and 1960s, categorised geographically: the Royal Court Theatre, Stratford East, out of town, experimental, and acknowledgement of the new drama appearing on radio and television. Lively and enthusiastic.

The Empty Space by Peter Brook (McGibbon & Kee, 1968)
Based on a series of lectures, this book discusses the relationship between the new uses of theatre space, and approaches to theatre as ritual, as political, as contemporary, and as vivid and immediate in performance.

The Second Wave – British Drama of the Sixties by John Russell Taylor (Eyre Methuen, 1971)
A sequel to the previous book, structured around chapters on individual playwrights, and those categorised by form – farceurs, social realists and the dark fantastics. Thorough and careful critical analysis and placing of each writer. Thirty playwrights discussed, all male. Very useful bibliographies of plays at the end.

Disrupting the Spectacle – Five Years of Experimental and Fringe Theatre in Britain by Peter Ansorge (Pitman Publishing, 1975)
A slim book based on a series of interviews in the theatre magazine *Plays and Players*, expanded into rather more in-depth discussion of some of the new work. Contextualised in relation to fringe group work – Portable Theatre, Inter-Action, the Arts Lab, the Welfare

State, lunchtime theatre – along with reference to influences from America. Ten writers discussed in some depth, all male.

Playwrights' Theatre – the English Stage Company at the Royal Court Theatre by Terry W. Browne (Pitman Publishing, 1975)
Short history of one of the most important generators of new writing, from its founding in 1957. Much detail about finances, repertoire, policies and quotes from participants. Includes invaluable appendices, one detailing costs, returns, etc., the other a list of the 250 plays so far produced. Of these, full productions accounted for eleven plays, and Sunday night one-offs for five plays by women.

Post-War British Theatre by John Elsom (Routledge & Kegan Paul, 1976)
An excellent summary of the theatrical landscape after the Second World War; the characteristic West End play, challenged by new styles of acting, the founding of the Arts Council and subsidy, the rise of the 'Fringe' and the young playwrights of the 1950s and 1960s.

Dreams and Deconstructions – Alternative Theatre in Britain edited by Sandy Craig (Amber Lane Press, 1980)
A book generated from within the enthusiastic theatre coverage given in *Time Out* magazine, for which seven out of the ten contributors wrote at the time. It includes essays covering the political ideologies behind the new work, feminism, community and ethnic theatre, children's theatre, performance art, venues, repertory companies, new ways of working, subsidy, lunchtime theatres and new writers. Based on close knowledge of the field as it was developing.

Stages in the Revolution – Political Theatre in Britain since 1968 by Catherine Itzin (Eyre Methuen, 1980)
Compendious summary of ten years of theatre (1968 to 1978). Brief chapters on grass-roots groups, the political organisations of the new theatres and groups, and some of the writers, their aims and intentions taken from policy documents and interviews. A chronology of productions lists 'the major productions of playwrights, theatre companies and theatres discussed', beginning with 1957. In an invaluable list of about 1100 plays, the breakdown on the basis of gender is a little complex but still quite revealing. Fifty-one individual women playwrights are credited. A further twenty-five plays are co-written by a man and woman playwright (John Arden and Margaretta d'Arcy), and sixty-eight collectively authored plays come from groups with women in

them. Finally, seven productions from the Women's Theatre Group self-evidently are group-authored by women.

Playwrights Progress – Patterns of Postwar British Drama by Colin Chambers and Mike Prior (Amber Lane Press, 1987)
An excellent survey of the postwar playwrights, analysed from a radical, left-wing perspective, linking drama and social and political context. Incorporates critiques influenced by feminism and debates within sexual politics. Section on 'Public and private' discusses women playwrights, and 'Feminist theatre', a chapter on Caryl Churchill, concludes the book with lively and thorough interpretations of her work.

Drama Today – A Critical Guide to British Drama 1970–1990 by Michelene Wandor (Longman, 1993)
A short guide to twenty years of new voices, established playwrights, gender and ethnicity, collaborative theatre processes.

1956 And All That – The Making of Modern British Drama by Dan Rebellato (Routledge, 1999)
A vigorous recontextualising which places post-war British drama in relation to theatrical history just after the war; including useful state-of-the-industry information, details about the developments of play publishing, and an illuminating examination of the subtextual presences of homosexuality before 1968. Provocatively questions and documents the ways in which *Look Back in Anger* has become the landmark for critics and commentators. An exhaustively useful and focused bibliography.

Theatre, gender, women and feminism

The Body Politic – Women's Liberation in Britain 1969–1972 compiled by Michelene Wandor (Stage 1, 1972)
First collection of British Women's Liberation writings, based on papers given at the first Women's Liberation Conference at Ruskin College in 1970. Includes pieces on women in the home, at work, in unions, pieces on motherhood, crime, and identity.

Innocent Flowers – Women in the Edwardian Theatre by Julie Holledge (Virago, 1981)
Carefully and originally researched, this book takes a women-centred look at Edwardian drama, from the enthusiasm for performing in Ibsen's

plays, to the groundswell of plays and sketches supporting the suffrage movement, to early all-women theatre companies. Includes three suffragette plays.

Still Harping on Daughters – Women and Drama in the Age of Shakespeare by Lisa Jardine (Harvester, 1983)
Scholarly and accessible challenge to crude 'feminist' (1) criticisms of Shakespeare's sexism, and (2) appropriation of his female characters. The book puts Shakespeare back in his century, by showing how his representations of women are part of a broader set of cultural issues. Jardine offers 'possibilities for reading the relationship between real social conditions and literary representation'. Excellent and stimulating.

Carry on, Understudies – Theatre and Sexual Politics by Michelene Wandor (Routledge, 1986)
Outlines the links between historical feminisms and radical theatre, delineates the post-1968 development of theatre and sexual politics, describing the most widely known companies, discussing the sexual and social division of labour in theatre, outlining the three basic feminist dynamics, and applying a brief, gender-based analysis to the work of a small number of men and women playwrights.

Making a Spectacle – Feminist Essays on Contemporary Women's Theatre edited by Lynda Hart (University of Michigan Press, 1989)
An excellent multicultural approach to theatre, feminism and work by women; mainly about American-produced theatre, but with thorough-going references to some British women writers. Includes theoretical discussions of the relationship between gender and the canon, music, and gay politics and aesthetics.

Once a Feminist – Stories of a Generation interviews by Michelene Wandor (Virago, 1990)
A series of interviews twenty years on, with women who were at the Ruskin conference. The women talk not only about what they remembered and have done since, but also about those parts of their lives which feminism did not always reach.

Performing Feminisms – Feminist Critical Theory and Theatre – edited by Sue-Ellen Case (Johns Hopkins University Press, 1990)
More stringently based theory, drawing in discussions of sexual representation, French psychoanalytic theory, class and ethnicity, gender-based reinterpretations of theatre history, the body as a site for the enactment of signs of gender, of sexual cross-referencing. Stimulating, American-based, wide-ranging theory.

An Introduction to Feminism and Theatre by Elaine Aston (Routledge, 1995)
A lucid and carefully guided tour around the thickets of academic definition. Aston traces the historiography of approaches to theatre by women/feminists, streamlines the complexities of French modernist theory, raises important questions about class and race, and presents some case studies of her own. Includes a strong selective bibliography for further reading.

The Routledge Reader in Gender and Performance edited by Lizbeth Goodman with Jane de Gay (Routledge, 1998)
The editors have collected an excellent basis for the study of gender and performance, presenting snippets of historical fact alongside speculative attempts to create a 'feminist' aesthetic, surveys of employment, comparative essays on other cultures, on dance, cinema, sexual representation and reception theory, and multi-media challenges. Again, an excellent and useful bibliography.

The Cambridge Companion to Modern British Women Playwrights edited by Elaine Aston and Janelle Reinelt (CUP, 2000)
In a transatlantic collaboration, the editors have compiled a historical survey of the twentieth century, including essays on Welsh, Scottish, Northern Irish, and black British women playwrights. The accounts of the plays are interwoven with references to theoretical discussions of the politics of location, feminism, language, body politics and lesbian performance.

Index

Abortion Act (1967) 30
AC/DC (H. Williams) 166–8
Actresses' Franchise League 116
Allen, Sheila 33
Almost Free Theatre 126, 127
The Amazing Equal Pay Show 124
Angry Young Men 66
Any Woman Can (Posener) 128
Arden, Jane 157–9, 190, 191
Arden, John 71–5, 79, 92, 94, 95
Arts Council 122, 130, 260
The Association of Community
   Theatre (TACT) 122
Association of Lunchtime Theatres
   122
Austen, Jane 132
Aveling, Edward 116
Ayckbourn, Alan 255–8

Babuscio, J. 140
Baker, Roger 128
Barber, John 127
Barrie, J.M. 49–50
Barthes, Roland 25
Beautiful Thing (Harvey) 225–7
Beckett, Samuel 34, 48–50, 76, 91,
   92–3, 95, 97
The Bed-Sitting Room (Milligan) 109
The Beggar's Opera (Gay) 103
Behan, Brendan 32
Behn, Aphra 23
Bent (Sherman) 185–7
Benton, Howard 168–9
Berliner Ensemble 33

Berman, Ed 126, 127–8
The Birthday Party (Pinter) 58–60
bisexuality 167
The Body Politic (Wandor) 119
Bond, Edward 87–90, 91, 93, 95,
   191
Brecht, Bertold 33–4, 148–53, 190,
   192, 220
Brenton, Howard 187–9, 190
The British Alternative Theatre
   Directory 131
British Communist Party 31
Brooke, Dinah 2, 127
Browning, Elizabeth Barrett 24
Burgess, Anthony 236

Cambridge University 34
Campaign for Nuclear Disarmament
   (CND) 29
The Captive Wife (Gavron) 30–1
Carry on, Understudies (Wandor)
   3–4
Cat on a Hot Tin Roof (T. Williams)
   105
censorship 24–5, 35, 91, 248, 250,
   251
Cheeseman, Peter 31
Chesterfield, Philip Dormer, Lord
   103, 111
Chicken Soup with Barley (Wesker)
   50–3
Christian Festival Light 123
Churchill, Caryl 95, 170–2, 181–5,
   190, 191, 221–2

Clark, Brian 168–9
Cleansed (Kane) 232–4
Clockwork Orange (Burgess) 236
Cloud Nine (Churchill) 181–5, 222
Co-operative Guild 116
Coningsby (Disraeli) 104
Conrad, Joseph 102
Contemporary Dramatists 131
Copenhagen (Frayn) 229–32
cross-dressing 21–2, 24, 78, 136–40, 233

Daily Telegraph 127
Daniels, Sarah 212–17, 220, 222
Delaney, Shelagh 32, 60–3, 91, 92, 93, 95, 96, 190, 191
Dench, Judi 32
Destiny (Edgar) 176–9
Devine, George 34
Disraeli, Benjamin 104
Divorce Reform Act (1969) 30
The Doll's House (Ibsen) 116
domestic settings 190, 214, 221, 237, 245; collision with urban violence 87–90; displacement in 58–9, 60; on the estate 225–7; gender roles 42, 51; invaded from within 82; personal/political aspects 151–3, 178–9; shifts in 76–7, 204–5; traditional/subversive 82–5; women in 27, 51, 71
drama, choice of 9–11; feminist/gay influences 127–30; form/content 7–8, 76, 96–7, 133, 192, 215, 236; funding for new 251–2; and gender differences 132–6, 247–8; as group-authored/group-sponsored 126–30; and method school of acting 76; new realism in 41–75; and performance/text repositioning 5–7, 8–9; and private/public shift 31–5, 76–7; realism/abstract absurdism in 95–6
Duffy, Maureen 159–62, 190, 191, 192
Dunn, Nell 202–7, 220, 221
Durrant, Sabine 260
Dyer, Charles 86–7

Each His Own Wilderness (Lessing) 67–9
Edgar, David 176–9, 190, 207–12, 220, 221, 229
Education Act (1944) 27
Eliot, George 132
Elsom, John 31, 32–3
An Enemy of the People (Ibsen) 116
English Stage Company 34
Entertaining Mr Sloane (Orton) 80–1
Equal Pay Act (1970) 30, 124

family 243, 248; alternative set-ups 206; centrality of 91; in crisis 48; disintegration of 50–3; inadequate 229; incest in 80–1; inclusion/exclusion of 249; Jewish 50–7, 92; maternal power in 60–3, 93, 94–5; non-appearance of 221; and outsider figure 55–7, 58–60, 87–90, 95–6, 226; overturning of conventions in 80–2; and personal/political aspects 36, 50–7, 125–6, 178–9, 183; post-War changes 27–8; sexual issues 29–30, 91, 92–5, 188–9; symbolic aspects 188–9; as transnational 58; types of 91–2; violence/fragmentation in 66, 235, 236–7, 251
The Feminine Mystique (Friedan) 30
feminism 23, 25, 117–19, 121, 127, 140–2; bourgeois 144–5, 185, 216, 219; and female transgressions 164–6; and feminine dynamic 146–7, 181, 183–5, 206–7; influence of 190–1, 221–2, 248; radical/cultural 142–3, 206, 207, 215, 216, 219; socialist 145–6, 184, 207; tensions of 202
Feminist Theatre Study Group 129
Fielding, Henry 103
Finer Report (1974) 30
Finney, Albert 107
Fowell, F. and Palmer, F. 110
Frayn, Michael 109, 229–32, 236
Friedan, Betty 30
Friel, Brian 197–9, 220
Fromanteel, Cameron, 1st Baron Cobbold 101

Gavron, Hannah 30
Gay, John 103
Gay Liberation Front (GLF) 119, 120–1
Gay Sweatshop 128
Gems, Pam 126
gender 199; amateur/professional divide 132; ambiguities in 21–2, 181–2; balance in 257–8; chronicling 187–9; conflict 170–2; and creativity 173–6; and cross-dressing 136–40; dynamics 242–3; function of 36–7; and identity 96, 244; imaginative divide 57, 96–7; imperative of 21–6; and the Left 176–9; and mysogyny 216; and playwriting 132–6, 246–8; power 48–50, 60–3, 90, 93, 94–5; questions concerning 17; reversals 15–21, 241; and sexual politics 115–21; and the sexual psyche 166–8; wrestling-ring metaphor 199–202
Gilder, R. 138
Greek myths 157, 158, 159–60, 217–19
Griffiths, Drew 136
Griffiths, Trevor 162–4, 168–9, 190, 191
the Group 31
Guarding the Change 108

Hamlet (Shakespeare) 17–21, 32, 241
Hardy, Thomas 101
Hare, David 164–6, 168–9, 173–6, 190, 191
Harvey, Jonathan 225–7, 236
Haymarket Theatre 127
heterosexuality 227, 228, 244
Holledge, J. 116, 139
homosexuals, homosexuality 30, 44, 119–20, 121, 140, 244; and coming out 86–7, 225–7; hatred of 162; military 77–80; persecution of 185–7; as unnatural 187; and violence 227–9
Hope, Bob 122–3
House and Garden (Ayckbourn) 255–8

Ibsen, Henrik 105, 115, 116
identity 64, 191–2, 248, 250–1; crisis in 30; and gender 96, 172; male 56, 164, 244
I'm Talking about Jerusalem (Wesker) 55–7
Inadmissable Evidence (Osborne) 100
Independent Theatres Council (ITC) 122
Independent Women's Theatre 116
individuality 93, 189
Institute of Contemporary Arts (ICA) 128
Ireland 197–9
Irving, Henry 105

Jardine, L. 137
Jellicoe, Ann 63–6, 76, 91, 92–3, 93, 97, 157, 158, 191
Johnson, Samuel 104
Jones, Henry Arthur 102

Kane, Sarah 232–4, 235, 236, 250
Kaplan, C. 134
Kensington Post 127
The Killing of Sister George (Marcus) 82–5, 92
King Lear (Shakespeare) 32
kitchen-sink theatre 41–8

Lady Macbeth syndrome 91–7, 151, 191, 212
language 157–8, 197–9, 220
Lay-By (multi-author play) 168–9, 190
Left Book Club 116
lesbians 82–5
Lessing, Doris 67–71, 91, 93, 95, 96, 190
Littlewood, Joan 31, 33, 34
Look Back in Anger (Osborne) 8, 37, 41–8, 80, 93, 94, 100
Loot (Orton) 81–2
Lord Chamberlain, and censorship 100–1, 105–11; duties/role of 98–101; historical background 99, 101–5
The Love of the Nightingale (Wertenbaker) 217–19

Lowe, Stephen 202–4, 220–1
Luckham, Claire 199–202, 220, 221
Luther (Osborne) 107
Lyttleton Theatre 1

McGrath, John 124
male gaze 206–7
The Man Who Came to Dinner 32
Marcus, Frank 82–5, 92, 93, 95
Marx, Eleanor 115–16
Masterpieces (Daniels) 212–17, 222
Maydays (Edgar) 207–12
men, and all-male environment 77–80; authority of 48–50, 93, 199–202; conventional view of 58, 60, 72, 73, 75, 175–6, 211, 218, 232, 234, 236; and crisis of masculinity/manhood 43–4, 47, 52, 66, 77–80; as damaged 57, 94, 170, 171, 180, 181; and dealing with emotions 220; and identity 56, 164, 244; and intellectual/ sexual potency 202–4; and the military 71–5, 77–80, 92; nihilistic view 227–9; and nude females 206–7; as progressive/hero 192; and property/ownership 170–2; representation of 245–6
Methuen 2, 131
Miller, Arthur 105
Milligan, Spike 109
Miss World contest 122–3
Monstrous Regiment 127
The Mother (Brecht) 148–53, 192
motherhood 168, 191, 212, 221, 243, 248; attack on 45, 46; centrality of 94–5; and female sexuality 65–6; as outside conventional structures 236; on a pedestal 148–53; as powerful 93–4, 158; and relationship with daughter 60–3, 94; and relationship with son 59, 67–9, 225–6; as sterile 165–6; as symbolic 96, 163–4
Mrs Warren's Profession (Shaw) 105

National Health Service (NHS) 27
New Left 29

Nichols, Peter 253–5
Nick Hern Books 131

Occupations (Griffiths) 162–4
Oedipus Rex (Sophocles) 102
Old Vic 32
O'Malley, Mary 179–81, 190, 191, 192
Once a Catholic (O'Malley) 179–81
Ophelia syndrome 173–6
Orlando (Woolf) 15–17, 241
Orton, Joe 80–2, 91, 95
Orwell, George 236
Osborne, John 8, 37, 77–80, 91, 92, 93, 94, 96, 100, 101, 106–8, 191, 221
outsiders 55–7, 58–60, 61, 62, 64, 69–71, 74, 87–90, 95–6, 167–8, 171, 191, 199, 204, 221, 226, 228, 229
Oval House community centre 122
Owners (Churchill) 95, 170–2

pantomime 24
Passion Play (Nichols) 253–5
A Patriot For Me (Osborne) 77–80, 93, 101
personal/political issues 36, 50–7, 69, 178–9, 181–5, 192, 207–12, 246, 249–50
Piggot, E.F.S. 105
Pinter, Harold 58–60, 93, 95
Play with a Tiger (Lessing) 69–71
Poliakoff, Steven 168–9
pornography 212–15, 216–17, 222
Posener, Jill 128
Post-War British Theatre (Elsom) 31, 32–3
Potter, Dennis 9
The Premise 108
psyche 41–8, 71, 166–8
public/private space 31–5, 76–7, 86, 220, 236, 245, 249
Punching Ladies 124

Ravenhill, Mark 227–9, 235, 236, 250
Red Ladder 125
Red Rag journal 119

Rickman, Alan 127
Rites (Duffy) 159–62
rites of passage 179–81, 221, 225–6
Robins, Elizabeth 116
The Romans in Britain (Brenton) 187–9
Roots (Wesker) 53–5, 94
Rowbotham, S. 23, 117
Royal Court Theatre 10, 34, 37
Royal National Theatre 10
Royal Shakespeare Company 106
Royal Shakespeare Theatre 10
Ruskin College (Oxford) conference (1970) 117, 119

St James' Press 131
Samuel French catalogues 131–2
Saved (Bond) 87–90
Scarborough, 11th Earl of 101
Serjeant Musgrave's Dance (John Arden) 71–5
7:84 theatre group 124, 149
sexuality 190; brutalism of 227–9, 235; family issues 29–30, 91, 92–5, 188–9; in family life 29; female views on 68; flexibility of 167; freedoms of 168–9; and gender/ gender roles 37; politics of 115–21; psyche 166–8; as subject in its own right 199; subtleties of 220–1
Shakespeare, William 8, 17–21, 241
Shaw, George Bernard 100, 102–3, 105, 110, 111, 115, 116
Sheldon, C. 140
Sherman, Martin 185–7, 190, 220
Shopping and Fucking (Ravenhill) 227–9
Simpson, N.F. 76
Slag (Hare) 164–6
Son of Oblomov (Milligan) 109
Sophocles 102
The Sport of My Mad Mother (Jellicoe) 63–6
Staircase (Dyer) 86–7
Standing Conference of Women Theatre Directors and Administrators 129–30
Stanislavsky 32

the state 48–50, 93
Steaming (Dunn) 202–7
Stoddart, Hugh 168–9
Strasberg, Lee 32
Sue, Eugene 1
Swinburne, Algernon 101

The Taming of the Shrew (Shakespeare) 8
A Taste of Honey (Delaney) 60–3
Teeth 'n' Smiles (Hare) 173–6
Thatcher, Margaret 192, 235
theatre, alternative 121–30; amateur/ professional gender divide 132; censorship in 35; as collaborative art 133–4; division of labour in 130–2; and function of gender 36–7; ghetto image of 247; post- War changes 31–5
Theatre Guild 116
Theatre Royal 31
Theatre Writers' Group (TWU) 122
Tibetan Inroads (Lowe) 202–4
Tilley, Vesta 139
Time Out 119, 127, 260
Tom Jones (Fielding) 103
Trafford Tanzi (Friel) 199–202
Translations (Friel) 197–9
Tree, Sir Herbert Beerbohm 102
Tynan, Kenneth 35, 115

Understudies (Wandor) 2–3
Unity Theatre 31, 116
utopias 57, 181–5, 236, 241

Vagina Rex and the Gas Oven (Jane Arden) 157–9
A View From the Bridge (Miller) 105
Virago 119

Waiting for Godot (Beckett) 48–50
Walpole, Sir Robert 103
The Wandering Jew (Sue) 1
Wandor, M. 117, 119, 123
Weeks, J. 120
Welfare State 27
Wells, H.G. 102
Wertenbaker, Timberlake 217–19, 220

Wesker, Arnold 50–7, 91–2, 96
Williams, Heathcote 166–8, 190, 191
Williams, Tennessee 105
Wilson, Snoo 168–9
A Woman's Work is Never Done 125
women, controlled by men 199–202; conventional view of 58, 60, 72, 73–5, 149, 175–6, 211–12, 218, 232, 234, 236; discontent amongst 30–1; as dramatists 23; and emancipation 67–9; ethical dilemmas for 179–81; excluded from theatre 22–3; and hatred of men/homosexuality 162; and identity 244; improved contraception for 28; influences of feminism on 23, 190–1; and language 157–8; as marginal 199; maternal power of 60–3, 93, 94–5; and myth 63–6; oppression of 157–9; post-War position 27–8; as powerless 216; as reactionary/ enemy 192; representation of 245; security/vulnerability of 206–7; and social outsider theme 69–71; as subject/not subject of plays 96; as symbol and reality 74–5, 162–4; and territorial control 159–62; theatrical presence of 136–40; as writers 132, 134–6, 249

Women's Liberation Movement (WLM) 23, 36, 117–19
The Women's Press 119
Women's Street Theatre Group 123–4
Women's Theatre Festival (1973) 126–7
Women's Theatre Group (WTG) 124, 126, 127
Woolf, Virginia 15–17, 241
Worker's Theatre Movement (WTM) 116
The World of Paul Slickey (Osborne) 106–7
Writers' Guild 122

You Won't Always Be On Top 108